KENNETH GRAHAME

KENNETH GRAHAME

KENNETH GRAHAME

LIFE, LETTERS AND UNPUBLISHED
WORK

BY

PATRICK R. CHALMERS

' You may indeed rest assured that Kenneth
will be more than a memory, that he will still
be a living presence and an enduring friend.'

ANTHONY HOPE

WITH 15 ILLUSTRATIONS, 2 FACSIMILE LETTERS
AND A PEDIGREE

METHUEN & CO. LTD.

36 ESSEX STREET W.C.

LONDON

First Published in 1933

.G76°7C

PRINTED IN GREAT BRITAIN

KENNETH GRAHAME

As song that follows song with burdens blithe
  As lovely are the lovely names of Thames
  That match green England to her garment-hems—
Medmenham, Mapledurham, Bablockhythe,
We say them and they say no little tithe
  Of June and slow, old mill-wheels dripping gems,
  Dog-roses, elms, in grave, green diadems,
Cuckoos and hay-cocks and the swish of scythe;

And we, who tell these river rosaries
And mention them among the nightingales,
Will speak of him who walked the Berkshire shore
And knew the Wind among the willow trees
And heard that Whisperer of Fairy Tales
And left his Thames one summer song the more.

P. R. C.

CONTENTS

LIST OF ILLUSTRATIONS

PLATES

ix

IN THE TEXT

INTRODUCTION

Who, if any one, ought to be another's biographer ? It is easy to say, and possibly right when said, that he who best knew that other is the man. And yet an intimate, maybe, is too near to see whom he would portray in true perspective and without an affectionate prejudice or so. Moreover, such a one sees but the view from an accustomed window. A new-comer may find other vistas and viewpoints. Or, possibly, he may not.

I but once met Kenneth Grahame. I went, on a summer day, to his house in Pangbourne upon an errand which in no way concerned him. He, among his roses, came round a corner of the garden to find that a stranger (myself) had come calling. He made swift excuse to the company ; he was going to the river, he was going to see the boats, ' the pretty boats ', he said, and he walked round the corner again. I have a remembrance of a massive, very tall figure in faultless grey flannels (they might have been cut for the Capitoline Jove), of an Olympian head, plentifully white-haired, of a clear and ruddy face and (as he disappeared) of a pair of shoulders to delight Savile Row.

Less than a year later it fell to me to be writing the life (that visible portion of it anyhow that lies between birth and death, between the terrestrial coming and the going) of the great virile gentleman who went down to the river upon that summer evening.

There are more ways, I suppose, than one of making a man's biography. Here is a sample mode that Kenneth Grahame said had much to recommend it. His scrapbook tells me that he found it ' pasted up in a village ale-house in 1885 '. He says that it is ' evidently the outcome of

sincere and genuine feeling stirred by what seemed an heroic
life and death into paying what poor tribute it could '.

A FEW LINES ON COLONEL BURNABY

' He like a soldier fell '

Our noble Colonel Burnaby, fought the battle brave,
But, with all his bravery, his own life he could not save.
He was born at Bedford, on the 3rd March, 1842,
And when only eighteen years of age, he was in the R.H.G. Blue.
He learnt many languages, and spoke many tongues,
And since he has been in manhood, see the brave acts he has done.
Then he has been promoted, of course he was not fixed,
For he was made a Captain in 1866.
And again that was not to be his fate,
For he was made a Major in the year 1878.
He was a brave fellow, he was not a lurcher,
See his journey through Turkey-in-Asia to Khor in Persia.
A more noble soldier, I should think was never seen before,
He was not like a short man,
For he stood six feet four.
A Brave man, and had an honourable heart,
But with all that, from this world he had to part.
Such a noble Colonel is seldom seen,
He fought for his country, and was a faithful servant to the Queen.
He to his fate, of course he had to yield,
Although he was wanted in the Conservative and Political field.
But poor fellow, he has gone before,
He came to his death in the Abu Klea War.

I suspect that some such artless broadsheet as this might
have been Kenneth Grahame's personal choice of biographies.

And I knew nothing of the man whose record I was
supposed to put down. Nothing at all beyond three things.
Firstly, that he had written a trio of books, *Pagan Papers*,
The Golden Age and *Dream Days*, on the contents of any
one of which I was able to take honours. And (a second
part of my firstly) that a fourth book stood to his credit
—*The Wind in the Willows*—which, though it had brought
money and fame to its author, I did not appreciate as
much as I appreciated the earlier three. Secondly, I knew
Kenneth Grahame to be a collateral of a famous Scottish

family because I had heard some one say so when I was at an age to think (even with Byron, Shelley and Swinburne to give me the lie) that professionalism in letters was a surprising pursuit for a gentleman born. I am told that Kenneth Grahame secretly held this same silly opinion ; it is fortunate therefore that the Muses have been (if on occasions only) too strong for him. Thirdly, I knew him to be a banker as well as an author and almost as successfully. This had interested me because I am a banker myself. On these three knowledges, then, I went to work.

And, at once, it seemed to me that no man who does not lead a public life has, literarily speaking, a life at all. An advocate, a statesman, a jockey, a soldier (as Burnaby above), an actor, such careers are crowded with ' copy '. And this career that I was to record was the career of a man who was sufficient unto himself. It seemed therefore to be more ' lifeless ' than most men's lives are. For Kenneth Grahame never made intimate friendships with his fellows. Men and women with whom his lot was cast respected him deeply, admired him greatly, loved him dearly even—and never knew him at all.

And yet I do not think that he was other than a happy man. But he lived within himself—though, to such solitaries as he, perhaps, ' The Friend of the Children comes out of the wood '.

His letters, with rare exceptions, are few, formally expressed and without emotion. Some two hundred thousand words cover his entire literary output.

As a writer he was prominent in the two literary sensations of his youth, the *National Observer* and the *Yellow Book*, yet, as a personality, he seems to have been entirely dissimilar to, and aloof from, those who were, respectively, his colleagues and contemporaries on the one publication or the other.

I went to the men who knew him best and, for all their goodwill, I came away little wiser than I was. But, by each, I had an impression of Kenneth Grahame confirmed, the impression that his books had given me, that here was,

in reality, the most companionable of men. That here was
a jovial scholar, a man infinitely kindly, a man of sane
commonsense, a man just and generous. That here was a
lover of good wit and good wine, one fond of a song and
of jolly company. Yet one who rarely, rarely, showed
himself outside his inner reserves. Reserves which some
called shyness, some a titanic inertia and which were,
probably, an ambrosial blend of both mixed with much
of a philosophical and phlegmatic acceptance of life as he
found it better suited to a Buddha than to a banker with
a balance to strike or to an author with a tale to tell.
Here was a man who desired neither the literary fame,
which was his in abundance, nor wealth. A man, it seemed,
who, had he a duty to do, did it with all his might and,
the duty done, was content to rest. He did not ride forth
looking for further dragons. And finally, I had the impression that here was a man whom Fate had thwarted,
a man who recognized, although without complaint, even
with equanimity, that he had asked differently of Life than
those things which Life had bestowed. This then was how
I saw my subject.

And at first sight I said that here was little enough to
make a book of, and I remembered that Kenneth Grahame
had replied when asked to write his reminiscences : ' Reminiscences ? I have none.' The creative artist, said I, painter
or author, lives in the imaginary world which he creates
and whither none can follow him to know of it other than
what the artist's own works tell. And I remembered also
what Mr. Stevenson had written concerning the author
of that classic dog-story, *Rab and His Friends* :

> 'They ken your name, they ken your tyke,
> They ken the honey from your byke ;
> But mebbe, after a' your fyke,[1]
>   (The trüth to tell)
> It's just your honest Rab they like
> And no' yoursel'.'

---

[1] Trouble.

Now while this is true, it is not quite true. It is of course
the author's books that are loved beyond the author. But
the author's personality is of interest also. Otherwise inquisitive strangers would not pry and peep about the homes
of poet laureates and their likes. And the usual Peeping
Tom or Tomasina would be far more intrigued by seeing
Mr. Masefield, for instance (digging in his potato patch),
pause to lower a pot of ale than they would be to see him
march in a scarlet gown to receive an honorary degree.
To lesser folk the victuals and drink of an Olympian are
ever of interest. Moreover quails and manna are the most-
quoted, and best-remembered, incidents in Exodus. For it
is the smaller things and the homelier that endear. William
Shakespeare was fined for poaching (though as a matter of
fact the venison he brought home was from the common
ground of Fulbroke and *not* from the manor of Sir Thomas
Lucy at all), and for that bit of humanity the man in the
street feels the nearer to Will. King Alfred is surnamed
' The Great '. And all that ordinary men care to know
of him is that he let a baking of girdle-cakes burn. A
thing that Kenneth Grahame, who had (this book will
show it) a high appreciation of cakes and ale, would
never have done. Therefore it is possible that the many
readers of *The Wind in the Willows* want to see the man
who wrote it in his ordinary, everyday life. And that
they are prepared to find the life of interest because
Kenneth Grahame lived it. So the life has been written,
the picture made.

The man who writes the life of another is much in the
position of the man who paints another's portrait. And
in all portraits you will find, I think, more background
than picture. Backgrounds are commonplaces ;—lots of
air, a book or so, even a shelf of books, a bit of blue sea
through an open window, a far-away landscape of hill and
down and wood, a columned portico, maybe, but neither
the nobility nor the loveliness of the sitter would be possible without them. And in the written picture of a man,

unless he is such a man as may be sculpted rough-hewn out of the immense granite of his achievements, the maker of the picture must trust in the trivialities of his background to show his subject to its advantage. The difference between the painted background and the written one is that the painter may use his fancy to any suitable extent while the writer must abide by the unassuming fact.

When this book was written I showed it to an acquaintance of Kenneth Grahame. This one said of my background, 'You assume too much, there is fancy here as well as fact.' I said, 'I assume nothing without evidence ; here and there that evidence is circumstantial but, if circumstantial evidence can hang a man, it can equally hang his picture.'

I will give an instance. I mention a song-thrush in the first chapter. I had heard it said that Kenneth Grahame had been 'born to bird-song'. A sparrow on the house-top does not sing nor does a starling upon the chimney. And a thrush was always Kenneth Grahame's favourite singer. I will give another instance. I have said that the first of the *Pagan Papers* appeared in the *St. James's Gazette.* The note of acknowledgement, in the first edition, states that the paper called 'A Bohemian in Exile' appeared in that evening daily. And that the other papers had appeared in the *London Observer.* Kenneth Grahame states, in an interview, that when Henley had seen his work he wanted *all* of it for the *London Observer.* It may therefore be assumed, I say, that 'A Bohemian' was the first of the *Pagan Papers* and that it was published in the *St. James's Gazette.* I do not however (a 'life' is not a law court) state in my text what is there on circumstantial evidence and what on the evidence of letters or on the lovingly remembered words of those closest to him.

While, as I have said, there are no great matters in the days of Kenneth Grahame, I have been fortunate in finding much manuscript hitherto unpublished in book form or at all. Its publication now is alone sufficient to make this

book of interest and my own words, moreover, not un-
reasonably long.

A reader judging Kenneth Grahame both from his own
writing and from my recording will say : ' Here was one
who in spite of his warmth of heart and his love of laughter
and good fellowship must walk aloof from his brother men,
while they for their part see him somewhat as men see a
mountain which they approach for a whole summer day
nor ever, so it would appear, draw the closer to.' Gulliver,
in Lilliput, was, perhaps, thus regarded.

Kenneth Grahame recognized that *aloneness* was, and
must ever be, his portion. His earliest and most youthful
jottings are these words of Caxton, written down and
written down twice over. They refer to the boyhood of
our English Edmund, saint, bishop and confessor :

' he lefte their felawshyp and went allone into a meadowe
and under an hedge he sayd his devocions. And sodeynlye
there apperyed tofore him a fayr chylde in white clothynge
which sayde, " Hayle, felawe that goest allone ! " '

Hail then, and farewell.

KENNETH GRAHAME

CHAPTER I

THE HOUSE WITHOUT A NAME

MARCH of 1859 leapt on Edinburgh like a tiger. The weather was black-easterly and striped with furious 'on-dings' of snow. Dawn on the 8th, however, came blue, but still bitterly cold, and, at 6 a.m., day was already smudging out the gas-lamps in the long grey streets. Dr. James Simpson, ' The Beloved Professor ' (of chloroform fame), had been expecting the summons that brought him, in choker and sealskin surtout, from Queen Street to Castle Street in the half-light. His duty there was to bring into the world a Grahame of the House of Clavers, which duty he duly accomplished at eight o'clock. He then came down the stair, congratulated the tall master of the house, addressing him, friendly and familiar, as ' James Cunning-ham ', and having accepted a cup of hot tea, would be hurrying home to his breakfast and his busy day.

Yet he paused on the doorstep of No. 32 to say two things. The first was that the new-comer would, he wagered, weigh eight pounds ; a good guess, for, when the former was put to scale, he pulled the finger down at eight pounds and three-quarters. And the second (spoken as he, raising his collar against the wind, glanced upwards at the bare and sooty almond tree, that tossed in the yard-breadth of front ' plat ') was that blossom-time would not now be long in coming. For ' The Professor ' was an optimist. He went, the wind in his long grey hair and the sun throwing his square-built shadow with importance before him.

I

Upstairs the girl who lay in the four-poster, a befrilled
arm about her newest possession, looked up at the window.
Over the opposite roofs the sky was blue and silver; upon
the almond tree, whose topmost twigs could lightly tap
upon her pane, a thrush, from Prince's Street Gardens,
sat singing. The mother sleepily accepted the song as a
happy omen. And the babe, because of that singer perhaps, found in due time the thrush to be a more acceptable
minstrel than any other bird. This though his nature
was to make him gentle to all singers, and lover of all
songs. Years afterwards some one in his company was to
refer to some one else as 'a minor poet'. The young
Grahame looked up. 'What do you mean,' he said, 'by
a minor poet? There is surely no such thing.' He paused
and seemed to be considering the question. Then he said
definitely : ' No, there is no such thing.' Conclusively he
added, ' Who ever heard of a minor thrush ? '

So Kenneth Grahame was born in Edinburgh at 32 Castle
Street, on the morning of the 8th of March 1859. His
father, James Cunningham Grahame, an advocate in the
city of advocates, had woo'd in 1852 and married in 1853
(carrying her off from a baker's dozen of suitors) Miss
Bessie Ingles, daughter of John Ingles, of Hilton, Lasswade.
In a family noted for its personal appearances, lovely Bessie
Ingles was distinguished, in and about her home, as ' the
bonny one '. She gave the world four children, Helen,
Thomas William (who left it at the age of 16), Kenneth
and Roland.

James Grahame, at heart a poet, had not the push and
impertinence that makes the successful lawyer. He loved
what was old and pleasant and easy and he shrank from
the obtrusive both in business and in social life. But he
was a man greatly beloved and, in the Parliament House,
his witticisms were repeated with those of Mackenzie,
Outram and other boon companions and excellent lawyers
of old. He was a keen Scot and he was proud to entertain his friends at Castle Street with such national dishes

as ' crappit heads ', ' collops ' or ' howtowdie '. He entertained in the days when claret had replaced usquebaugh ;
and James Grahame's claret was notable in a town where,
and at a time when, men knew what claret ought to be.
And as a good citizen of Edinburgh, James Grahame was
proud to be living in the house that faced the house wherein
Sir Walter Scott, some twenty years earlier, was wont to
entertain a like company to a like fare.

James Grahame admonished his children that they should
picture to themselves, they flattening their noses' ends on
the dining-room window-pane, how the Laird of Abbots-
ford might have been seen to walk out upon the very
causey opposite to their own young eyes, the deer-hound,
Maida, leaping and baying about him and Marjorie Fleming, ' pet Marjorie ' herself, maybe cocking on the Laird's
broad shoulder. But before the third child, Kenneth, became of an age to flatten his nose and see, of Fancy, Marjorie,
Maida and the Wizard, James Grahame had ' flitted ', wife
and bairns and bag and baggage, from Castle Street and its
romantic associations.

In 1860, Argyllshire and the Campbell country seeking
a Sheriff Substitute to administer the Queen's laws within
their wide and wild borders, James Cunningham Grahame
was, in spite of all clan tradition, chosen for the post.

And thus Kenneth missed a boyhood in a City of Dreams,
of History and, in the Canongate of those days over which
Edinburgh exalted herself in bridges, the Horrors of Hell.
But until the end of his life the glamour of the house
opposite remained with him. Walter Scott was his literary
hero and *The Talisman* was the bedside-book that Kenneth Grahame laid down at last that he might go whither
the man who made it had gone just one hundred years
earlier, almost to a summer night. Walter Scott went
forth to the lapses of Tweed, Kenneth Grahame to the
lulling of old Thames.

Nevertheless Kenneth, the name was his at the Church
of St. Giles in June 1859, although his Edinburgh days

were brief days, was, is, the son of the aristocrat of cities,
and of a society where wit was better thought of than
wealth and where a great man is still, so I am told, esteemed
above a millionaire.

So the Grahames, in the May month of 1860, went to
pitch tent in the shadow of the Macallum Mohr,—James
Grahame, his young and lovely lady, and their three children.
There was a house in building for the Sheriff Substitute at
Inverary, but things moved slowly in the Duke's country
and the Grahames must wait the time of a Campbell contractor, for three years must they wait it, before their fine
new house was ready for them.

The family journeyed from Edinburgh to Glasgow by
rail. Long years afterwards, when Kenneth was interpreting childhood for childhood, an interested friend asked him
of his own young youth, inquiring what first he remembered of it ? He answered, ' Shiny black buttons, buttons
that dug into dusty, blue cloth.' Thus was a first-class
railway carriage, from ' The Caly ' station through to
Buchanan Street, recollected. His recollections of a drive
in a four-wheel cab, with straw on the floor of it, were not
so vivid, but he surely recalled, he said, a blunt-nosed,
fussy little paddle-boat that, *chuff-chuffing*, took the travellers fussily to Ardrishaig. And at Ardrishaig he and his
abode for three years while still, at Inverary, the Campbell contractor put one leisurely grey stone a-top of another.

At Ardrishaig there was much to make a little boy a
lover of boats and of the little water creatures that run in
the sea-pools and among the brown kelp that goes popping
so finely under a small foot. For at Ardrishaig the boats,
and the bearded men in blue jerseys, went in and out to
the fishing, the grey gulls cried and wheeled, and bare-
headed lassies, their hard faces as brown as their own
brown creels, sat at home, like Penelopes, for ever thread-
ing lug-worms and mussels on to bait-hooks.

There was a smell of tar and fish and green sea water.
There were masts and brown sails, wild ' gleamy ' sunshine

and continual rags of warm rain. Enough to make any
boy wistful of boats. And that wistfulness was with the
boy Kenneth till the end. Even the peaceful river-craft
of peaceful Thames had their fascination. To his last
summer evening he would walk, a kenspeckle figure, the
lesser holiday folk head-turning to see him, and sit awhile
watching the argosies that come and go at Whitchurch.
And there, not a week before he must leave his friend,
Father Thames, to lip over the lasher without him, a young
lady, of whom he was also the friend, found him and sitting
by him in silence presently said half to herself:

> ' I remember the black wharves and the ships
>   And the sea-tides tossing free;
>   And the Spanish sailors with bearded lips,
>   And the beauty and mystery of the ships
>   And the magic . . .'

' Why, yes,' said the man who was still the boy, ' I first
heard that, it must have been hot from the workshop, in
—oh, bother the date—but my father cried it aloud to
us in a very suitable place of brown sails, blue water
and Highlanders, just for the sake of that " magic of the
sea ".'

' And that would probably have been at Ardrishaig,'
said I, when these words of his were told to me.

At Ardrishaig a boy went to bed and heard, just at the
nid-nodding, the romantic whistle of the newfangled steamers
that blew up their horns of Elfland and, to the same enchanted note, he might wake of a morning and run to the
window and see. There was but one road in Ardrishaig.
Yet at either end of it interest awaited Youth and the joy
of life. If you went east the road you might pick the
very ' green rushes O ' that the poet has sung of. If you
went west the road you came to the cockatoo who sat
outside Mrs. Jenkins's, and finally, the cockatoo calling
after you, you came to the pier and the shop where par-
liament-for-tea was sold (a delicious, sticky, golden-brown
gingerbread) ; ' conversation sweeties ' also.

There was the ' mussle rock ' where the fishermen howked the blue-black, limpetty shells for the fishing, for the fingers of the hook-baiting lassies ' up by '. There was Rory MacGilp with the blue jersey, the bluer eyes and the very brown face. Rory it was who gave the two little boys, Willie and Kenneth, two little boats ' like birds on the wing '. These boats Rory had christened respectively, *The Ocean's Bride* and *The Canty Quean*. By precedence of days Willie claimed, the more poetically called, *Ocean Bride*. But Kenneth's *Canty Quean* was a right good ship until she ' cowpit ' and went, on her beam ends, away east on the flood. A black day indeed. But at Ardrishaig, and afterwards, there were dogs to be consolers. There were ' Bhodach ' and ' Chaillach ', the two varmint Cairns from Colonsay, a gift of the lineal descendant of

> . . . Colonsay's fierce lord
> Who pressed the chase with gory sword—

the lord who presently died in so fascinating and suitable a manner. Were not, then, Bhodach and Chaillach, direct links with Bannockburn and the Bruce, dogs to be proud of ?

And thus at Ardrishaig the months moved on until, wearying of a life in temporary lodgings, James Grahame, in May 1863, ' flitted ' his family to Inverary where he might, at long last, superintend the final touches to the new home. And now that it was finished he must admit that the Campbells had made a good job of it. They had omitted nothing except a name and this omission James Grahame readily forgave, taking pleasure in devising lovely titles under which the new home would duly get its warming. He would quote thereon his father's friend, George Outram, Edinburgh advocate and afterwards Editor of the *Glasgow Herald* :

> ' Is the house warm yet ? Is the house warm yet ?
> It aye becomes the cosier the longer that we sit ;
> An' though it's like an oven we will never steer a fit
> Though we ask at ane anither—Is the house warm yet ? '

THE GRAHAME CHILDREN
AND THEIR FATHER
KENNETH SEATED

ELIZABETH GRAHAME
MOTHER OF KENNETH

By right of birth and of official position the Grahames were accepted without question by a county society which valued itself above rubies. Bessie Grahame, writing to ' My dear Mamma ' on the 2nd October 1863, mentions (a casual allusion) that she and her husband had dined the other evening ' at the Castle '. The ducal condescension that, by dinner invitation, endorsed her, that set local seal upon her social status, is accepted as the matter of no importance. Mrs. Grahame mentions her fellow guests, ' a lot of county people, the Malcolms, the MacNeils '. Among them is ' a nice Lady Emma, the Duke's sister ', and ' a Mr. Arthur ' who, because he was ' very quiet ', she supposes to be in holy orders. She has however a complete success with Lord ' Lorn ' not because of her own bright eyes but because, she modestly concludes, he learns that she is the sister of her brother David. And young Lord Lorne is ' very enthusiastic about David's boating achievements ' and is thrilled to know that Mrs. Grahame is sister to the Ingles he so admires at Eton. (David Ingles was in the Eton Eight and a mere marquis was less than the dust under David's rowing-shoes.) Bessie Grahame moreover tells her Mamma that the young ladies at the Castle ' are not yet of a flirtable age ' and that one of them ' wears brown stockings '. And that, next day, she took ' Nelly ' (doubtless her own little daughter Helen) up to the Castle to see the ' little girls '. But, ' of course they never spoke to each other '. The Duchess however promises that she would order her gardener ' to help with the flower beds at the new house '. So the call was not entirely a vain civility. And ' the new grates are coming in and Mr. Cleghorn has brought me such a pretty present from Germany for the house— an inkstand of black marble and bronze, also two candlesticks of the same '. But, alas, the white broom that came from Hilton (Bessie's birthplace) is dead, but, on the other hand, the Hilton roses, which were cut down as dead too, ' have all sprouted again '. A nice chatty letter this such as young ladies to-day have lost the art of.

Those who knew her said that Bessie Grahame's laugh was one of her chiefest charms. She laughed joyously and made no secret of it. Mr. Saxmundham, in *The Diary of a Sportsman*, has told of a summer dinner-party at ' the Castle '. In ' bustles ', whiskers and the austere light of day the guests stood, with ceremony arrayed, in the drawing-room waiting a delayed announcement of dinner. There came a scamper of feet in the corridor (obviously not those of the butler) and there entered, with a door-bang and a pattering rush, a small and dishevelled child who squealed, in a passion of temper and tears, ' Mamma, Mamma, forbid Henrietta to feed my rabbits with green food, she'll give them (the squeal climbed the scale to *crescendo* and tailed out into a shrill and long-drawn agony) *pot-bell-ee-e.*' There was a shocked silence. Then Bessie Grahame laughed, ringing-clear and joyful and as like ' an irreverent angel ' as the diarist can imagine. But he does not say what ' Mamma ' did about the rabbits.

Bessie Grahame's new home, the home, clearly, so much in her mind, was a big granite house, swept about by green lawns, bright borders of posies, and ' weel happit ' at the back of it, by fine trees. For the Campbells are the true tree-lovers and larch, spruce, silver-fir and pine, they tell you, will come at a crying of ' Cruachan '.[1] From his night-nursery window, in this intriguing new house, a little boy might see the sugar-loaf of Duniquoich, a high hill clouded upon, bottom to top, with the true and evergreen pine. And to front the day-nursery windows was blue Loch Fyne where the porpoises play and the hunting terns and herring-gulls stoop, the day long, *cloop*, at the herring. But better than the splashing gulls and the blue water were the red squirrels that scampered and scraped and, sitting up, sometimes six at a time, made the lawn a very kingdom of Puck.

But, early in 1864, tragedy came to the house without a name. Bessie Grahame took scarlet fever and presently

[1] The rallying-cry of the clan Campbell.

the fever took her and she was gone, slipping out on the west wind of a mild spring day. ' It's all been lovely,' she whispered, like a child home from a party.

And the day she went, Kenneth was down with a similar sickness. He beat it, but only by a hair's breadth. His father and his grandmother, in the frantic futility of the distracted, heaped his cot with toys. Yet the child, already in the borderland, seemed to see and, responding to the call of childhood, wavered on his further way and finally turned back to life, to Life the Toyshop. To a world where *on s'amuse*. Or, in Kenneth's case, to a world where one entertains other people.

But, with Bessie Grahame, went the day of the house without a name. The Grahame children were taken south to live with their grandmother who had left Midlothian for the middle Thames. Mrs. Ingles lived at The Mount, Cookham Dene. Little boys are fickle but, at Cookham, Kenneth gave his heart for all time to the river. But next summer the children went to Scotland, paying their father a long visit and returning, leisurely to Cookham, a year later.

On the way south, Stirling was visited. Among the attractions of Stirling was a toy-shop. In the window was a large bounce-y ball of many colours. During the days of the Grahames' visit to Stirling that ball became the very moon to Kenneth. On any whither he would go by way of the window. One day a kindly relative, of his careless good nature, led the children within and bid them buy each a plaything. Kenneth's choice was no choice at all, it was natural selection. But the relative, now he came to think of it, considered that a large bounce-y ball in a small room, in a railway carriage. . . . He pointed out the beauties of bricks and even of Mr. Noah. He offered this, he urged that. ' Would you not like——? ' ' Oh, look, isn't *this* nice, Kenneth ? ' Kenneth gnawed the elastic of his Glengarry bonnet and remained adamant. The old lady who kept the shop, seeing how matters lay, coaxed diplomatically with,

' See here, sir,' and ' It's a bonny horsie this, is it no ? '
Kenneth hardly heard her. At length the elder person
acknowledged defeat. He nodded to the old lady who
' raxed ' down the big bounce-y ball. She happ't it up in
' a bit paper '. She handed it to Kenneth saying as she
did so, ' I shall always honour you, sir, because you've a
mind o' your own.'

And Kenneth remembered and he, among many compliments, appreciated this one all his life.

And so south again to Cookham Dene and the summer
Thames. At The Mount there was a big bare-empty room.
It was known, for no remembered reason, as the Gallery.
It became the children's room, a Land of Youth. Within
it was a world welded entirely to the heart's desire. In that
world, I am told, was ' an imaginary City '. Who shall
doubt that its walls were of jasper and that the glamour of
it was to build the Golden Town at the end of the Knights'
Road ?   That its unforgettable pageantry was, afterwards,
to awake anew the Boys of Heaven, their ' tiny red caps
upon their thick curls ' to walk in gay, in cobbled streets,
for ever beneath a fleckless blue ?

The City was meantime kept strictly, in the Gallery.
Except on Sunday. On Sunday it became mentionable
beyond the Gallery door, but only upon the way to church,
but only if out of earshot of elder persons. Then, on the
dusty churchward mile, the previous week passed under
close review, then all mortals encountered, Sunday to
Saturday, in a world of workaday, were weighed in the
balance. Those found worthy were forthwith proposed and
elected freemen of the City. Those found wanting—was
there not a savage pleasure, in excluding them, in hearing
the golden barriers clash to and those without a prey to all
regrets ?

But the Gallery had many mansions, had room for swifter
moving, more mundane things, things closer to hand than
the rose-tinted towers of the City. In the Gallery were
read, elbows down on bare boards, Sir Samuel Baker on the

sources of the Nile, and Mr. Ballantyne's *Dog Crusoe and
His Master*. The Nile, though no rival to the Thames, yet
was inspiring in the art of whip-making, the sort of whip
wherewith the faltering Bisharin is urged on through the
sandstorm. And *Crusoe*, though no patch on Don, the
curly-coat retriever, yet served as an introducer to the
lassoing and ' creasing ' of mustangs, to the thunderous
stampede of the bison, to the wigwam and the war-path.

And the wigwams of the Grahames were again to be
folded ; for presently the family must move to Cranborne
in the pinewoods of Windsor. Granny Ingles (she was
affectionately called so) made a home there not only for her
grandchildren but for her bachelor son who had been
appointed to a curacy at Cranborne. For Bessie Grahame
gone, James Grahame saw but little of his young family.
He allowed his loss to crush him. He resigned his office in
Argyllshire to live abroad and there bide his own time.
But it was not for another twenty years that Time took
him.

Meanwhile, at Cranborne, Kenneth became the pupil and
friend of Cranborne's scholarly vicar. There is a portrait,
an impression perhaps is the better word, of the latter, in
The Golden Age. He ' brandishes an aorist ' over his pupil's
head and gives him tea in the garden.

In those schoolroom days Kenneth Grahame was a little
boy of a grave and kindly courtesy, a courtesy beyond his
years. He hated to give unnecessary trouble and to that
end he was mindful to leave his bedroom tidy and to be as
reasonable about his clothes and their neatness as could
be expected. A contemporary letter says that ' Kenneth
is punctilious about brushing his teeth '. Another letter
says that ' Kenneth is a reasonable boy in everything
except his unbounded generosity '. His grandmother's
servants adored him. And it was at Cranborne, so writes
his sister, that Kenneth ' began to spout poetry, first
Shakespeare, then Macaulay's Lays, then Tennyson '. The
vicar, it seems, had been fortunate in the ground he sowed

and sound in the rotation of his crops.   Kenneth is remembered as marching through the *sough* of a pine-wood shouting down the voices of wood and wind with :

> ' But hark, the cry is Auster
> And lo, the ranks divide
> And the great lord of Luna
> Comes with his stately stride—'

One may fancy him, the ' fourfold shield ' clanging upon ' ample shoulders ' until it should please the wearer to discard it and recall, familiar to his mouth, ' Harry the King, Bedford and Exeter ' or ' Blow, bugle blow, set the wide echoes flying.'

And, at Cranborne, Kenneth being now nearly ten years old, it was decided that he must go to boarding-school.   We may imagine, I think, that he accepted the situation as an *Edward,* as an optimist.

CHAPTER II

' TEDDY'S '

KENNETH entered St. Edward's School, Oxford, in 1868. He was not ten years old and he and St. Edward's began life almost together. He was among the first fifty of the Saint's *alumni* and the school stood, when Kenneth came to it a new boy, in New-Inn-Hall Street. Shortly afterwards ' Teddy's ' was in occupation of the earlier of those fine buildings, in the Woodstock Road, where it has since flourished so exceedingly. Kenneth was one of a handful; to-day over three hundred boys answer the roll-call. St. Edward's, each summer of nowadays, sends an ' eight ' to Henley and in sport and scholarship she can bear comparison with any or all of the foundations.

Kenneth was an ' Edwardian ' until 1875. He became head of the school, he became captain of the Rugby XV, he was in the eleven. With his love of boats and of blue-ruffled Thames water he must have regretted that, in 1870, say, no ' eight ' existed for him to stroke to victory. In after years, recounting his school triumphs, he was careful, so he said, to mention ' fact without frivolous detail '. If pressed as to the frivolity he would reply that he referred to the ' almost Hobsonian ' poverty of choice, to which, doubt-less (said he), was owing his youthful laurels and wild-parsleys.

One of Kenneth's few ' Edwardian ' contemporaries remembers ' Grahame ', in his later schooldays, as a tall, good-looking lad, a dandy in his dress, and nobly simple in his choice of a phrase. When asked by a friend how he intended to be attired on the morrow—' " Gaudy " Day '— he replied, it is remembered, with a splendid simplicity, ' To-morrow I shall be superb.'

13

As a schoolboy Kenneth had the same gifts of wit and repartee which made him, in later life and when in the, all too rare, mood, so brilliant a host, so diamond a guest and so spritely-dangerous an opponent in argument. I have a picture of Kenneth in debate. He is a hobbledehoy with a cracking voice. He creaks rather than speaks, but, as usual, to the point. A school Debating Society discuss whether ' this house is justified in a belief in ghosts '. A visiting undergraduate, with a hyphened name the second syllable of which is Blood, has opened the debate in a windy and long-sustained justification of credulity. At length he sits down. But, or ever the leader of the opposition is up in answer, young Grahame, on the back benches, is upon his legs. ' Mr. President, sir,' he squeaks, ' ghosts may not have flesh and bones on their side—they at least have Blood.'

And one more youthful *mot*, a holiday one, is remembered. Some dull family friends, kindly folk who, of their garden's plenty, gave surplus vegetables to their neighbours, were on the agenda. ' They have their points,' declared some one at the dinner-table. ' Have they ? ' said Kenneth doubt-fully. ' Well, dear,' he was told, ' they gave us this excellent asparagus.' ' *Pointes d'asperges*,' Kenneth is said to have retorted as he helped himself.

But I have in his own handwriting, a story of his very early schooldays whereto are joined certain reflections, com-forting to a boy who is habitually at the bottom of a form. I quote from a speech prepared, doubtless, for some occasion of prize-giving.

' . . . . I cannot help noticing that when a distinguished general, a famous statesman, or other deservedly successful and popular personage, honours a school by consenting to give away the Prizes, he is fond of informing his admiring audience that he, for his part, strange to say, never reached any giddy pre-eminence in his school lists, was rather an idle dog than otherwise, and ranked very low in the opinion of all the masters. " And look at me now ! " he seems to

say, though of course he does not use those actual words.
For my part, I have always thought this mental attitude
of the Distinguished Person not exactly a prudent one, to
put it mildly.   Dr. Johnson, who was a very sensible man,
says somewhere or other—at least I think it was Dr. Johnson
—that a man should never tell a story, however witty and
amusing it may be, of which the point, the ultimate point,
is against himself.   Because, he adds shrewdly, though
people may be greatly amused, and laugh heartily, at the
time, yet—yet—they *remember it against you*.   Now, how
would it be, just as an experiment, next time such a person
addresses you on those lines, telling you perhaps that, for
his part, he never rose beyond the Lower Third, you were
to remark blandly, " Why, of course not ! " or " What about
it ?   Where did you expect to be ? " or words to that effect.
This would not exactly please the general or statesman, of
course, in fact it would probably annoy him very much.
But what of that ?   You are not there to amuse him.   It's
his business to amuse you—if he can.   And it might do him
good.

   ' Those of you who are determined to become great
generals or statesmen, by the sheer process of remaining
doggedly in the Junior Second, should pause and remember
that we cannot all be great statesmen or generals.   There
aren't enough of such jobs to go round.   Turn your thoughts
elsewhere.   There is many a hard-working, honest—at least
fairly honest—millionaire, many a fashionable physician,
prominent barrister, or successful dramatist, who is only
waiting to resign his position to you as soon as you have
gently but firmly signified your intention of occupying it.
And of course the first question he will ask you will be,
whether you ever succeeded in getting out of the Fourth
Form.   Moreover, strange as it may seem, it is not so easy
as you may think for the most ambitious youth to attain
his ends by sticking to the bottom of the form.   Let me
give you a little reminiscence of my own, which dates from
the first few days of my arrival at this school—the old school,

3

I mean, of New-Inn-Hall Street days. The Junior form, or class, was in session, so to speak, and I was modestly occupying that position, at the very bottom, which seemed to me natural enough, when the then Headmaster entered— a man who had somehow formed an erroneous idea of my possibilities. Catching sight of me, he asked sternly, " What's that thing doing down there ? " The master in charge could only reply that whether it was crass ignorance or invincible stupidity, he wotted not, but there it was. The Headmaster, who was, I was persuaded, a most illogical man, and could not really have studied that immortal work, the *Republic of Plato*, in which the principles of ideal Justice are patiently sought out, merely remarked that if the thing —meaning me—was not up there or near it, pointing to the head of the form, before the close of work, it was to be severely caned ; and left the room.

' Well, you can imagine my feelings. I was a very little chap—not yet ten. I was not accustomed to be caned— that is, beaten. I never had been beaten. I had been doing my best, and at home I had not been considered an absolute fool. And there I was, up against it in the fullest sense of the word ! It was not surprising, perhaps, that I shed some bitter tears. But what happened ? No one of my colleagues started forth, as I half expected, to champion the cause of youth and innocence. Instead, they all proceeded to display an ignorance and a stupidity, on even the simplest matters, which seemed unnatural, even for them. The consequence was, that I presently found myself, automatically it really seemed, soaring, soaring—till I stood, dazed and giddy, at the top of the form itself, and was kept there till my friendly colleagues thought the peril was safely past, when I was allowed to descend from that bad eminence to which merit had certainly not raised me. It was from that moment, I think, that I first began to realize that I was never very likely to become either a successful general or a leading statesman.

' You see therefore that the path to success is not easy,

'I WAS A VERY LITTLE CHAP'

even by a steady neglect of the educational side of school
life. Some of you may therefore say, " I will try other
methods. Hang it all, why shouldn't I try and get into
the Sixth ! " Well, it is a great thing to have arrived at
the Sixth, even if you are unable to maintain your position
there for as much as a whole term. But you must remember,
that the Sixth are very great men. To hope to reach the
giddy height of the Sixth is like wanting to begin life as a
Cabinet Minister. No, it might be more prudent to have
a modest aim—say about the middle of the Fourth. The
advantage of that is, that nobody will be jealous of you,
and as people will think you more stupid even than you
really are, they will always be ready to lend you a helping
hand. Let us suppose, then, that Jones, as we will call
him, goes forth into the world from the giddy eminence of
the Lower Fourth. He looks round for somebody to give
him a leg up, and he sees Smith, whom he remembers in
the Sixth, and who, of course, by now holds some distinguished position. He writes to Smith. Smith says,
condescendingly, " Ah yes, Jones ! I remember him well.
Such a good fellow, Jones. Not a genius, of course, like
some fellows. Poor Jones ! We must give him a leg up."
He does so, and in due course Jones finds himself occupying
a position not very inferior to that of Smith. And soon,
by giving his mind to it, Jones succeeds in doing Smith
out of his job, and wangling it for himself. That is one
way of doing it, almost as good as the general's way of
dodging education altogether.

' But I perceive by the pained expression on the Headmaster's countenance that I am becoming rather—shall we
say—morbid. I am talking the sort of stuff that during
the War was called, I think, Defeatism. So I will now ask
you to try and forget everything I have said as speedily
as possible. . . .'

Fortunate also is it that there exists a Kenneth Grahame
paper, ' Oxford through a Boy's Eyes,' which appeared
posthumously in *Country Life*. Follows here the MS. (it

differs slightly from the printed word) of this happy article, this picture of Oxford, and of a school, of sixty years ago. And the reader will observe how the last paragraph bears out the Brummel of 1874—' to-morrow I shall be superb '. For the boy was father to the man and Kenneth Grahame, by physical advantage and personal preference, was always a credit to his tailor.

' The main difficulty that confronts me in setting down these random recollections of a now very distant past is to avoid the excursions, the tempting bypaths, that start into sight and appeal to me at every step of my progress. For instance, I tried to begin in brisk and strictly historical fashion by stating that on or about Michaelmas Day, 1868, a bright and eager (sullen, reluctant, very ordinary-looking) youth of nine summers sprang lightly (descended reluctantly, was hauled ignominiously) on to the arrival platform of the Great Western Railway Station at Oxford ; and at once I was arrested by those magic words Railway Station.

' Can anything be more eternally immutable than Oxford Station ? Paris, Berlin, Vienna, have built, and re-built, and built again, their monumental stations. Hundreds of feet below the surface of London, stations have sporadically spread after the manner of mushroom spawn. I have even lived to see Waterloo Station re-constructed and re-built. But Oxford Station never varies, and to-day is exactly as it flashed upon my eager vision in '68. That it has been re-painted since then I know, for I was once staying in Oxford when this happened, and used to go specially to gaze at the man told off for the job, and admire his deliberate brushwork and the lingering care with which he would add a touch and then step back to admire it. But even then, when he had at last done, the station looked exactly as before.

' What a tribute this is to the station itself and its designer ! Had there been anything needed to achieve perfection, this, of course, would have been added long ago. But nothing has ever been added, so nothing can have been

needed, and Oxford Station, in its static perfection, will be
there to greet him as now, when the proverbial stranger
comes to gaze on the ruins of Christ Church from a broken
arch of Folly Bridge.

' But we must be getting on. Our hero then, still under
the feminine control he was about to quit for the first time,
was propelled into—what ?—why, a fly, of course, for there
was nothing else to be propelled into or by. All England
at that period lay fly-blown under the sky, and flies crawled
over its whole surface. Whatever station you arrived at, a
fly crawled up to you and then crawled off with you.
Oxford's flies were no worse than other people's—a fly must
not be confused with a growler or four-wheeler, though of
course it had four wheels all right—flies were solid and roomy
and had often seen better days in private service. Some
years later, however, there descended on Oxford an extra-
ordinarily shabby collection of what must have been the
worst and oldest hansoms ever seen. What town had
scrapped and passed them on to us I never knew. It could
not have been London, because the beautiful " Shrewsbury-
Talbot " type, which revolutionized the London streets,
had not yet been designed. Aeons passed, however, and
these unspeakable survivals crumbled into dust, such fragments as archaeologists could preserve being deposited in
the Ashmolean alongside the dodo and Guy Fawkes's
lantern ; and, at last, to make amends, Heaven sent Oxford
hansoms that were clean, smart and pleasant to look on ;
cane or straw-coloured, upholstered in light grey, suggesting
jinrickshas, skiffs, anything both swift and cheerful to look
at : and these endured until historic times—until, in fact,
the advent of the all-devouring taxi.

' But this will never do. We haven't even started. On,
then, my noble steed (a Tartar of the Ukraine breed !).
Past the castellated County Buildings, which a young friend
of mine once, being up for the first time and bound for the
House, mistook for Christ Church and insisted on being
deposited there ; past (on the other side) the ugly and quite

uninteresting church of St. Something-Le-Baily, long ago
swept away and replaced by a little public garden : a sharp
turn to the left, and New-Inn-Hall Street burst on the
enraptured view.

' People who gaze on New-Inn-Hall Street as it now is
must not imagine that things were always just so. On the
left, or west side, first you had the buildings composing the
Hall itself, the " Tavern " of Verdant Green's days, where
the buttery was open all day ; then, the grounds and solid
Georgian vicarage of St. Something-Le-Baily aforesaid—a
pleasant jumble. On the right or east side were little two-
storeyed white gabled houses, of the sort common enough
in Oxford then, and of which a few specimens still remain,
running up to the old, fifteenth-century, back gate of Frewen
Hall. Then came St. Edward's, a stone-built mansion of
two storeys, reaching to the end and then " returned ", as
architects say, for its own depth and a trifle over. While
the " flyman " is being paid, let us briefly polish off the
rest of New-Inn-Hall Street.

' There was no opening through into George Street then.
The street turned at a right angle and ran right up to the
" Corn ", this " leg " being now christened St. Michael's
Street. Lodging-houses, and a few private residences, one
of which was soon to be taken over by the School for Headmaster's quarters, Oratory, and a bedroom or two, made up
the rest of it. Altogether a pleasant, quiet street, central
and yet secluded.

' Mr. Simeon once told me that he could never find out
anything about the house's previous history. Although
Oxford climate and Oxford stone had worked together to
give it the characteristic of all Oxford stone-built houses
older than a certain date, I fancy it must have been a little
late for the antiquarian. Quite roughly I should date it
about Queen Anne. One entered by a pleasant low, wide
hall, recessed to one side, on which lay the then Headmaster's
sitting-room, soon to become a senior classroom. To the
right, one passed through a low but well-lighted eastward-

facing room used as a dining-room and supplied with trestle tables, at the head of each of which, during meals, sat a " Big Boy " (there was no " Sixth " in those troglodytic days). We neophytes were always placed next to one of these great men, the idea being that they would watch over our table manners and deportment—" the juniors, Mr. Weller, is so very savage "—and the theory seems a sound one, always supposing that the Big Boy has any manners himself.

' Through the dining-room again, and completing the building in that direction, lay the School Room, a handsome room of some style, running up the full height of the building to a coved ceiling, such ornamentation as it had being classical and " period ". I suggest that it may have been of rather later date than the rest, and that the designer may have had in mind a music-room. But this, of course, is mere conjecture. Here were desks, allotted to our private ownership, and it also served as a general playroom when we were " confined to barracks ". And hence one emerged, by swing doors, into the playground.

' This must have been, at one time, a pleasant garden, running north for the whole length of the house and bordered, eastwards, by the wall of its neighbour, Frewen Hall. Perhaps there were trees in it then, and there still remained, in the receding " waist " of the house, under the dining-room window, some scanty flower-beds, where the horticulturally minded were allowed, and even encouraged, to employ their grovelling instincts. The rest was gravel, with one or two gymnastic appliances. Northwards from the entrance hall, one master's room (I think), the staircase, and then kitchen, pantry, and other offices ; rambling, stone-flagged, in the ancient manner. Some sort of stable, or garden, gateway gave issue on the street northwards ; but this was never used, and I only happen to remember it because on my first Guy Fawkes Day we boys attempted a private bonfire, thinking, in our artless way, that in Oxford bonfires were the rule rather than the exception. The authorities, how-

ever, thought otherwise, and firemen and police battered at
the stable gate aforesaid till explanations ensued and till,
I suppose, somebody was squared as usual.

'Upstairs, I recall little. It was rabbit-warrenish, and
we were distributed in bedrooms, five or six or thereabouts
apiece. There was also a master's sitting-room, a cheerful
bow-windowed room, overlooking the playground. Thither
I was shortly summoned, and met a round and rosy young
man with side-whiskers, who desired, he said, to record my
full name for some base purpose of his own. When he had
got it he tittered girlishly, and murmured, " What a *funny*
name ! " His own name was—but there ! I think I won't
say what his own name was. I merely mention this little
incident to show the sort of stuff we bright lads of the late
'sixties sometimes found ourselves up against.

'The canings came along in due time. But after I had
seen my comrades licked, or many of them, the edge of my
anticipation was somewhat dulled.

'We used to play cricket under difficulties on Port Meadow
(this must have been in the following year). The sole
advantage of Port Meadow as a cricket pitch was the absence
of boundaries. If an ambitious and powerful slogger
wanted to hit a ball as far as Wolvercote, he could do so if
he liked ; there was nothing to stop him, and the runs would
be faithfully run out. The chief drawback was that the
city burgesses used the meadow for pasturage of their cows
—graminivorus animals of casual habits. When fielding
was " deep ", and frenzied cries of " Throw her up ! "
reached one from the wicket, it was usually more discreet to
feign a twisted ankle or a sudden faintness, and allow some
keener enthusiast to recover the ball from where it lay.

'But this expeditionary sort of big-game hunting ceased,
so far as cricket was concerned, when we got the use of the
White House cricket ground, since devoted to the baser uses
of " Socker " on half-holidays. This was a satisfactory and
well-kept little ground, and I never remember any complaints about it. How football fared I entirely forget.

' Now for what I may call our extra-mural life, apart from games. During lawful hours we were free to wander where we liked, and it was my chief pleasure to escape at once and foot it here and there, exploring, exploring, always exploring, in a world I had not known the like of before. And when I speak of footing it, I am reminded that pious pilgrims now visit Merton Street to gaze on the only survival of the cobblestone or kidney paving of medievalism ; but in the time I speak of, most of the Oxford streets were as cobbled as Merton. The High, to be sure, was macadam, and no trams yet squealed their way down its length to a widened Magdalen Bridge. But the Broad was all cobble, so, I fancy, was St. Giles, and most of the lesser streets, including Brasenose Lane.

' Why I drag in Brasenose Lane, like Velazquez, at this particular point, is that I have reason to remember its cobbles well. We loved to pass with beating hearts along that gloomy *couloir*, pause on its protuberant cobbles, and point out to each other the precise window behind which, on that fatal Sunday night, the members of the Hell Fire Club (Oxford Branch) were holding their unhallowed orgies when the blackest sinner of the crew expired on the floor in strong convulsions, while, outside, a strayed reveller was witness of the Devil himself, horned and hoofed and of portentous stature, extracting the wretched man's soul slowly through the bars, as a seaside tripper might extract a winkle from its shell with a pin. There was always a thrill waiting for you in that little street ; and though much of its terror has passed away, especially since they asphalted it, I should not much like, even at this day, to pass along Brasenose Lane at midnight.

' I said just now that we were free to wander where we liked ; but there were " bounds ", mystic but definite, and these we must never overstep—first, first because it was so easy for us to be spotted in our school caps, and secondly, because we didn't want to. These bounds chiefly excluded districts like St. Ebbes, St. Thomas's (except for church), the Cattle Market, Jericho, and their like, and there was little temptation to go exploring in such quarters. One result, however, of these bounds has been, in my own case, slightly comical. Though before I was ten I knew all the stately buildings that clustered round the Radcliffe Library like my own pocket, as the French say, it was only in comparatively recent times that I even set eyes on Paradise Square or looked upon the Blue Pig in Gloucester Green. And even as I write these words I hear rumours that the Blue Pig, like so much that is gone or going, is threatened with demolition. This seems to be a case for one of our modern poets to speak the word and avert the doom. Browning once wrote a poem which (he said) was to save the Paris Morgue from a similar fate—though I don't think he succeeded in doing so. Please, Mr. Masefield of Boar's Hill, will you not save our Blue Pig?

' Two things struck me forcibly when I began my explorations. The first was the exceeding blackness of the University buildings, which really seemed to my childish mind as if it was intentional, and might have been put on with a brush, in a laudable attempt to produce the " subfusc " hue required in the attire of its pupils. Of course, one must remember that in those days there was not so much of the architectural " spit and polish " that now goes on during the Long. A man could then go down in June with the assurance that he would find much the same Oxford awaiting him when he returned in the autumn. Now it is otherwise, though the climate sees to it that, in a term or two, things are much as before.

' Perhaps the things most remarkable at that time for their exceeding nigritude and decay were the Sheldonian Caesars. Those who now pause to study their (comparatively) clean-cut features can form little idea of the lumps of black fungoid growth they once resembled. It is the original Caesars I am referring to, of course—not the last set—a comparatively fresh and good-looking lot. In the closing words of " A Soul's Tragedy " the speaker observes :

" I have known *four* and twenty leaders of revolution."
Well, I have known *three* sets of Sheldonian Caesars : and
perhaps, with luck, I shall yet know a fourth.

' The Sheldonian should really be more careful of its
Caesars. It uses them up so fast—almost as fast as old
Rome herself did. There must be some special reason for
it. Perhaps it is the English pronunciation of the Latin in
which the Public Orations are delivered. No patriotic and
self-respecting Caesars could be expected to stand that—
and they don't. They flake, they peel, they wilt, in dumb
protest. Or can it be the Latin itself ? But no, that would
be unthinkable.

' The other most abiding impression that I then received
was from the barred windows, the massive, bolted and
enormous gates, which every college had, which were never
used or opened, and which gave these otherwise hospitable
residences the air of Houses of Correction. The window-
bars, of course, were not the chief puzzle. The Mid-Victorian
young were dangerous animals, only existing on sufferance,
and kept as far as possible behind bars, where one need not
be always sending to see what baby is doing and tell him
not to. The porter's lodge system also has much to say
for itself. But those great and lofty double gates, sternly
barred and never open invitingly, what could they portend ?
I wondered. It was only slowly and much later that I began
to understand that they were strictly emblematical and
intended to convey a lesson. Among the blend of qualities
that go to make up the charm of collegiate life, there was
then more than a touch of (shall I say ?) exclusiveness and
arrogance. No one thought the worse of it on that account :
still its presence was felt, and the gates stood to typify it.
Of course, one would not dream of suggesting that the
arrogance may still be there. But the gates remain.

' As to the exclusiveness, I have nothing to complain of
personally. The only things I wanted to get at were certain
gardens, and I never remember being refused entry, though
this might very well have happened to a small boy, always

such an object of suspicion. It was really better than at home, where, of course, one had friends with beautiful gardens, but they usually meant formal calls and company manners, and perhaps tedious talk of delphiniums and green fly and such. Here, one strolled in when one was in the mood, and strolled out when one had had enough, and no one took the slightest notice of you. It was an abiding pleasure, and to those who made it possible for me I here tender, *ex voto*, my belated thanks.

' After the colleges came urban joys, and specially the shops in the High. There were more of these then than now, as Oriel had not " come through ", nor had Brasenose emerged into air and light, and both these colleges were shop-eaters. Then there was the market, always a joy to visit. It seemed to have everything the heart of man could desire, from live stock at one end to radiant flowers in pots at the other. It is still one of the pleasantest spots I know, and when I have half an hour to spare in Oxford, or when one of her too frequent showers sends me flying to cover, I love to roam its dusky and odorous corridors, gazing longingly at all the good things I am no longer permitted to eat.

' Before leaving the High, where fashion used to sun itself, I should record that there was still a good deal of dressiness in Oxford. It was a sad falling off when I found myself, a generation or so later, discussing with Mr. Hall, in his shop in High Street, the decadence of the times, and the good old days when one never appeared in the High except in some sort of toilette—and sometimes a good deal of toilette! And as we talked, there would enter to us a customer, wearing, as Sergeant Buzfuz has it, the outward semblance of a Man, with hatless and touzled head, wearing a shabby Norfolk jacket with belt flying loose. . . .'

Still remembering ' Teddy's ', Kenneth Grahame has, elsewhere, said of his old school:

' The two influences which most soaked into me there, and have remained with me ever since, were the good grey

Gothic on the one hand and, on the other, the cool secluded reaches of the Thames—the " Stripling Thames ", remote and dragon-fly haunted, before it attains to the noise, ribbons and flannels of Folly Bridge. The education, in my time, was of the fine old crusted order, with all the classics in the top bin—I did Greek verse in those days, so help me ! But these elements, the classics, the Gothic, the primeval Thames, fostered in me, perhaps, the pagan germ that would have mightily shocked the author of *The Sabbath.*' [1]

At St. Edward's, in 1873, Kenneth Grahame became for the first time a published author. He had written to order (and without much inspiration) an essay on ' The good and bad effects of Rivalry '. But it was, nevertheless, the best of those ' shown up '. And it was therefore printed in the *School Chronicle* to encourage, as the pedagogue editor tells, ' a care in composition '. The essay states, truly enough, that it is ' one of the most difficult things in the world to feel kindly towards a rival '. It is signed ' K. Grahame '. And the reward of print for ' care in composition ' may have turned the author's fancy, for the first time, towards Parnassus ? A fancy destined to lie fallow for ten years.

But, in 1875, Kenneth being seventeen, it was decided that he should leave ' the school that faces the Berkshire hills ', proceed to London and there, presently, enter the service, ' from 10 to 4 ', of the Old Lady of Threadneedle Street. And a kindly Old Lady enough was she and, allowing Kenneth high place in her famous house, never once looked askew at Thalia the Muse, she who came visiting him upon the premises, albeit that ' it is one of the most difficult things in the world to feel kindly towards a rival '.

[1] James Grahame, the poet ancestor of Kenneth Grahame ; see also p. 44.

CHAPTER III

FALLOW GROUND

KENNETH'S nomination to a clerkship in the Bank of England, referred to in the last chapter, did not become operative until the end of 1878. It was on the 1st of January 1879 that he came to Threadneedle Street for the first time, walking from his Bloomsbury lodgings to the City through a choky yellow fog—a fog of a density that seems to-day to be, happily, extinct, a fog then known as a ' London Particular '.

Of what did the boy think as he went to his new work? Who shall say? But Kenneth Grahame was always too big for less than a philosophical view of life. He had begged to be allowed to go to the University, vowing that he would live, while up, with economy and, a degree taken, that he would make very good in one or other of the learned professions. Possibly he had dreamed of a Fellowship, of a cloistered life for ever with books and scholars, for ever with old Oxford faces, old friends, old oak, old wine ; for ever with young Youth, green gardens, even flowing water, even flowing hours. But those in authority had decided against Oxford on the ground of expense. So Kenneth walked into the future chosen for him and saw thereof no further than his nose.

However, some years later, in half-holiday mood, and upon a summer day, he is able to write with resignation, even cheerfulness, of the obsequies of one's ambitions :

' After those nearly vertical rays outside, the copse, once its shelter is gained, is an instant relief and a most blessed refreshment. A little heaven of shade, it is stored with

28

everything a sensible man can ask on a tropical day : everything, that is, but beer, which, indeed, must not be so much
as thought of, if reason be to hold her seat in a distracted
globe. In the open, the Lybian air not more adust, up to
the dry lip of the gaping chalk-pit, is a stretch of sheep-
cropped sward, and thereover the heated atmosphere broods
flickering till the quiet distance is all a-jostle and a-quake ;
but here are peace, seclusion, a sweet-breathed wind, couch
of bracken, swaying shelter of beechen green. Here might
one lie and doze, and muse, and doze again, the most contented animal under the sun, the whole long, lazy afternoon
—if only one could command the needful habit of mind.
But to bring the green thought to the green shade—to
go work-forgetting being world-forgot—holiday-making in
rabbit-land, to take on a rabbit's considering-cap—that is
just what none of us, slaves as we are of every tricksy
maggot in the over-fermented brain, may look to do.
Once here, for instance, I had meant to dismiss with a
backward jerk of the thumb the disagreeable entity I had
dragged up with me, and, casting the body's vesture, to
commune trancedly with the woodland spirit, till it slipped
its bark and leaf and blade, even as I my flesh and bones,
and we twain were twain no more. But my petulant Ego
will have none of it ; he has a humour of aggressiveness
to-day : and he takes the most disgusting way there is of
showing it, by persistently recalling a certain past that I
would resign to any dealer in marine stores on very easy
terms. All pasts are hateful—one or two distinctly more
hateful than others ; and an Ego that on a day like this
goes on reminding you of your own peculiar burden is—
to say the least—no gentleman. But I can pretend to take
no notice : making believe very much, I can sprawl on
the bracken, and seem to ignore him. He hates that. I
hear him muttering and growling in my ear, but fainter—
fainter—fainter ! It is plain that I have fobbed him off
for good.

    ' Then . . . ! There is a rustle in the last year's leaves

that still cling round the edge of the wood ; the young
bracken-shoots are quivering and shaking : and yet the
rabbits—I have it from one of themselves—have all gone
to an At-Home to-day ! With a sinking heart I watch a
tiny procession come forth into the open. Woe is me !
I know the faces in it, every one. The bearers are dead
days ; bespangled some, and some in plain russet, and
many draggled and smirched, but all averse and resolute,
grimly set towards the lip of the chalk-pit. And the stark
little forms they carry, I know them too. Old hopes all
of them, some pathetically deformed, others of comelier
build and hide and hue, but, of all, the gauzy, transparent
wings are folded straight and close. Their hour has come.
Stark and cold, with no banner nor march-music, but in
sad undecorated silence, they are carried out for committal
to the chalk-pit. I watch the vanguard pass, and without a sigh ; schoolboy hopes these, comically misshapen,
tawdry and crude in colour—let the pit receive them, and
a good riddance ! But those poor little corpses at their
heel—*they* are tight and trim enough, some of them at
least. And their pinions are brave and well set on, and
might have borne them fast and far. Who left these stout
young fledglings to perish ? Starvation and neglect are
ugly words, in truth. Is it even now too late ? With
downcast faces the bearers pace on, and the chalk-pit
engulfs their burdens one by one.

' Let them go. Who cares ? This beechen shade would
not be cooler, the brave summer day no longer by an hour,
had every one of them lived to wing it in triumph up to
the very sun. Achievement ever includes defeat : at best
I should only have found myself where I am now—with a
narrowing strip of sun and sward between me and the vast
inevitable pit a-gape for us each and all. And the grapes
are sour ; and the hopes are dead ; and the funeral is
nearing its end. Only one little corpse is left ; and the
very bearers seem to beweep their trifling burden. Some
hues of life seem even yet to flush the frail limbs and the

delicate features; the glorious wings are still tinctured with an iris as of Paradise. Not that one! Let me keep that just a little longer! Surely it cannot be dead? Only yesterday I nursed its failing little frame awhile. Take all the others, only leave me that! In vain. The small bearers avert their faces, and the dainty ephemerid, involved in the common doom, follows its mates over the chalk-pit's edge into the still-unravined grave.

'The sun is low by this time and strikes athwart: a cool wind wanders up the valley; the rabbits are dotting the neighbour field, intent on their evening meal; and—did somebody mention beer? or did I only dream it with the rest? It is time to have done with fancies and get back to a world of facts. If only one could! But that cry of the Portuguese Nun wails ever in the mind's ear: "I defy you to forget me utterly." Well, one can but try. It will be easier, now that they are really buried all. Hail and farewell to the short-lived dead! The pyre is out, the supreme valediction over and done.'

But to go back to winter. Because of the fog Kenneth had allowed ninety minutes for his mile-and-a-half walk eastward and arriving, punctually at ten o'clock, he found himself without a chief to report to and as yet, the only man in his department. An hour later he was to learn from a youthful colleague in a frock-coat and flourishing whiskers, the first principle of Finance. Which is that a London Particular excuses all things dilatory in a banker and especially is it indulgence, extenuation and ample justification for an extra hour in bed and a leisurely break-fast. But this was in 1879 and Kenneth had left school over two years earlier. He had meanwhile been a voluntary seeker for clerical experience in the Westminster offices of his uncle, John Grahame. Uncle John Grahame was a parliamentary agent and, at Westminster, Kenneth began to take an interest in the more gentlemanly of party politics as practised by Mr. Disraeli and the Marquis of Salisbury.

4

He lodged in Bloomsbury Street where later he was joined by his brother Roland who, as Kenneth, was also to obtain a clerkship in the Bank of England.

Kenneth paid twenty-five shillings a week for a bedroom and a sitting-room (the latter he shared with Roland) and for that sum his landlady gave him meals which, he writes (out of his love for a nobly sounding adjective), were ' sumptuous '. He was often, however, in those days, a dinner guest at his uncle's house in Sussex Gardens. A lady, who was then a little girl and, as such, recollects her cousin Kenneth's regular coming to Sunday dinner, said recently in half-apology, that all she could remember of him was that he was ' tall and kind to us children and nice to look at '. She added, ' Oh, yes, and we were always glad, all of us, to see his face at the door.' And the last, I think, would be, of the many ways a man is remembered, the best way of all.

The Grahame boys had been, in their schooldays, frequent visitors at Sussex Gardens during the Christmas holidays. Then had been wonderful nights at Drury Lane ; then had Mr. Bilson (head clerk to Uncle John) been given afternoons off that he might take ' the young gentleman ' to the Zoological Gardens or the Tower. ' Seeing things ', such excursions were called.

In the summer holidays the Grahames, when not at Cranborne, came now and again to Portsmouth, where their maternal uncle, Commander Ingles, carried out his naval duties and occasions. Kenneth's younger cousin, Reginald Ingles, writes of the (in comparison) big Kenneth of those holidays that : ' He was the nice one who was always kind and whom we were always delighted to see and to go out with. He never ticked us off and was always ready to help us in little things.'

It was at Portsmouth that Kenneth began a life-long love for, and intimacy with, line-of-battle ships. The *Hercules*, his uncle's ship, was in dry dock and what more natural and delightful than that the Ward-Room should invite the two boys, Kenneth and Reginald, to step up the gangway and come below to breakfast ?

Brass-work winked, whiskered marines sprang clashing to the salute. Clean-looking, clean-shaven, bare-foot men did things with mops and pails and paint pots—even with muskets. A white gull sat at the peak, and several of its mates upon the railing. There were the guns (just like in Captain Marryat) which Kenneth and the youthful Reginald called ' cannons ' until the gunnery-lieutenant told them differently. And lastly there was an aroma (no lesser word would do) of hot coffee (Kenneth was to become a specialist in coffee) and devilled kidneys. It was a glorious breakfast. Certainly it beat the breakfast of *Tom Brown* at the Coaching Inn. And it finished with (piping hot, plump, golden and smooth as cream) the first omelette that Kenneth had ever eaten. Unforgettable all. And, ever afterwards, Kenneth was expert in omelettes. Also in fighting-ships and, his life long, he was at home in a Ward-Room and never would he miss an opportunity of going on board anything that possessed a white ensign and a funnel.

Years after that blue August morning on *Hercules,* Kenneth Grahame and a friend visited an American flag-ship that lay off Portland Island. A rumour went abroad that the author of *The Golden Age* was at that very moment under the Star Spangled Banner. Those of the ship's company whose kits did not include a copy of that small yellow volume (there were, I am told, only a few such kits) pro-duced autograph books and fountain pens. And when *Golden Age* title-pages, *ad infinitum*, had had Kenneth Grahame's endorsement and blessing, the autograph hunters came into action. The pretty ships lay in port for some further days, the Stars and Stripes fluttered seductively, but Kenneth Grahame lazily forebore to set further foot on any unit of that brave Fleet.

But in the days of Uncle John's office in Westminster, in the early days of the Old Lady, Kenneth Grahame wrote nothing of the kind that attracts autograph hunters. His brain lay fallow as far as concerned literature, he was by day busy at the Bank of England, his spare time of an evening he gave to ' the Volunteers '. He was tired, moreover, when he came home to Bloomsbury Street and he had little time or little taste for society.

His cousin, Reginald Ingles, who, as Kenneth before him, went, in 1877, to school at St. Edward's, tells how Kenneth gave up one of his infrequent ' days off ' to come to Oxford and look him up. He writes of that visit and of other days, thus :

' You know how pleased a boy is when some relation comes to see him at school—and very few ever came to see me ? I *was* delighted to see K. and I thought him such a nice, kind sort to come and such a nice-looking chap. He played in a cricket match for a bit. I remember it quite well. He stood at the wicket with his bat up in the air—not on the ground (some cricketers *did* in those days)— and put up a good innings and hit some fine slogs. He was most *awfully* nice to me. After I left school, when I was sixteen, I saw more of him. Father was promoted Captain and was doing the long course at Greenwich Naval College. We lived at Blackheath and I used to come to London sometimes and spend an evening with Kenneth and Roland at their diggings in Bloomsbury Street. They were both in the Bank of England then and both in the London Scottish—Kenneth was a Sergeant and very keen on drill and fencing. I remember their sitting-room well. Kenneth was always so kind when I went there. After dinner they smoked Honey Dew tobacco and nice briar pipes. And Kenneth made coffee. He was particular about coffee and he used to grind the beans and put the coffee in a brown earthenware coffee-pot with an earthenware strainer. It *was* good coffee that Kenneth made. Both he and Roland were very moderate drinkers, but sometimes we had a glass of hot whisky-and-water before I went home. Kenneth always treated me just as an equal,

though I know now that I was rather young and foolish.
We used to talk a lot and discuss the ordinary topics that
young fellows do discuss. And once Kenneth took me to
dine at a small Italian restaurant in Soho and we had
about ten courses for 1s. 6d. and drank Chianti out of a
basket bottle and, afterwards, he took me to the Lyceum
to see Faust. It *was* decent of him. And, once at Bloomsbury Street, I remember Kenneth lending me a long churchwarden clay pipe with red sealing-wax on the stem. It
was one of his treasures—that churchwarden. But I
unfortunately broke the bowl off by tapping it on the
fire-grate to knock the ash out. Kenneth, though he
looked just slightly annoyed, was awfully nice about it
and said that it did not matter a bit. But he was always
like that.'

The letter that I have quoted from was written by Major
Ingles after his cousin's death. There have been, I suppose,
finer appreciations of Kenneth Grahame than this one.
Yet I fancy that it would be the difficult thing for any
artist of words to give a more lovable picture of a young
man or big boy (Kenneth was little more than a big boy
on the night when his pet churchwarden lost its head)
than this unstudied letter gives.

But the young years going, the young years coming
brought the inevitable bubbles of Helicon to the top of
the ink-pot, even the official ink-pot, at last. There came
into practical being a small ledger book, no doubt originally
bound for the baser uses of the Bank and its balances,
wherein the young clerk began to write down his fugitive
thoughts and fragments of the kind of verse that poetical
young men, especially healthy and contented young men,
do write.

Just how far a biographer may make free with a man's
private poetry I do not know. It seems as wrong as to
photograph, in the nude, little children who must presently
be old enough to blush. But the latter outrage is perpetrated daily, and without offence. So I will quote briefly,

from this old ledger's contents, for the sake of some of its youthful beauty, which is the excuse of all people who expose the very young to the plate. But before quoting from the young Grahame's personal Muse I will give a fragment of verse, two fragments of verse, which are not his but which have served him, on the initial page of this his very personal book, as motive of his own thoughts, as introduction to his own budding imagery. The first quatrain on the first sheet is Matthew Arnold. I can fancy that to Kenneth, pent and impatient in Threadneedle Street of a jolly summer day, the muffled roar of City traffic in his ears, may have come a recollection of these apposite lines. And that he, opening the brand-new ledger that lay at his elbow, of a sudden, of a whimsy, scribbled them down for the love of them, thereby not only making an idle apprentice of himself but spoiling the Old Lady's property :

> ' In the huge world, that roars hard by,
> Be others happy if they can !
> But in my helpless cradle I
> Was breathed on by the rural Pan ! '

The thrush that piped on the Edinburgh almond-tree ? I wonder.

And how, in a further impatience, he remembers Herrick and he writes :

> ' Born I was to be old
> And for to die here ;
> After that, in the mould
> Long for to lye here.'

So much then for preface. And now, on the note of that introduction, young Kenneth goes on to say on his own account :

> ' Life's a sad sepulchral song
> Chanting of an unseen choir
> Rising, falling, ever higher
> Striving up through clouds of wrong ;
>   Life's a long
> De Profundis from the mire.

'Life's a jumble and a maze
Where we trip and blunder ever,
Halt performance, high endeavour,
Panting strife and withered bays :—
Pass the days—
Rest, at last, from fret and fever.'

And, over the leaf, I find, written probably on some foggy November afternoon :

' Worn and depressed by harrying troubles I dreamt that I sped south over the sea, to a sunny isle far South in the Atlantic. There, existing many days in the balmy present, alone, new life and strength flowed silently in with every minute of warmth and peace. Till it happened, one odorous night, that I sat watching the large Southern stars while the ocean chimed with lazy rise and fall in the bay below. Then first, and suddenly, my thoughts flew back to the far-away northern island, arena of strife and all the crowd of petty vexations. Now, how small they all seemed ! How simple the unravelling of the baffling knots ! How orderly and easy the way to meet them and brush them by ! So that I, sitting there in the South, seemed to be saying to my struggling self in the North, " If I were you, how easily would I make my way through these petty obstacles ! and how helpless and incapable you are in a little strait ! " And myself in the North, put on defence, and seemed to reply : " And if I were you, so would I—with your fuller knowledge, fuller strength. As it is, perhaps on the whole I do my best." And myself in the South, in justice forced to assent, returned, " Well yes, perhaps after all you do your best— a sorry best, but as much as can fairly be expected of you." Then I woke, startled at the point to which my dream had led me.

' Will it be just like this again ? Sitting one day on the dim eternal shore, shall I look back, see and pity my past poor human strivings ? And say then, as now, " Well, perhaps, little cripple, you did your best, a sorry one though, you poor little, handicapped, human soul " ? '

And, next in order, I come to these thoughtful and quiet lines :

'Let by-gones be by-gones ? Very well, dear, e'en have it so,·
The more that we cannot help it ; the hurrying years that go
Make by-gones only too quickly and I can't, if I would, say no.
But indeed, could I bid old Time turn round and halt the flying
    minute,
I would have it all back, each quarrel of old (never mind who was
    first to begin it !)
And you with your tempers and tears and sulks—for the sake of
    the sweet that was in it.'

And, now he writes, in this fallow time of his, this period of literary preparation when 'not one solid step' has been made :

'Of the friends that make so great a part of our life, relentless Time makes two bodies—the living and the dead—which are the dearer ? The latter perhaps,—for *very* living still are they to us. For though, through circumstance and the sorry, sordid rubs of life, the former may start away, or pale and change till they are perhaps even actively hostile, derogatory, scornful and love sickens and grows cold, still the dear dead always approve ; their sympathies are sure.

'But there is yet a third class—with whom shall we reckon them ? Hardly with the former, more nearly with the dead, though occupying still a limbo of their own, whirling in a dim, Purgatorial circle. The friends of our youth, nearer then than brothers, one in sympathy.

'These live somewhere yet in the flesh,—might be seen and talked with, if we would. But we will not have it, at least yet. Because of the very height of the ideals we shared together, we cannot face them yet, while *not one solid step* has been made. Still, one always hopes that when the Peak of Ararat is reached, we may meet again on the old footing ; but not till then ; that would be unbearable.

'Meanwhile, that time never comes—not here, at least.'

So much then I have taken ; yet the ledger's entries are not all to the dark, or debit, side of life. Here's for lightness then and the *mot juste* :

'Ordinary people, I notice, use a singularly small vocabu-

lary and a scant selection of words. " Awful ", " jolly ",
" beastly " are adjectival examples and serve the ordinary
for the expression of a very wide range of emotion, the
hearer being expected to supply the *nuance* or degree necessary on each occasion of their use. This seems to me a
poor compliment to pay to a listener, to expect him to be
at the trouble of supplying, so to say, inflections to your
own rude roots and, being based on laziness (or, that is, a
refusal to be at the trouble of thinking of the right word), it
ranks among the major incivilities of life.'

And, I turn over and on the next page, I find :

' T'other day I was about to cross the Channel—the usual
crowd at the quay. A lady approached me in evident
distress—a pretty woman too. " Sir," she said, " my
husband disappeared from my side ten minutes ago and I
can perceive no trace of him—and now my black poodle
has slipped his collar and escaped ! " " Madam," said I,
severely, " you are most unreasonable. I can supply the
place of your husband to a limited extent, but I'll be hanged
if I'll play at being a black poodle for any one." '

This, I am sure, is an entirely fictional episode. In the
practical fact, Kenneth Grahame, a dog-lover, would have
been prompt with help to restore the latter fugitive to its
friends. In support of this I quote from a letter written
later by one who knew him well.

' I remember Kenneth's pain and indignation when, in
an old French *conte*, after the final transformation scene had
restored all characters " under spells " to their original
shapes, an unfortunate camel, that had been figuring very
modestly and helpfully as a wooden tub, was overlooked
and never put on camelhood again.

' Personally, from an imperfect sense of justice and a rooted
dislike for camels, I should have felt inclined to let the matter
slide, but Kenneth Grahame, the Great Lover, was fully prepared to love that camel and to see that it got its rights.
And if you can love a camel you can love anything.'

Now it is noticeable that not one of these scribblings,

these early rumours, can be read as finger-posts indicating
that Road of Gay Adventure, that Kingdom of Youth,
whereon and wherein the writer was presently to win his
spurs. Yet, in his correspondence of this period, the little
of it that exists (he was unfortunately not a writer of letters),
he finds his similes in Toyland, he finds the child a person
of interest. ' Yes ' (he writes in a private letter), ' I think
that children think long thoughts and the record of one such
thought touches a thousand chords. But while one is
young one seems tremendously unique ! '

And in a letter, to a girl about to be married, after pointing out the uselessness of ' straining my voice by shouting
good wishes to cloudland ' he says of himself that he is shaking with influenza and that he feels like Shem or Japhet out
of a nursery Ark, ' left by a careless child on the carpet,
trodden on by a heavy-footed nursemaid and badly mended
with inferior glue. I hope to see you soon however—if my
glue does not come undone.'

But, when not serving in the Bank, in those days Kenneth
Grahame was either enthusiastically serving with the
London Scottish or giving his spare time to social work in
the East End. At Toynbee Hall he was known and loved
by all who met him there. A shy man he fought off his
shyness and sung, extremely badly (so he said) but to large
audiences, the extremely sentimental songs of the period.
Moreover, as the occasional chairman of sing-songs, he
would announce the names of numbers, at which he must
have shuddered, without a visible tremor. He fenced, he
boxed, he played billiards.

Toynbee Hall, Stepney, was new ; it was a place of intellectual and physical recreation for the East End poor and
was under the trusteeship of the Universities Settlements.
Kenneth Grahame continued to be associated with its good
work for many years and long after he attained to literary
fame. Dame Henrietta Barnett, the doyenne of Toynbee
Hall, wrote lately of the delight, the self-congratulatory-
delight with which she first read some of the papers which

'LONDON SCOTTISH'

were to make *The Golden Age.* ' I had always,' she writes,
' guessed something of the beauty and poetry of his character
even though the Mr. Grahame that I best knew seemed
outwardly but a young City man with a dutiful consideration
for his poorer neighbours.   Imagine my keen personal joy
when I recognized, from his writings, that he really *had* the
nature that I had romantically ascribed to him ! '   I have
mentioned that Kenneth Grahame was a shy man, his
reserved nature required a strict schooling to compel it to a
duty towards a caste not his own.   It came easy to him
to be generous with his money, but it was a sacrifice to give
personal service to what was squalid and unscholarly.   And
his sense of duty (this virtue of his) sometimes brought him
its own strange rewards.   A lady, herself a desperate keen
worker in Stepney, once took advantage of Kenneth
Grahame's incapability of saying ' no ' to a heart-appeal.
She pursuaded ' that kind young Mr. Grahame ' to give a
reading, or a talk, to her pet class of girls.   Now while a
gathering of East End boys or young men is easy to handle
it is not always so when the gathering is of the ' female of
the (same) species '.   And the good looks of ' kind young
Mr. Grahame ' were possibly accentuated by his bashfulness.
He was alone with the literature class.   Whereupon the
class, climbing, when necessary, on chair and table, pre-
cipitated itself over him and kissed him soundly, at the
same time chanting, to the tune of *Men of Harlech*, ' What
is one among so many ? '   The ' talk ' was never delivered.
    And Kenneth Grahame has said that the incident made
him keener than ever before on ' the Volunteers '.
    The London Scottish of the time, its grey kilts, its bonnets,
its drum-major, especially its drum-major, was one of the
sights of London.   The kilt is a becoming garb.   And,
speaking of it, Kenneth has said that when he left Scotland
as a child he brought with him a kilt.   And he cherished it
secretly for years, and wore it ' until I discovered that my
legs came too far through for Saxon prejudices—narrower
then than now '.   But long-legged Kenneth in the philabeg

was a credit to the regiment. And the regiment likewise was a credit to him, for he loved it and was soon a sergeant and a first-class ' drill '. But there remains now small record of a military career of nearly fifty years ago. Yet in a letter addressed to the late Mr. Traill, he makes it evident, I think, that his regiment was on duty on Queen Victoria's Jubilee Day in 1887. I quote the letter *in extenso*.

' Bank of England,
' *June* 1887

' DEAR MR. TRAILL,—I am obliged to you for all that you say in your letter and I will *make* the time to let you have what you, so agreeably, ask me for and this before your return to England. I am happy to know that you are enjoying the " mountain solitudes " far from the " court-sutlers " and " Occasions " to which you refer ! I was on duty during the whole short summer night prior to the Great Day. Before we moved off, which we did at 6 a.m., D. N. walked round us. Roland said, that if he, D. N., wanted to lean on his sword and wipe away a tear, he'd have to stand on tiptoe to do so ! A General Officer, with many decorations but no taller than is our D. N., was with the latter—un-officially, I think. It was reported later that this soldier was no other than Sir Frederick Roberts, but I don't vouch for it.[1] As the informal inspection inspected myself, D. N. tipped a sort of a wink at me and said to the other, in his best English, " Here's a braw Highland laddie, sir." Answered he, " Biggest, ain't always best, D.—*as you and I know* ! " It was a great day, full of music, marching, and much true and affectionate loyalty and patriotism.

' I am,
' Yours most sincerely,
' KENNETH GRAHAME '

The ribbon of the London Scottish bound the flowers that those who best loved Kenneth Grahame brought to him at the last.

[1] In 1887 Lord Roberts held a command in the East, but it may well have been that he was in England for the Queen's Jubilee.

CHAPTER IV

' ONE OF HENLEY'S YOUNG MEN '

BUT the ledger, Kenneth Grahame's private nursery garden, expanding, overflowed. And on an evening in 1886 the young bank clerk, dining in Soho, became acquainted with a hirsute and handsome man of middle age. The two were seated at neighbouring tables. The elder was loudly spoken, irascible and merry of wit. The last was a sure way to the younger man's approval. He, overhearing a sally, smiled in sympathy with it and caught his elder's eye. They finished the evening together and, well satisfied with each other's society, they exchanged cards.

The hairy diner was Frederick James Furnivall, an eccentric, rebellious, singularly hard-working, singularly ill-requited man of letters and the highest living authority on Shakespeare. Dr. Furnivall was at that time engaged on works founded on his formation, in 1874, of the New Shakespeare Society. And in Kenneth Grahame he discovered a voluntary but invaluable assistant. Also an affectionate and life-long friend. For both were interested in social work, both loved boating, the Thames at Royal Richmond, picnics, cold gooseberry fool and a song—*Twickenham Ferry* for choice. But Kenneth, for all his love of the River, never drank Thames water and Dr. Furnivall did—with impunity and by the tumblerful.

And Youth was, moreover, at that moment ready to accord to Middle Age a certain amount of mild hero-worship. Mild because Kenneth Grahame never gave way to enthusiasms for men or things. But he had taken, secretly so far, to that ' fatal facile drink ', Scribbler's Ink. And, in Threadneedle Street, in the volunteers, in his own family

43

and among his friends he had found, as yet, no one with a similar failing, no one to whom he could confide these first literary chickens of his. Chickens of whom he was both ashamed and proud. And here was this fine new friend, a man of letters himself, a light in the literary world, quite ready to spare a moment to look at the ledger. Furnivall was off-hand and a little contemptuous, but he was, on the whole, encouraging. Accustomed to the best the best meant nothing much to him. Certainly, said Furnivall, Grahame ought to show his stuff to Editors. But he did not recommend the medium of verse. And so I think that a beautiful poet of the lighter sort, an Austin Dobson maybe, was strangled at birth. For the few lyrics that Kenneth Grahame has left behind him show the exquisite touch of a master of the minor keys.

And why would it not be so ? Kenneth Grahame has said of his ancestors that, though respectable, ' they nevertheless once produced a poet—my great-grand-uncle James Grahame, author of *The Sabbath* and similar works. The title of his principal production saved him, upon an occasion, from Glasgow justice (though Lord Byron was a little nasty on the subject, in *English Bards and Scotch Reviewers*), but the family never repeated the experiment and I have never read his works.'

' A little nasty ' means, of course, the following :

> ' Lo ! the Sabbath bard,
> Sepulchral Grahame, pours his notes sublime
> In mangled prose, nor e'en aspires to rhyme,
> Breaks into blank the Gospel of St. Luke
> And boldly pilfers from the Pentateuch ;
> And, undisturbed by conscientious qualms,
> Perverts the Prophets and purloins the Psalms.'

To which my lord appends the further appreciative footnote : ' Mr. Grahame has poured forth two volumes of cant, under the name of *Sabbath Walks* and *Biblical Pictures*.'

Nevertheless James Grahame, an amiable man and pleasing poet, published subsequently *The Birds of Clyde* and other

GREAT-GRANDMOTHER GRAHAME
(MRS. ARCHIBALD GRAHAME OF DRUMQUHASSLE)

GRANNY INGLES
(MRS. DAVID INGLES)

work. But his reputation rests on his *Sabbath*. He began
life as an advocate in Edinburgh ; but he had small success
at the Bar and, being ' of a melancholy and devout ' temperament, entered Holy Orders and retired to a curacy near
Durham, where he died in 1811.

And as to the peccadillo that demanded ' Glasgow
justice ' ? ' Sepulchral Grahame's ' great-grand-nephew has
held his peace and I will hold mine.

The ' Sabbath Bard ' had a pretty sister called Jean. She
married, at the age of sixteen, her cousin Archibald Grahame
of Drumquhassle, Barrowfield and Dalmarnock, a man then
over sixty. Jean's yellow hair was her crown and her glory.
It is told that her husband, anxious to have a portrait
of his young wife, approached Henry Raeburn on the matter,
who, it is said, declared that he had not sufficient gamboge
to do her justice. And, for that reason or another, Mistress
Jean did not get her portrait painted until she was both
thirty and a widow. And even then there were difficulties,
since the artist employed took a very natural scunner to
the widow's cap she wore. And so she was painted, like
any tinker lass, with a black silk kerchief about her pretty
head, as may be seen by the picture which is in this book.

But, between uncle and nephew, it is not, perhaps, too
long a step from the *Birds of Clyde* to the wind among the
willows at Cookham and the small riverside dwellers of
Thames ? And that poetic heredity was high in Kenneth
this fragment of his own goes to prove :

TO ROLLO

Untimely taken

Puppy, yours a pleasant grave,
Where the seeding grasses wave !
Now on frolic morns the kitten
Over you, once scratched and bitten—
Still forgiving !—plays alone.
You, who planted many a bone,
Planted now yourself, repose,
Tranquil tail, incurious nose !

Chased no more, the indifferent bee
Drones a sun-steeped elegy.
Puppy where long grasses wave,
Surely yours a pleasant grave !

' Whom the gods love '—was this why,
Rollo, you must early die ?
Cheerless lay the realms of night—
Now your small unconquered sprite
(Still familiar, as with us)
Bites the ears of Cerberus :
Chases Pluto, Lord of Hell,
Round the fields of asphodel :
Sinks to sleep at last, supine
On the lap of Proserpine !
While your earthly part shall pass,
Puppy, into flowers and grass !

And now, under advice, Kenneth Grahame began to submit to the dailies, and the weeklies, and the monthlies, the earlier of those floral artifices—so poetical, so quaintly affected and so of-the-period—which were to be famous afterwards as *Pagan Papers*. Of these days, when he was knocking (per proxy of the G.P.O.) at editorial doors, he has said that ' five out of six of my little meteorites came back to me '. Sometimes, nevertheless, they were returned rather reluctantly, or so it seemed :

' DEAR SIR,'—(writes the Editor of the *Cornhill Magazine* on 18th September 1888) ' your little paper is too short and slight for the *Cornhill*, but the humour it exhibits has struck me as being exceptional and leads me to hope that I may again hear from you.

' Yours faithfully,

' JAMES PAYN '

Of the next half-dozen ' meteorites ', however, the sub-editor of the *St. James's Gazette*, receiving a sample, was attracted by two minor things. The first was the unusual clarity of the handwriting in which an eighteen-hundred-word article, ' A Bohemian in Exile ', was transcribed. For in the 'eighties the typewriter, still a rarity, was practically unknown in free-lance journalism. So a legible long-hand went far with sub-editors and other readers of manuscripts. And Kenneth's hand was ever a clerkly one. Too much so some thought for any ultimate success in the courts of Mammon. An old Scotch ledger-clerk in Threadneedle Street had said of it, doubtfully rubbing his nose, ' It's no' the hand o' a principal, young Grahame.' And perhaps it was not. But it was as clear as print and this facility and the intrigue attaching to the fact that ' The Bohemian ' was written upon Bank of England note-paper, induced the sub-editor, reaching for a rejection-slip, to ' read the thing first anyhow '. He did, and, recognizing it as ' nice fresh stuff ', he passed it along for proof.

A day of April weather had inspired ' The Bohemian '— April in Threadneedle Street. A continuance of blue-and-white skies and a Bank of England pigeon that said *rocketty-coo* on the window-sill, was responsible for a rather similar paper, entitled (out of the very private ledger and the poems of Mr. Matthew Arnold) ' The Rural Pan '—the Faunus who had breathed on Kenneth's ' helpless cradle '.

' The Rural Pan ' was, is still, a delicate, adequate and poetical piece of work. Indeed, had it not been for Dr. Furnivall and his advice, verse, not prose, might well have been its vehicle. The author, recognizing this and hoping therefore that it might appeal to a poet (such as was the maker of The Infirmary verses), sent ' The Rural Pan ' to W. E. Henley who edited the new *National Observer* (lately *The Scots Observer*, of Edinburgh), a weekly that had, till now, heard no word of young Mr. Kenneth Grahame and his works.

Some days later Kenneth read the scribble (in violet ink) of a furious driven pen which invited him to call at ' the office ' and added, in a postscript, ' any Tuesday after four '. On the forthcoming Tuesday, calling, he found that in ' Pan ' he had turned up trumps and that his literary fortune was, if he so wished it, made.

5

Lame and an invalid himself, Henley appreciated good looks in others as highly as he did good writing. And in this new man of his he recognized the one and the other. As editor of the *National Observer*, Henley was surrounding himself with the young talent of a day to equal which, in the profusion of its portents and literary prodigies, one would require to look back to the day of Elizabeth.

Nor has there been seen so plenteous a day since. Its morning broke with Stevenson as star, its evening closed perhaps, with the advent of young Mr. Kipling. When, a year or so afterwards, *Pagan Papers* was published, a reviewer condoled with the author on being ' only one in a crowd, only one in a whole generation who turns out a " Stevensonette " as easily and as lightly as it rolls a cigarette '.

Meanwhile William Ernest Henley was not a man who did things by halves. He bade Kenneth Grahame become his regular contributor ; he demanded of him, first with cajolery and finally with curses, that he should make letters his profession, that he should let The Old Lady go hang. The new recruit refused to hear of such a thing.

Kenneth loved a life that was easy and placid and, at the same time, secure. An Oxford Fellowship would have given him, perhaps, the career that he was most fitted for, the scholar's life that he would have best preferred and best adorned. But the Bank of England gave him security, present and future, and was to add thereto, very shortly, place and responsibility.

And though, as a whole-time author, he might no doubt have amassed a fortune, it would have been to him a fortune made against his collar and his convictions. One who knew him well said lately of him that he looked on the art of letters as the gentlemanly recreation of a scholar and never as the brain-wracking and brow-slapping resource of a breadwinner. So Kenneth Grahame, the banker, obeyed the inevitable urge of ink only since, and only when, it was inevitable. He held himself to be a spring, he said, and not a pump.

And Henley, genius and wild-man-of-the-woods, stamped at him and cursed him and then, for a time, was content to let the spring flow provided always that it flowed into his bucket. And then, of a happy day, the ' urge inevitable ' woke up the child in the ' helpless cradle ' of Kenneth Grahame's heart and bid it write first of, and then for, childhood. The essay that is known as ' The Olympians ' was the earliest of these waking dreams.

Henley was proud of his paper and its Imperialism, proud too of his contributors, though these, he said, almost outnumbered his readers. He spoke of the former still as ' gentlemen of the *Scots Observer* ', much as the first Duke of Marlborough was accustomed to refer to his troopers of the Guard as ' Gentlemen of the Life Guards '. These ' Scots Observers ' and their friends were accustomed to gather, ' an uproarious Valhalla ' under the rampant chairmanship of Henley, for conversation and refreshment at Verrey's Restaurant upon a Friday evening.

From the *Christian Science Monitor*, of Boston, I am able to quote a fragmentary description of one of those *noctes* of the early 'nineties :

' It was in those days a mixed and versatile group of men that gathered around William Ernest Henley, in London. Diverse in temperament and achievement, Henley was the cord that bound them together, he and the fact that all were writing, more or less, for the *Scots Observer* or the *National Observer*.

' Most of these men earned their living by their pens, but there were a few of the group to whom literature was a wellloved, but a leisure-hour, occupation. They held positions with regular salaries, and they wrote in the evening or on Sunday. I always fancied that I could distinguish those who had salaried positions ; who were not obliged to live by their pens. They looked more comfortable ; they ate their food in a more leisurely way ; they were readier to praise than to blame, because literature was to them a delightful relaxation, not an arduous business.

'Among these leisure-hour gentlemen of the pen was a
tall, well-knit man, who moved slowly and with dignity,
and who preserved, amid the violent discussions and alter-
cations that enlivened the meetings of the group, a calm,
comprehending demeanour accompanied by a ready smile.
And yet this temperate, kindly-looking man had also a
startled air, such as a fawn might show who suddenly found
himself on Boston Common, quite prepared to go through
with the adventure, as a well-bred fawn should do under
any circumstances, but unable to escape wholly from the
memory of the glades and woods whence he had come.
He seemed to be a man who had not yet become quite
accustomed to the discovery that he was no longer a child,
but grown-up and prosperous. Success did not atone for
the loss of the child outlook. Every one of us has his
adjective. His adjective was—startled.

'There were so many men in this group, so many strangers
were continually coming and going, that it was some time
before I learnt who this gentleman of letters was. I
addressed a question to my neighbour at one of the dinners.
"Who is that man?" I asked. My neighbour replied,
"Kenneth Grahame. He wrote that jolly thing about
children called, 'The Olympians', last week. Henley
thinks very highly of him. He's something in the Bank
of England.'

Kenneth Grahame has written affectionately of his old
chief :

'My personal recollection of W. E. Henley is vivid enough
still—perhaps because he was so very vivid himself. Sick
or sorry—and he was often both—he was always vivid.
The memory of this, and of his constant quality of stimula-
tion and encouragement, brings him best to my mind.

'The Henley I am speaking of is the Henley of the *Vanity
Fair* Portrait, not of the Nicholson one. Good picture as
that is, I had lost sight of him before it was painted, and
it does not recall him to me.'

'A GENTLEMAN OF THE *SCOTS OBSERVER*'

And of Henley (whom he calls Burly) as a conversation-
alist Robert Louis Stevenson, another of ' Henley's young
men ', has said :

' Burly is a man of a great presence ; he commands a larger
atmosphere, gives the impression of a grosser mass of
character than most men.   It has been said of him that his
presence could be felt in a room you entered blindfold ;
and the same, I think, has been said of other powerful con-
stitutions condemned to much physical inaction.   There is
something boisterous and piratic in Burly's manner of talk
which suits well enough with this impression.   He will roar
you down, he will bury his face in his hands, he will undergo
passions of revolt and agony ; and meanwhile his attitude
of mind is really both conciliatory and receptive ; and after
Pistol has been out-Pistol'd, and the welkin rung for hours,
you begin to perceive a certain subsidence in these spring
torrents, points of agreement issue, and you end arm-in-arm,
and in a glow of mutual admiration.   The outcry only serves
to make your final union the more unexpected and precious.
Throughout there has been perfect sincerity, perfect intelligence, a desire to hear although not always to listen, and
an unaffected eagerness to meet concessions.'

The Monitor uses the simile ' fawn ' in reference to Kenneth
Grahame.   I cannot reconcile this reconstruction of so
essentially manly a man as the young London Scottish
sergeant must have looked among the *fin-de-siècle* highbrows.
But Mr. Graham Robertson writes of Kenneth Grahame
(rapidly becoming one of the lesser lions) in those early
days : ' He was living in London where he looked all
wrong—that is to say, as wrong as so magnificent a man
could look anywhere.   As he strode along the pavements
one felt to him as towards a huge St. Bernard or Newfound-
land dog, a longing to take him away into the open country
where he could be let off the lead and allowed to range at
will.   He appeared happy enough and made the best of
everything, as do the dogs, but he was too big for London
and it hardly seemed kind of Fate to keep him there.'

And yet he found beauty in London and has told of it in this urban pastel :

' A welcome magician, one of the first real suns of the year, is transforming with touch of alchemy our grimy streets, as they emerge from under the pall of another soot-stained winter ; and the eye, weary for colour, bathes itself with renewed delight in the moving glint and flutter and splash of hue. The buses whirl up, and recede in vivid spots of red and blue and green ; tawdry house-fronts are transmuted into mellowest shades of blue-grey and tawny ; or, freshly painted, throw up broad masses of dazzling white. A butcher's cart, a child's Tam-o'-Shanter, a mounted orderly jogging from Pall Mall—all join in the conspiracy of colour ; and woman everywhere, realizing what she was created for, flecks the canvas with pigments unknown to the dead and buried year. The artist, meanwhile, crouching under the park-railings, rubs in the white round the widow's cap, brings out the high lights on the green sod, and adds corners of the proper droop to the mouth of the orphan in his old masterpiece—" Her Father's Grave ".

' Do but give a glance up, and you are whirled away from the roaring city as though it had never been. From turquoise at the rim to the hue of the hedge-sparrow's egg, it melts through all gradations, the wonderful crystalline blue. In the liquid spaces pigeons flash and circle, joyous as if they sped their morris over some remote little farm-stead, lapped round by quiet hills ; and as they stoop and tumble, the sunlight falls off their wings in glancing drops of opal sheen. He of the chalks is portraying, with passion-ate absorption, the half of a salmon on a plate ; with special attention to the flesh-tints at the divided part. A vision of glancing ankles—a susurrus of chatter—a girls' school trips by, with restless eye and quick turns of head. Some are quite pretty—all are young and fresh as the morning —and O, that wave of red hair that flaps on one cool white neck ! It disappears up the street, beckoning, provoking, calling ever, a flag of dainty defiance. The artist wriggles

over on his other leg, and grimly touches up six cannons
vomiting flame on as many impossible horsemen ; the
Charge of Balaclava, as rigid artistic tradition has handed
it down.

' The golden afternoon wears on ; and the London haze,
by this time enveloping, mellows every crudity and sharp
edge with an illusion of its own.   Through the park-railings
one can catch, here and there, vistas of warm dim distance,
broken by sparkle of water, or dotted by far-away red coats ;
is it really a bit of London then, or do we peep for a moment
into the park of some old-time château, and see the skirts
of a *fête-champêtre* in a France that died with the last
century ?   But little effort of imagination is needed to make
the change of time and scene complete.   Small as the effort
may be, the artist does not make it ; he is busy transforming, by the addition of a beard, by the excision of a medal
or two, the portrait of Lord Wolseley into that of the Duke
of Saxe-Coburg.

' The shades begin to fall, street-lamps twinkle into
existence one by one, and the artist himself disposes his
six candle-ends along the border of his creations with an
eye to chiaroscuro.   Stepping with a grace that is scarcely
English, a woman passes slowly, tall and lithe, magnificent
in every line and contour.   A sinuous and splendid animal,
she satisfies the eye as a perfect expression of the eternal
type.   Lilith is abroad—the enduring, the unchangeable ;
and as she glances with assurance under the hat-rims of men
already hastening westward in steady stream, one can
picture her, with little outward change, treading old-world
pavements in famous cities long since dead.   Neither type
nor specimen has any special appeal for the Academician,
who, prone on his stomach, is inscribing, in sprawling
characters, the cheerful legend, " I do it for my daily
bread."

' The darkness closes round with completeness ; and
dainty broughams, whirling dinner-wards, flash back the
successive lamplights from their polished sides.   Hansoms,

speeding all one way, dot the gloom with specks of red from the little hole at the back of each lamp. To some they suggest the lights of the great liners, as one has seen them at night, far out at sea ; to others the lambent eyes of huge beasts, surprised in the recesses of some vast cavern. To the R.A. they only seem to suggest Beer. There is " four-arf " written all over him as he gathers together his chalks and candle-ends, and struggles to his feet ; and there is no hesitation at all as to the path he shall take. For him—in another minute—the cool feel of the pint-pot's rim as he tilts it well on to his nose ; and all that is artistic in him shall blossom and expand to the soothing smell of sawdust and of gin.'

It was the day of the ' Kailyard '. But Kenneth, Scot as he was, had no inclination to exploit the Scottish accent and the facile, Scottish love of sentiment. ' You have a Scotch name, Mr. Grahame,' said a cheeky young lady to the rising writer at an evening party where the Arts were predomi-nant, ' you are a banker and a journalist—both extremely Scotch things to be—but you have not a Scotch accent. Why ? ' ' I left it in Edinburgh when I came to London,' Kenneth told her. ' Oh, but can't you imitate it ? I love a Scotch accent like that of Mr. —— and Mr. ——.' And she named two cultivators of literary kail. ' At school I was kicked for just that apeing.' ' Oh, but you look too big to be kicked.' ' No man,' said Kenneth, ' is too big to be kicked for imitating the Scotch accent.'

I think that Kenneth Grahame is the only Scot, of con-temporary note in letters, who escaped a notoriety—and a beating of clubs—at Mr. T. W. H. Crosland's witty pen. It was *The Unspeakable Scot* that scotched the Kailyard and finally killed it. Mr. Crosland's text was that Hadrian had had ' the excellent sense to build a wall for the purpose of keeping the Scotch out of England '. *The Unspeakable Scot* was a provocative book and a successful book, and its largest sales were in Scotland. But, without any like advertisement, Kenneth Grahame was now definitely arriving.

The Kailyard suggests vegetables. Mr. Alan Lidderdale, a son of the Governor of the Bank of England under whose auspices Kenneth had entered the household of the ' Old Lady ', writes of the rising author and of a ride in a Victorian Covent Garden market-cart thus : ' Years ago Kenneth told me how late one night, after a very cheerful dinner, he, in full evening dress, walked out into Piccadilly, and seeing a vegetable cart making its way eastward, ran after it, and climbing up behind, made himself comfortable among the vegetables. He was then overcome by an " exposition of sleep ". He woke in broad daylight. He was still in the cart, which, now empty, was moving down Piccadilly in the opposite direction. That is all. It was one of the regrets of Kenneth's life that he never knew what happened in the interval.'

In 1893 *Pagan Papers* was published by Matthews and Lane, John Lane who, at the Bodley Head, was shortly to publish the *Yellow Book*.

Henley took a personal interest in the publication of the *Pagan Papers*. Kenneth, writing to his publishers, in September 1893, says, ' Henley asks me to let him see a set of sheets of the book before it appears. He is anxious to see how it turns out.'

Pagan Papers, a little book of 160 pages, was (in first edition) a reprint of Kenneth's essays published in the *National Observer*. It was published on terms of a royalty of 10 per cent. for the first 200 copies sold and of 20 per cent. on further sales. The author, asking for these terms, writes : ' I don't call this a grasping proposal—especially from a Scotchman.' To the essays were added ' The Olympians ' and those other five items of childhood which were afterwards to make a part of *The Golden Age*. ' A Bohemian in Exile ' likewise became, by courtesy of the *St. James's Gazette*, a pagan paper. ' A quite grotesquely ill-fitting title, by the way (says a review in *Great Thoughts*)

—for it was in the pages of Mr. Henley's ever-English organ that its contents made their first appeal.' The reviewer goes on to say:

' Indeed, much of the best prose of the day is to be found in the same columns, and it would be a lasting disgrace to patrons of English journalism if rumour's lying tongue was for once proved correct and the *National Observer* sunk into the limbo of the forgotten. Not that the paper's sentiments for a moment inspire sympathy. Its views are not our views, nor its manners our manners, and yet . . . how far duller would our week-ends be had we not the *National Observer* to correct our faults and to chasten our follies. The almost too perfect, too elaborated prose of Mrs. Meynell, since republished in *The Rhythm of Life*, first appeared in these ultra-Conservative and ultra-refined pages.

' Mr. Kenneth Grahame, the author of *Pagan Papers*, is of a very different type from Mrs. Meynell—so different, that to compare them were impertinent. A lover of all the varied delights of life, Mr. Grahame shows, even while he is most palpably young, that he has lived his years to the utmost. Joy in the fields and in books, in boating and in old authors, in tramps over the open downs, and in poets, is his, and one gets from his diverse subjects a sense of the greatest gusto, and a feeling that here one is in touch with a writer complete and virile to his finger-tips.'

The *Papers* were an immediate success. There was no dissenting voice in the chorus of praise. Although, here and there, a reviewer complained of the ' plethora of good things ' that the young men of 1893 were writing. Thus, for instance, the *Daily Chronicle's* young man :

' " Ods quillets and quiddities " how monstrous clever we all are ! When Goethe said—

> " Niemann will ein Schuster sein,
> Jedermann ein Dichter,"

the implication was that men who might have been good cobblers insisted on being bad poets instead. Well, there was no great harm done. No one was compelled to read the poetry, and those cobblers who stuck to their last, if economics be not a vain fable, earned a proportionately better wage. But the trouble to-day is that the poetry is not bad, but good—much more excellent, probably, than the boots which the same men would have turned out, cobbled they never so wisely. It is well worth reading. It deserves to be admired, to be loved ; but we are all so busy writing, admiring and loving our own poetry, that even while we skim it and praise it we feel it to be a superfluity. When every man is his own Shakespeare, there will be nothing left for it but to burn all libraries, make education a penal offence for a century or so, and then begin literature afresh. Music depends upon an audience. When the world is all orchestra, the deaf alone will have even the will to hear.'

And, here and there, a reviewer expressed ignorance of the author. ' Of Mr. Kenneth Grahame I know nothing,' says the *Queen*, ' but he appears to be one of Mr. Henley's clever young men. His book proves him to be one of Mr. Henley's *very* clever young men.' The *Queen*, however, goes on to mar a fine effort by finishing the paragraph thus : ' There is plenty of good writing in these smart newspaper sketches.'

And the *Pall Mall Gazette* says : ' These *Pagan Papers* are by Mr. Kenneth Grahame ; have you heard of him, gentle reader ? No ? No more have we.' But the P.M.G. presently becomes lyrical. ' His accomplishment is astounding,' it says, ' an occasional affectation apart, his style is a delight, so high is its vitality, so cool its colours, so nimble and various its rhythms.' But the critic cannot quite go the course and tails off sadly with ' inoffensive and wellbred '. And he dismisses ' The Olympians ' and kindred essays, so acclaimed by his contemporaries, as ' full of insight and humour '.

The *Literary Echo* fears that the title, *Pagan Papers*, may deter readers, with growing families, from making their acquaintance. ' This we should specially regret,' it says.

The *Scotsman* declares (on a rather similar note) that ' any one who likes showy pictorial writing may read *Pagan Papers* with pleasure '. This although ' they do not manifestly appear to be the work of a Christian '. And the *Westminster Gazette* tells its readers that ' you may expect much of Mr. Kennith (*sic*) Grahame '. They have not been disappointed.

Looking over these old reviews, for the most part so warmly welcoming, I wonder how the author received them, his first-fruits of attainment ? Did he walk to Threadneedle Street, more head-in-air than usual, eager and flushed in the joy of achievement ? I think not. Such manifestations were not his way. Yet he could not have been entirely indifferent. He must have enjoyed the only genuine thing that cannot be bought for money—the whole-hearted praise of one's fellows bestowed whole-heartedly upon the children of one's brain.

Though the short essays, which alone compose the later editions of *Pagan Papers*, had met, on publication, with the high approval of the reviewers, they had been a little overshadowed by the attention paid to ' The Olympians ' and the handful of kindred articles that made the tail-piece of the new book. The young banker-author became recognized at once as an authority on childhood and what pertains to childhood. Indeed, the publication of ' The Olympians ', in the *National Observer*, had thrown the shadow of this authority before him. And it is not surprising therefore to find Kenneth Grahame, himself among the critics, ' doing ' the children's book page, the Christmas books, for a London daily paper, in December 1899. He notices, kindly and conscientiously, some two dozen works. Alas, with the exception of Mr. Vere Stacpoole none of the writers reviewed are writers of to-day. And many of their publishers are no longer publishing, even their names I cannot say are names that once I knew. But these books are but the pegs on which is hung ' the fabric of a fairy-tale ' :

' When the Ark took the ground at last with a bump, shivered throughout her length, careened a trifle, and saw the gurgling floods drop inch by inch down her pitchy sides, all her leg-cramped, wing-cramped, neck-and-trunk-cramped crew, forgetting the sulks, cliques, and quarrels inevitable to the voyager, burst hilariously forth into the sunlight, and with many a squawk, squeal, trumpet, and snort went gaily galumphing about their respective businesses. Alone among these forgetful ones, the kindly domestic pigeons, gratefully remembering—with their cousin the dove—the many home comforts of the snug old ship, resolved upon some memorial of the excursion, whenever they should have the necessary time and money. So as soon as things were a bit settled and running in the old grooves once again, they set to work and erected a stout pole ; and on the top of that they set up their first house—a miniature Ark, *ex voto*, with a sliding roof painted wavy red, two straight rows of black windows, a flat promenade all round for fine weather, and at each of the four corners a little round tree, of the evergreen tribe, seeing that their foliage was shavings painted green. There had always been lots of shavings in odd corners of the Ark, and, of course, plenty of green paint, as befitted a well-found ship ; so in the tedious days when the world was a flat watery waste, they had got in the habit of making these trees, just for fun.

' Of course as time went on architect-pigeons worked out what they called improvements in design. To mitigate the force of tempests, pigeon-arks were built shorter and shorter, and broader and broader, still keeping, however, their roof, windows and promenade. At last a genius-pigeon arose who boldly demolished corners altogether, and the Ark became the dove-cot of the present day. But this is the dove-cot's architectural history, and the history, too, of the first play-ark, as distinguished from the original bluff-bowed old coaster.

' To return, however, to the first memorial pigeon-ark. This was stoutly built, with a broad promenade, and was much admired by the other animals, who often wished they had had the wit to think of such a memento themselves. A ladder led up to it, and Shem, Ham, and Japhet were not too proud to stroll up of a cool evening and sit about, dangling their legs over the edge and remarking how homelike it all felt. Some of the animals, too, would drop in promiscuous, when business was slack—stout, bow-legged, skipperhippopotamuses, pensive giraffe-captains of the foretop, or maybe a monkey-cabin-boy or two. And by degrees many a knotty point came to be talked over and settled up there ; for there were plenty of threads to be picked up and old traditions set on their legs again, in the new order of things.

' They settled the size and colour of the spots on wooden horses ; they laid down the lines of the first (and last) box of bricks. They decreed that cotton-wool smoke should for ever puff cloudily out of wooden locomotives ; they inserted wonderful red and blue threads inside glass marbles. They decided on the particular purple tint always used for the rings round ninepins ; and they eternally fixed the plastic curves of the monkey that restlessly jerks on a yellow stick. They settled—as who should know better ? —how pirates were to be played ; and the rules for hunting down the various wild beasts of forest and plain were easy to compile when the actual animals themselves were at hand with advice and assistance. They fixed the scrunchingpoint of bulls'-eyes and barley sugar, and composed the mottoes to be printed on peppermints. And lastly, they resolved themselves into a special committee for drafting a code and a scheme and a syllabus for the eternal fairytale, that should hold till the sun was shrunken and dim, and it was too cold to do anything but build big fires and sit round them and tell stories. A pinch of fairy godmother, both the invited and uninvited kinds—a youngest prince of three, a youngest princess of nine—dragons for the driving,

caves for the password, bullion for the beating heart and
wary sword. Riddles to guess, with a castle for prize
money; forests to pierce, with a princess worth winning
deep in the murky heart of them. Relations and guardians,
gnomes and sprites, on the hostile or tricksy side; on the
other, fairies generally, animals always, friendly and helpful.
Ogres in sugar-plum-castles, essential rings in eagles' nests—
of these and many another thread the web was woven, and
the texture has never been questioned or discussed since
the date of the original committee.

' Do writer-people still weave them as of old, these
tapestries? Or have all possible combinations of the hues
and the threads in the old loom become exhausted? Well,
it is not often that one meets a bit of the real antique work
nowadays.

' Perhaps it is on this very account that the later pioneers
in fairy scholarship, recognizing in this very fixity something
more natural, have advanced the daring theory that as it
cannot possibly be we who invented Fairyland, Fairyland
must have invented us. According to this thesis of theirs,
we only exist by the favour of fairies. Having pleased, in
a whimsical moment, to invent us (Lord only knows why),
they have us at their mercy, and, as soon as they are tired
of thinking about us, or want a new amusement—puff !—
we shall go out and *that* story will be over. Fortunately,
fairies, as all records agree, are loving, irrational, and not
easily wearied ; and, after all, humanity must possess many
humorous points for the outsider that escape the encaged
observer within. So we may, perhaps, count upon another
month or so yet in which to read a fairy book or two, and
even to criticize them.'

Twenty years later the writer was to allow himself to be
' drawn ' on, more or less, the same subject. A reader of
The Wind in the Willows (Professor G. T. Hill of London
University) inquiring, by letter, of the only man likely to
know, as to who cleaned up Mole End in Mr. Mole's absence

and, similarly, who fed his goldfish, received the following seriously-minded reply :

> ' *Bohams,*
>> ' *Blewbury, Didcot,*
>>> ' *Berkshire,*
>>>> ' *24th September* 1919

' DEAR SIR,—The very natural inquiries contained in your kind letter which reached me this morning are probably best answered by a simple reference to the hopelessly careless and slipshod methods of the author whose work you are criticizing. But it may perhaps be pointed out in his defence, that Mole, though unmarried and evidently in rather poor circumstances, as incomes go nowadays, could probably have afforded some outside assistance say twice a week or so, indeed, living as he did, it would be almost a necessity. He probably then had a char-mouse in for a few hours and her dinner on certain days, and the animal would have cleaned up his whitewashing mess in a perfunctory sort of way ; then, finding that her weekly pittance was no longer forthcoming, quite naturally and properly would have taken her services elsewhere, though from kindness of heart she might have continued to give an occasional eye to the goldfish.

' In support of his theory, I would ask you to observe that our author practises a sort of " character economy " which has the appearance of being deliberate. The presence of certain characters may be indicated in or required by the story, but if the author has no immediate use for them, he simply ignores their existence. Take this very question of domestic service—however narrow poor Mole's means may have been, it is evident that Rat was comfortably off— indeed I strongly suspect him of a butler-valet and cook-housekeeper. Toad Hall, again, must have been simply crawling with idle servants eating their heads off.

' But the author doesn't happen to want them, so for him they simply don't exist. He doesn't say they are *not* there ; he just leaves them alone. To take another instance—the wretched fellow, ignorant as he is, must have known perfectly well that the locomotive on which Toad escaped required the services of a stoker as well as an engine-driver, but he didn't happen to *want* a stoker, so he simply ignored him.

' I think you will find that this same character-economy runs through all the classic old fairy-tales and our author probably thought that he was sinning (if sinning at all) in very good company. The modern method leaves so little to the imagination of the reader that it describes with insistent particularity the appearance of the taxi-driver who did *not* say " Thank you " to the heroine when she gave him 3*d*. above the legal fare from South Audley Street to Waterloo. Our author would have treated a taxi exactly as he would treat a Magic Carpet (which indeed is just what it is) and would not have given the taxi a driver at all. And this is right, for not one passenger in a hundred is ever conscious of the presence of a driver at all. They only see at the end a paw thrust out into which they drop something, and the taxi vanishes with a snort. Probably Magic Carpets had drivers too, but the authors of old saw that they were unessential to their stories, and ignored them.

' Yours very truly,

' KENNETH GRAHAME '

But in 1893 Mr. Mole and his friends were not born. Even the *Yellow Book* was not just yet, would not be till next year, in fact. Kenneth Grahame, though arriving, had not actually arrived. His days of best beguilement were yet to be. A reviewer had said of him : ' Mr. Grahame is not yet an individual, not yet, at any rate, a character. He is simply an excellent specimen of a latter-day type.'

And of these ' latter days ' he has himself said :

' Mr. Henley was the first Editor who gave me a full and a frank and a free show, who took all I had and asked me for more ; I should be a pig if I ever forgot him.'

CHAPTER V

THE YELLOW BOOK

In April 1894 was hatched the most famous ephemeron of all literary ephemera. Its covers, suitably enough, prophetically enough, wore the ephemeral primrose of the May-Bug and the *Yellow Book* was its name.

On a tipsy (the adjective is not mine) February night Mr. John Lane, of the Bodley Head, gave a dinner-party, at the Devonshire Club, to certain of the *literati*. Among the last were Mr. John Davidson, the poet; Mr. Henry Harland, novelist, of U.S.A., lately arrived in London, and that infant magician of black-and-white magic, Mr. Aubrey Beardsley. There, conceived on champagne and enthusiasm, the *Yellow Book* leapt, *cap à pie*, from the callow pate of the latter, an erotic Minerva from the brain of an immature Jove. The great idea was seconded by Mr. Davidson, and the company carried it with acclamation. Even the host (financier, presumed, and paymaster) was so struck by the originality of the proposition that he appointed, on the spot, Mr. Harland as editor (because, so they said, he was more elevated than anyone present) and, then, as was only fair and right, he named Mr. Beardsley art editor and ordered another magnum of Pommery.

Thus was the *Yellow Book* born. Its aim was to shock deliciously. Its object was to lead the *fin-de-siècle* and startle a Victorian London, bored to death with five decades of flannel petticoat, by a new and delicate impropriety. It succeeded at once, in both object and aim, succeeded beyond the most extravagant dreams of its promoters and its publisher.

From an article written forty years afterwards, by Mr.

Albert Parry, I give a brief picture of that almost genius, Henry Harland, who sat (on the whole with parochial propriety) in the editorial chair at the Sign of the Bodley Head :

' Harland liked to imagine himself a wild Bohemian and a rakish woman-fancier. He was proud of the premature streak of grey in his black disordered hair. He wore his hair longer than any of his Paris and London friends. He paraded the goatee and the gesticulating habits that made him seem more French than any of his French acquaintances. He emphasized his preoccupation with style by his preference for pyjamas as his writing garb at home. He tried to look, and sound, unconventional at the Bodleian editorial offices of Lane. In his rooms in Cromwell Road he arranged literary dinners, after which he would sit on the floor and mete out your-eyes-remind-me-of-the-moon-rising-over-the-jungle compliments to the women. He said that he abhorred sentimentality and that he fled from Marie Corelli as from the measles. But the fact remained that a real sin shocked him. He could not stomach the Murgerish love affairs and the hashish habits of Ernest Dowson in Soho. He winced, trying not to show it, when English and French poets and artists boasted in his presence of their entanglements with married women. In his stories appearing regularly in the *Yellow Book* and collected into two volumes (*Grey Roses*, 1895, and *Comedies and Errors*, 1898) there was not the least suggestion of indecency.'

The Cromwell Road dinners were a feature of the *Yellow Book*. On these Saturday evenings it was Kenneth Grahame's practised hand that broke the eggs that made the omelette, himself doubtless, invoking to his handiwork some echo of that initial omelette, eaten on H.M.S. *Hercules*, and in so different a company, long days ago.

Miss Netta Syrett, a contributor to the *Yellow Book*, writes :

' I used to meet Kenneth Grahame at the Harlands and, though I never came to know him well, instinctively I liked him. I can only describe the impression he gave me as *solid* and that not only in the physical sense. He answered my idea of a *man* and I suppose half consciously (I was young for my age and much of what I heard and saw at the Harlands was uncomprehended) I was comparing him with the more or less effeminate young men I met there. He was sane and normal and I should like to have known him better. But he was shy and being shy myself then I found him difficult to talk to. I liked his sense of humour and his complete freedom from the affectations which so puzzled me in the other men of the set. I remember sometimes enjoying these evenings and sometimes not at all. Everything depended on the moods of the host and hostess, both of whom were erratic and, when bored, made little effort to disguise their feelings. If but a few people were present one heard Harland and Beardsley discussing drawings, gossiping about John Lane and criticizing recent contributions. Harland was an incalculable creature of moods, at one moment sneering and unjust and the next serious and appreciative. I remember being at the flat when there were present only two or three other people, one of whom was Kenneth Grahame. The post arrived and brought the MS. of John Davidson's well-known *Ballad of a Nun*. Harland read it aloud to us, making mock and scoff of it. I could see that his bad taste in so doing quite hurt K.G. —whatever he may inwardly have thought of the Nun and her ballad ! Kenneth was (as I have said) good looking but always a little conscious of his *height*, or at least, I used to think it was this that made him want to get into a corner ! And he liked to talk of his work—if he knew you were not likely to gush about it. He was immensely pleased once when I had the cheek to say that I did not like his little girls, that they were not *real*, like his boys. He never spoke much unless he had something to say ; he never said anything unkind *about* anybody, or *to* anybody, except through his inability to be insincere. We knew the Beardsleys— brother and sister—well. Mabel Beardsley was beautiful, really lovely, like an orchid, pale with red hair and a tall graceful figure. She was as brilliant as Aubrey, deeply read and full of knowledge. Aubrey was remarkable to look at, tall and thin ; he had a straight fringe, beautiful long hands and was spotlessly clean and well groomed. One was *impressed* by his cleanliness. I knew he was a genius the moment I saw his drawings. His line is the most beautiful I ever saw, apart from Chinese and Japanese work. It was a gay world then. Piccadilly was charming, all the houses had flowers in window-boxes and striped awnings over balconies. And the *Yellow Book* set—it was gay too ; very gay, very witty, very brilliant. It was like a flame flashing up and then going out—too brilliant to last, too unreal, too artificial. And in the set we all admired Kenneth tremendously and the appearance of one of his articles would be hailed as an event and discussed at length next Saturday night.'

At this time Kenneth had left Bloomsbury Street and was living in a tiny top flat on Chelsea Embankment. Thither came to take tea with him, on the 5th of May 1894, his sister and Miss Mary Richardson. Miss Richardson has given her impressions of the tea-party and of her host. She says :

' It was like climbing the stairs of a lighthouse, there was no lift and the dirty stone staircase swept up in endless spirals. When we got to the top we were out of breath and I remember that we stood and fanned ourselves with the Royal Academy catalogue (we had come on from Burlington House) before we rang the bell. I had never met Kenneth Grahame, except in *Pagan Papers*, and I was ever so anxious to see if he was a suitable author for so delightful a book. He opened the door to us himself and my first impression was of relief. For he was just as I would have had him be. And though, I suppose, I did not take him all in at a glance, this is how I remember him. He was tall—well over six feet—and fine looking ; he was well proportioned and carried himself like a drilled man (was he not a " London Scot " ?) and he had a magnificent head. His grey eyes were rather widely open and his expression was one of the most kindly. He was not exactly handsome but distinctly striking to see. The Scotch adjective " kenspeckle " describes him better than any other, I think. He had too a sort of young dignity which well became him. But, oh, he was altogether too big for his little flat ! He made tea and poured it out for us himself and we all sat at a tea-table in the window. It was a beautiful afternoon and the view over Kenneth's beloved Thames, with the green of Battersea Park beyond, was a lovely one. I was very interested to find that he knew about my brother, and remembered his two " National " winners of so long ago.[1] He collected those hollow glass rolling-pins that sailors brought home to their sweethearts—or else smuggled brandy in. He showed some of these to us, holding them lovingly. He had a Chippendale bureau of which he was very proud. He had bought it as a bargain and it had, he said, belonged to the great Duke of Wellington. I said, " What fun if you found a secret drawer in it containing dispositions and dispatches ? " He beamed like a regular boy. " What a jolly idea ! " he said, and then his face fell and he added, " Alas, if one may believe gossip, the drawer would be more likely to contain *billets-doux* and love-letters." " But, Mr. Grahame," said I, " possibly love-letters might be more interesting than dispatches ? " " Very likely," said he, " but neither I, nor, I hope, any one else, would think it *right* to read them." And, though he spoke in fun, I am sure that that, in fact, would have been Kenneth Grahame's attitude had the contingency arisen ! After tea he read to us, because we plagued him to do so, the proof sheets (I think they were) of " The Roman Road ". He read beautifully. I have always remembered that tea-party.'

Kenneth had, through life, a boy's (or a magpie's) love

[1] Miss Richardson is sister of the late Maunsell Richardson— ' The Cat '—who, among many other winning rides, rode Disturbance and Reugny to victory in the Grand Nationals of 1874 and 1875.

of a secret hoard. When, after his death, his bureau was searched for some business papers, just such a collection of ' treasures ' was disclosed as that one he had hidden in the secret-drawer of *The Golden Age*. ' Treasures ' gathered not only in youth but in manhood : a set of Maunday Money, a handful of small sea-shells, minute models of *filets-bleux* (Breton fishing-nets), the Rules of Roulette (in miniature), a coloured prayer-card of Tobias and the Angel—anything that was gay and tiny and bright pleased him—all his days.

It may seem surprising that, normal and public-spirited, Kenneth Grahame should have cast off the *National Observer* and its weekly Imperialism for so iconoclastic a quarterly as the *Yellow Book*. But, early in 1894, the *National Observer* had ceased to exist, W. E. Henley becoming editor of the *New Review*. And therefore, from now on, Kenneth divided his work, roughly, between Henley's *New Review* and Harland's *Yellow Book*.

Henry Harland, permitted, by John Lane, to exercise his complete discretion as to whom he invited to contribute to the new infant in yellow, had recognized that Kenneth's clear, and completely sane, prose would lend a balance to his own flibbertigibbet pages. And so Harland saw to it ; and the first contribution of the late ' gentleman of the Scots *Observer* ' was the brilliant ' Headswoman ', afterwards published as a Bodley Booklet. The *Dundee Advertiser* called it ' a sweet thing in fiction ', and the *Star*, claiming that Mr. Grahame ' here tweaks the nose of St. Woman's Rights ', adds (and how pleased must the *Star* young man have been with his alliteration !) ' seldom is the whipped white of a whim served in such English '.

Kenneth Grahame, now appointed to *Yellow Book* regularity, published there the balance of his *Golden Age* essays. Also three papers which, strangely enough, he never thought to put into book form. The most individual of these three he called ' The Inner Ear ' and, since I choose to see in it some throwback to great-grand-uncle James Grahame and *The Birds of Clyde*, here it is :

'To all of us journeymen in this great whirling London mill, it happens sooner or later that the clatter and roar of its ceaseless wheels—a thing at first portentous, terrifying, nay, not to be endured—becomes a part of our nature, with our clothes and our acquaintances ; till at last the racket and din of a competitive striving humanity not only cease to impinge on the sense, but induce a certain callosity in the organ, while that more sensitive inner ear of ours, once almost as quick to record as his in the fairy tale, who lay and heard the grass-blades thrust and sprout, from lack of exercise drops back to the rudimentary stage. Hence it comes about, that when we are set down for a brief Sunday, far from the central roar, our first sensation is that of a stillness corporeal, positive, aggressive. The clamorous ocean of sound has ebbed to an infinite distance ; in its place this other sea of fullest silence comes crawling up, whelming and flooding us, its crystalline waves lapping us round with a possessing encirclement as distinct as that of the other angry tide now passed away and done with. The very Spirit of Silence is sitting hand in hand with us, and her touch is a real warm thing.

'And yet, may not our confidence be premature ? Even as we bathe and steep our senses refreshingly in this new element, that inner ear of ours begins to revive and to record, one by one, the real facts of sound. The rooks are the first to assert themselves. All this time that we took to be so void of voice they have been volubly discussing every detail of domestic tree-life, as they rock and sway beside their nests in the elm-tops. To take in the varied chatter of rookdom would in itself be a full morning's occupation, from which the most complacent might rise humble and instructed. Unfortunately, their talk rarely tends to edification. The element of personality—the *argumentum ad hominem*—always crops up so fatally soon, that long ere a syllogism has been properly unrolled, the disputants have clinched on inadequate foothold, and flopped thence, dishevelled, into space. Somewhere hard by, their jackdaw

cousins are narrating those smoking-room stories they are
so fond of, with bursts of sardonic laughter at the close.
For theology or the fine arts your jackdaw has little taste ;
but give him something sporting and spicy, with a dash of
the divorce court, and no Sunday morning can ever seem
too long. At intervals the drum of the woodpecker rattles
out from the heart of a copse ; while from every quarter
birds are delivering each his special message to the great
cheery-faced postman who is trudging his daily round overhead, carrying good tidings to the whole bird-belt that
encircles the globe. To all these wild, natural calls of the
wood, the farmyard behind us responds with its more cultivated clamour and cackle ; while the very atmosphere is
resonant of its airy population, each of them blowing his
own special trumpet. Silence, indeed ! why, as the inner
ear awakes and develops, the solid bulk of this sound-in-
stillness becomes in its turn overpowering, terrifying. Let
the development only continue, one thinks, but a little longer,
and the very rush of sap, the thrust and foison of germina-
tion, will join in the din, and go far to deafen us. One
shrinks, in fancy, to a dwarf of meanest aims and pettiest
account before this army of full-blooded, shouting soldiery,
that possesses land and air so completely, with such an entire
indifference, too, towards ourselves, our conceits, and our
aspirations.

' Here it is again, this lesson in modesty that nature is
eternally dinning into us ; and the completeness of one's
isolation in the midst of all this sounding vitality cannot
fail to strike home to the most self-centred. Indeed, it is
evident that we are entirely superfluous here ; nothing has
any need of us, nor cares to know what we are interested
in, nor what other people have been saying of us, nor
whether we go or stay. Those rooks up above have their
own society and occupations, and don't wish to share or
impart them ; and if haply a rook seems but an insignificant
sort of being to you, be sure that you are quite as insignificant
to the rook. Nay, probably more so ; for while you at

least allot the rook his special small niche in creation, it is
more than doubtful whether he ever troubles to " place "
you at all. He has weightier matters to occupy him, and
so long as you refrain from active interference, the chances
are that for him you simply don't exist.

'But putting birds aside, as generally betraying in their
startled, side-glancing mien some consciousness of a feather-
less unaccountable tribe that may have to be reckoned with
at any moment, those other winged ones, the bees and their
myriad cousins, simply insult one at every turn with their
bourgeois narrowness of non-recognition. Nothing, indeed,
could be more unlike the wary watchful marches of the
bird-folk than the bustling self-centred devotion to business
of these tiny brokers in Nature's busy mart. If you happen
to get in their way, they jostle up against you, and serve
you right ; if you keep clear of the course, they proceed
serenely without so much as a critical glance at your hat
or your boots. Snubbed, hustled, and ignored, you feel,
as you retire from the unequal contest, that the scurrying
alarm of bird or beast is less hurtful to your self-respect
than this complacent refusal of the insect to admit your
very existence.

'In sooth, we are at best poor fusionless incapable bodies ;
unstable of purpose, veering betwixt hot fits and chill,
doubtful at times whether we have any business here at
all. The least we can do is to make ourselves as small as
possible, and interfere as little as may be with these lusty
citizens, knowing just what they want to do, and doing it,
at full work in a satisfactory world that is emphatically
theirs, not ours.

'The more one considers it, the humbler one gets. This
pleasant, many-hued, fresh-smelling world of ours would
be every whit as goodly and fair, were it to be rid at one
stroke of us awkward aliens, staggering pilgrims through
a land whose customs and courtesies we never entirely
master, whose pleasant places we embellish and sweeten
not at all. We, on the other hand, would be bereft indeed,

were we to wake up one chill morning and find that all these practical capable cousins of ours had packed up and quitted in disgust, tired of trying to assimilate us, weary of our aimlessness, our brutalities, our ignorance of real life.

' Our dull inner ear is at last fully awake, fully occupied. It must be a full three hundred yards away, that first brood of ducklings, fluffily proud of a three-days-old past ; yet its shrill peep-peep reaches us as distinctly as the worry-worry of bees in the peach-blossom a foot from our head. Then suddenly—the clank of a stable-bucket on the tiles, the awakening of church-bells—humanity, with its grosser noises, is with us once more, and at the first sound of it, affrighted, the multitudinous drone of the under-life recedes, ebbs, vanishes ; Silence, the nymph so shy and withdrawn, is by our side again, and slips her hand into ours.'

Henry James, himself an occasional contributor to the *Yellow Book*, writes, in a private letter : ' I haven't sent you the *Yellow Book*—on purpose. I say on purpose because although my little tale which ushers it in (" The Death of the Lion ") appears to have had, for a thing of mine, an unusual success, I hate too much the horrid aspect and company of the whole publication. And yet I am again to be ultimately, conspicuously, associated with the second number. It is for gold and to oblige the worshipful Harland.'

Now what were the horrors to which Mr. James refers ? I have lately read the whole dainty troop from one yellow cover to another, thirteen volumes, and found nothing to shock my susceptibilities, nothing. Even in Aubrey Beardsley's morbidly rococo ladies I can find little suggestion, perhaps because Mr. John Lane himself strictly censured the pictures in his paper, sometimes, I am told, snatching his young art editor's inspirations out of the very jaws of the press ! Here and there, in the prose, postures a nymph with harmless ' wine-red hair ', and I found one who inscribed on her alpenstock the names, not of mountains

conquered, but of men. So, *pace* Mr. Henry James, it
seems that we were all very easily shocked in 1894.

Everybody who was anybody in letters contributed, at
least once, to the *Yellow Book*—except Mr. Kipling, except
Mr. Anthony Hope, except, remarkably, Mr. ' Saki ' Munro.
The quarterly ran for three years and then it died of inanition
rather than the ridicule it began to inspire. Harland was
wont to explain all attacks upon it by ascribing them to the
brilliant men of other papers whose contributions, offered
at the Bodley Head, he had not considered quite brilliant
enough for *Yellow Book* use. Yet Mr. Seaman, now Sir
Owen (who could have had no such cause for mortification
or jealousy), led the scoffers ; in his parody of John Davidson's *Nun* (which he calls *The Ballad of a Bun*) these verses,
for example, occur :

> ' . . . A Decadent was dribbling by,
> " Lady," he said, " you seem undone ;
> You need a panacea ; try
> This sample of The Bodley bun.

> ' It is fulfilled of precious spice
> Whereof I give the recipe ;—
> Take common dripping, stew in vice,
> And serve with vertu ; taste and see." '

And, later in the lyric,

> ' The seasons went and came again ;
> At length the languid Public cried :
> " It is a sorry sort of Lane
> That hardly ever turns aside " . . .'

He also said, in another parody of another *Yellow Book* bard :

> ' I know it's
> Not given to many poets
> To frame so fair a thing
> As this of mine to Spring
> Indeed the world grows Lilliput
> All but
> A precious few, the heirs of utter godlihead,
> Who wear the yellow flower of blameless bodlihead ! '

But before the 'languid Public' cried a halt the paper had ceased to be the slogan of emancipated Youth, had ceased to mark a movement and had become, as Mr. Arthur Symons wrote of it, 'little more than a publisher's magazine'. It had printed nothing that has remained except those Kenneth Grahame chapters that chronicle *Harold* and his brothers and sisters. But the contribution, from the same pen, called 'Long Odds' since it made, in July 1895 (so said, royally, the *Queen* newspaper), the quarterly number of the *Yellow Book* 'notable not only in contemporary literature but in all', I will here reproduce :

'For every honest reader there exist some half-dozen honest books, which he re-reads at regular intervals of six months or thereabouts. Whatever the demands on him, however alarming the arrears that gibber and grin in menacing row, for these he somehow generally manages to find time. Nay, as the years flit by, the day is only too apt to arrive when he reads no others at all ; the hour will even come, in certain instances, when the number falls to five, to four—perhaps to three. With this same stride of time comes another practice too—that of formulating general principles to account for or excuse one's own line of action ; and yet it ought not to be necessary to put forward preface or apology for finding oneself immersed in *Treasure Island* for about the twentieth time. The captain's capacities for the consumption of rum must always be a new delight and surprise ; the approaching tap of the blind man's stick, the moment of breathless waiting in the dark and silent inn, are ever sure of their thrill ; hence it came about that the other night I laid down the familiar book at the end of Part the Second—where vice and virtue spar a moment ere the close grip—with the natural if commonplace reflection that nineteen to six was good healthy odds.

'But somehow I was in no hurry to take the book up again. The mental comment with which I had laid it down had set up a yeasty ferment and a bubble in my brain ; till at last, with a start, I asked myself how long was it since

I had been satisfied with such a pitiful majority on the side of evil ? Why, a certain number of years ago it would have been no majority at all—none, at least, worth speaking of. What a change must have been taking place in me unsuspected all this time, that I could tamely accept, as I had just done, this pitiful compromise (I can call it nothing else) with the base law of probabilities ! What a totally different person I must have now become, from the hero who sallied out to deal with a horde of painted Indians, armed only with his virtue and his unerring smoothbore ! Well there was some little comfort in the fact that the fault was not entirely my own, nor even that of the irresistible years.

' Frankly, in the days I look back to, this same *Treasure Island* would not have gone down at all. It was not that we were in the least exacting. We did not ask for style ; the evolution of character possessed no interest whatever for us ; and all scenery and description we sternly skipped. One thing we *did* insist on having, and that was good long odds against the hero ; and in those fortunate days we generally got them. Just at present, however, a sort of moral cowardice seems to have set in among writers of this noblest class of fiction ; a truckling to likelihood, and a dirty regard for statistics. Needless to say, this state of things is bringing about its inevitable consequence. Already one hears rumours that the boy of the period, instead of cutting down impalpable bandits or blowing up imaginary mines and magazines, is moodily devoting himself to golf. The picture is a pitiful one. Heaven hath blessed him, this urchin, with a healthy appetite for pirates, a neat hand at the tomahawk, and a simple passion for being marooned ; instead of which, he now plods about the country playing golf. The fault is not his, of course ; the honest heart of him beats sound as ever. The real culprits are these defaulting writers, who, tainted by realism, basely shirk their duty, fall away from the high standard of former days, and endeavour to represent things as they possibly might have happened. Nineteen to six, indeed! No lad of spirit will put up with this sort of thing. He will even rather play golf; and play golf he consequently does.

' The magnificent demand of youth for odds—long odds, whatever the cost!—has a pathetic side to it, once one is in a position to look back thereon, squinting gloomily through the wrong end of the telescope. At the age of six or seven, the boy (in the person of his hero of the hour) can take on a Genie, an Afreet or two, a few Sultans and a couple of hostile armies, with a calmness resembling indifference. At twelve he is already less exacting. Three hundred naked Redskins, mounted on mustangs and yelling like devils, pursue him across the prairie and completely satisfy his more modest wants. At fifteen, 'tis enough if he may only lay his frigate alongside of two French ships of the line; and among the swords he shall subsequently receive on his quarter-deck he will not look for more than one Admiral's; while a year or two later it suffices if he can but win fame and fortune at twenty-five, and marry the Earl's daughter in the face of a whole competitive House of Lords. Henceforward all is declension. One really has not the heart to follow him, step by dreary step, to the time when he realizes that a hero may think himself lucky if he can only hold his own, and so on to the point when it dawns on him at last that the gods have a nasty habit of turning the trump, and have even been accused of playing with loaded dice— an aphorism any honest boy would laugh to scorn.

' Indeed, the boy may well be excused for rejecting with indignation these unworthy sneers at the *bona fides* of the autocrats who, from afar, shift the pieces on this little board, and chuck them aside when done with, one by one. For he but sees the world without through the chequered lattice of the printed page, and there invariably the hero, buffeted though he may be of men, kicked by parents and guardians, reviled by colonels and first lieutenants, always has the trump card up his sleeve, ready for production in the penultimate chapter. What wonder, then, that the gods appear

to him as his cheerful backers, ready to put their money
on him whatever the starting price ? Nay, even willing to
wink and look the other way when he, their darling, gets
a quiet lift from one of themselves, who (perhaps) may
" have a bit on ? " Meanwhile, to the wistful gazer through
the lattice, his cloistral life begins to irk terribly. 'Tis full
time he was up and doing. Through the garden gate,
beyond the parish common, somewhere over the encircling
horizon, lie fame and fortune, and the title and the bride.
Pacific seas are calling, the thunder of their rollers seems
to thrill to him through the solid globe that interposes
between. Savages are growing to dusky manhood solely
that he may flesh his sword on them ; maidens are already
entangling themselves in perilous situations that he, and
he alone, may burst the bonds, eliminate the dragon, and
swing them forth to freedom and his side. The scarlet
sunsets scorn him, a laggard and a recreant ; behind them
lie arrogant cities, plains of peril, and all the tingling adventure of the sea. The very nights are big with reproach, in
their tame freedom from the watch-fire, the war-whoop,
the stealthy ambuscade ; and every hedgerow is a boundary,
every fence another bond. From this point his decadence
dates. At first the dice spring merrily out on the board.
The gods throw, and he ; and they again, and then he,
and still with no misgivings ; those blacklegs know enough
to permit an occasional win. All the same, early or late,
comes that period in the game when suspicion grows a sicken-
ing certainty. He asked for long odds against him, and
he has got them with a vengeance ; the odds of the loaded
dice. While as for that curled darling he dreamed of, who
was to sweep the board and declare himself the chosen,
where is he ? He has dropped by the roadside, many a
mile behind. From henceforth on they must not look to
join hands again.

'Some there are who have the rare courage, at the realizing
point, to kick the board over and declare against further
play. Stout-hearted ones they, worthy of marble and brass ;

but you meet them not at every turn of the way. Such
a man I forgathered with by accident, one late autumn, on
the almost deserted Lido. The bathing-ladders were drawn
up, the tramway was under repair ; but the slant sun was
still hot on the crinkled sand, and it was not so much a
case of paddling suggesting itself as of finding oneself barefoot
and paddling without any conscious process of thought.
So I paddled along dreamily, and thought of Ulysses, and
how he might have run the prow of his galley up on these
very sands, and sprung ashore and paddled ; and then it
was that I met him—not Ulysses, but the instance in point.

' He was barelegged also, this elderly man of sixty or
thereabouts ; and he had just found a *cavallo del mare*, and
exhibited it with all the delight of a boy ; and as we
wandered together, cool-footed, eastwards, I learnt by
degrees how such a man as this, with the mark of Cheapside
still evident on him, came to be pacing the sands of the
Lido that evening with me. He had been Secretary, it
transpired, to some venerable Company or Corporation that
dated from Henry VII ; and among his duties, which were
various and engrossing, was in especial that of ticking off,
with a blue pencil, the members of his governing body, as
they made their appearance at their weekly meeting ; in
accordance with the practice dating from Henry VII. His
week, as I have said, was a busy one, and hinged on a Board
day ; and as time went on these Board days raced up and
disappeared with an ever-increasing rapidity, till at last
his life seemed to consist of but fifty-two days in the year
—all Board days. And eternally he seemed to be ticking
off names with a feverish blue pencil. These names, too,
that he ticked—they flashed into sight and vanished with
the same nightmare gallop ; the whole business was a great
humming zoetrope. Anon the Board would consist of
Smith, Brown, Jackson, &c., Life Members all ; in the
briefest of spaces Smith would drop out, and on would
come Price, a neophyte—a mere youngling, this Price. A
few more Board days flashed by, and out would go Brown

7

and maybe Jackson—on would come Cattermole, Fraser,
Davidson—beardless juniors every one. Round spun the
unceasing wheel; in a twinkling Davidson, the fledgling,
sat reverend in the chair, while as for those others—!
And all the time his blue pencil, with him, its slave, fastened
to one end of it, ticked steadily on. To me, the hearer,
it was evident that he must have been gradually getting
into the same state of mind as Rudyard Kipling's delightful
lighthouse keeper, whom solitude and the ceaseless tides
caused to see streaks and lines in all things, till at last he
barred a waterway of the world against the ships that per-
sisted in making the water streaky. And this may account
for an experience of his in the Underground Railway one
evening, when he was travelling home after a painful Board
day on which he had ticked up three new boys into vacant
places which seemed to have been hardly filled an hour.
He was alone, he said, and rather sleepy, and he hardly
looked at the stranger who got in at one of the stations,
until he saw him deposit in the hat-rack—where ordinary
people put their umbrellas—what might have been an
umbrella, but looked, in the dim light of the Underground,
far more like a scythe. Then he sat up and began to take
notice. The elderly stranger—for he was both gaunt and
elderly—nay, as he looked at him longer he saw that he
was old—oh, so very old! And one long white tuft of hair
hung down on his wrinkled forehead from under his top
hat,—the stranger squatted on the seat opposite him, produced a note-book and a pencil—a *blue* pencil too!—and
leaning forward, with a fiendish grin, said, "*Now* I'm going
to tick off all you fellows—all you Secretaries—right back
from the days of Henry the Seventh!"

' The Secretary fell back helplessly in his seat. Terror-
stricken, he strove to close his ears against the raucous
voice that was already rattling off those quaint old Tudor
names he remembered having read on yellowing parchment;
but all was of no avail. The stranger went steadily on, and
each name as read was ruthlessly scored out by the unerring

blue pencil. The pace was tremendous. Already they were in the Commonwealth ; past flew the Restoration like a racehorse—the blue pencil wagged steadily like a nightmare —Queen Anne and her coffee-houses—in a second they were left far behind ; and as they turned the corner and sped down the straight of the Georgian era, the Secretary sweated, a doomed man. The gracious reign of Victoria was full in sight—nay, on the stranger's lips was hovering the very name of Fladgate—Fladgate whom the Secretary could himself just remember, a doddering old pensioner—when the train shivered and squealed into St. James's Park Station. The Secretary flung the door open and fled like a hare, though it was not his right station. He ran as far as the Park itself, and there on the bridge over the water he halted, mopped his brow, and gradually recovered his peace of mind. The evening was pleasant, full of light and laughter and the sound of distant barrel-organs. Before him, calm and cool, rose the walls of the India Office, which in his simple way he had always considered a dream in stone. Beneath his feet a whole family of ducks circled aimlessly, with content written on every feature ; or else, reversing themselves in a position denoting supreme contempt for all humanity above the surface, explored a new cool underworld a few inches below. It was then (he said) that a true sense of his situation began to steal over him ; and it was then that he awoke to the fact of another life open to him should he choose to grasp it. Neither the ducks nor the India Office (so he affirmed) carried blue pencils, and why should he ? The very next Board day he sent in his resignation, and, with a comfortable pension and some reminiscence (perhaps) of that frontage of the India Office, crossed the Channel and worked South till he came to Venice, where the last trace of blue-pencil nightmare finally faded away.

' "And are you never bored ? " I tenderly inquired of him, as we rocked homewards in a gondola between an apricot sky and an apricot sea.

' " During the first six months I was," he answered, frankly ; " then it passed away altogether, even as influenza does in time, or the memory of a *gaucherie*. And now every day lasts as long as a year of those Board days of old, and is fifty-two times as interesting. Why, only take this afternoon, for example. I didn't get over here till two, but first I met some newly-arrived Americans, and talked for a cycle with them ; and you never know what an American will be surprised at, or, better still, what he will not be surprised at ; and if you only think what that means—— Well, presently they left (they had to get on to Rome), so I went up to the platform over the sea and had oysters and a bottle of that delightful yellow wine I always forget the name of ; and aeons passed away in the consumption. Each oyster lasted a whole Board day, and each glass of yellow wine three. Then I strolled along the sands for a century or so, thinking of nothing in particular. Lastly, I met you, and for some twelve months I've been boring you with my uninteresting story. And even yet there's the whole evening to come ! Oh, I had lots of leeway to make up when I came over here ; but I think I shall manage it yet—in Venice ! "

' I could not help thinking, as I parted from him at the Piazzetta steps, that (despite a certain incident in the Underground Railway) here was one of the sanest creatures I had ever yet happened upon.

' But examples such as this (as I said) are rare ; the happy-starred ones who know when to cut their losses. The most of us prefer to fight on—mainly, perhaps, from cowardice, and the dread of a plunge into a new element, new conditions, new surroundings—a fiery trial for any humble, mistrustful creature of use-and-wont. And yet it is not all merely a matter of funk. For a grim love grows up for the sword-play itself, for the push and the hurtle of battle, for the grips and the give-and-take—in fine, for the fight itself, whatever the cause. In this exhaltation, far from ignoble, we push and worry along until a certain day of a mist and a choke, and we are ticked off and done with.

' This is the better way ; and the history of our race is
ready to justify us. With the tooth-and-claw business we
began, and we mastered it thoroughly ere we learnt any other
trade. Since that time we may have achieved a thing or
two besides—evolved an art, even, here and there, though
the most of us bungled it. But from first to last fighting
was the art we were always handiest at ; and we are generally
safe if we stick to it, whatever the foe, whatever the weapons
—most of all, whatever the cause.'

The yellow sands finally ran out in 1897. But they had
been running down ever since Beardsley had retired (to the
secret relief of his editor who grudged him his youth and
his early fame).

And so the primrose ephemeron, that had fluttered so
bravely, became ' spent gnat ' and floated, on the current
of events, first out of fashion, then out of existence. Such
gold as was in the yellow had been of Kenneth Grahame's
minting.

CHAPTER VI

ATTAINMENT

BUT, though the *Yellow Book* was gone, before it went Kenneth Grahame had arrived at a literary renown. And to keep pace with his position in letters and in Threadneedle Street, he had quitted his eyrie above the Chelsea Embankment to become a householder in Kensington Crescent. To keep his house he engaged a certain Sarah Bath, a martinette, and an outspoken lady of surpassing honesty. She had looked after a gentleman in the Temple before Kenneth secured her. She specialized in bachelors. She regarded her new employer from two points of view. The Mr. Jekyll, who went to the Bank of England, of him she approved ; the Mr. Hyde, ' who wrote bits in the papers ', she mistrusted. She openly said that literary men were ' loose fish '. ' I suppose bankers are gold fish ? ' riposted her master.

Sarah waited at table and was always ready to take a part in the conversation. A dinner guest, a man of law and ignorant of Sarah's past, compared politely the luxury of his host with the lack of it at his own chambers. He added that he would like to see all the Temple bed-makers hanged. He was surprised when Sarah, over his shoulder, said grimly, ' I wouldn't hang round *your* neck, Sir, were it ever so.'

It was at Kensington Crescent that Kenneth Grahame, banker and dilettante in letters, awoke one morning to find himself an author and celebrated.

In 1895 John Lane had published for him *The Golden Age*, a little book on the borderland between Prose and Poetry, bound in yellow buckram, and enhanced with a design by Mr. Charles Robinson.

It was a collection of eighteen articles about children.

It included the half-dozen of similar essays previously produced in *Pagan Papers*. Its success was instantaneous and remarkable. The reviewers and critics were unanimous in praise. To read the more laudatory of the critiques makes the Song of Solomon seem as a Commination Service. The poorest notice comes from the *Saturday Review* critic. But even he, I imagine, meant well when he said of *Harold* and *Edward, Charlotte* and the serene *Selina*, ' there could be few better entertainments for a wet afternoon '.

Kenneth's most important lauder was Algernon Charles Swinburne. The poet was no weekly reviewer, and printed praise of his was therefore as sensational a thing as could befall a book. I think that if Mr. Kipling sat down to-day and wrote at some length an appreciation of a new author, that his unbending would scarcely cause the commotion that Mr. Swinburne's condescension (in two columns) gave rise to. This condescension was accounted, in leading articles, pulpits and other places, not so much as a generous eulogy of a book about Innocence by Mr. Kenneth Grahame but as a sign, in a renegade bard, of grace and of repentance for a past best described by Sir Owen Seaman (in the ' Dolores ' manner) :

> ' Panatheist, bruiser and breaker
>   Of kings and the creatures of kings,
> I shouted on Freedom to shake her
>   Feet loose of the fetter that clings ;
> Far rolling my ravenous red eye,
>   And lifting a mutinous lid,
> To all monarchs and matrons I said I
>   Would shock them—and did.

> ' O delights of the time of my teething,
>   Félise, Fragoletta, Yolande !
> Foam-yeast of a youth in its seething
>   On blasted and blithering sand !
> Snake-crowned on your tresses and belted
>   With blossoms that coil and decay,
> Ye are gone ; ye are lost ; ye are melted
>   Like ices in May.

'Hushed now is the bibulous bubble
     Of "lithe and lascivious" throats ;
Long stript and extinct is the stubble
     Of hoary and harvested oats ;
From the sweets that are sour as the sorrel's
     The bees have abortively swarmed ;
And Algernon's earlier morals
     Are fairly reformed.

'I have written a loyal Armada,
     And posed in a Jubilee pose ;
I have babbled of babies and played a
     New tune on the turn of their toes ;
Washed white from the stain of Astarte,
     My books any virgin may buy ;
And I hear I am praised by a party
     Called Something Mackay ! '

Mr. Swinburne's most quoted words in this ' babble of
babies ' were that *The Golden Age* was ' well-nigh too
praiseworthy for praise '.   He confesses that *Harold* was
his favourite of Kenneth's four dream-children.   In this
preference he is not original.   But he goes on to say briefly
that *Harold* (and, says Mr. Swinburne, a more deliciously
life-like child was never begotten of fancy) would have been
' a good playfellow for Shakespeare's *Mamillius* '.   The idea
is an intriguing one.   *Harold* has an imagination which is
his chief charm.   Its mission is to cause a creeping of the
flesh.   Had the small *Mamillius* been given half a chance
his fancy might have caused a creeping of the flesh
also, perhaps adding to that a further chattering of the
teeth :

Hermione.   ' Pray you, sit by us and tell's a tale.'

Mamillius.   ' Merry, or sad, shall't be ? '

Hermione.   ' As merry as you will.'

Mamillius.   ' A sad tale's best for Winter.   I have one of
sprites and goblins.'

Hermione.   ' Let's have that, good Sir.   Come on, sit down.'

Mamillius.   ' There was a man——'

Hermione.   ' Nay, come, sit down ;   then on.'

Mamillius. ' Dwelt by a churchyard ;—I will tell it
softly ; yon crickets shall not hear it.'

Hermione. ' Come on then, and give't me in mine ear.'

Alas, of course, the entrance of *Leontes* and others stops the
story. But compare *Harold's* tale of the burglars with the
' sprites and goblins ', with the above beginning. I think
that I see, with Mr. Swinburne, a brotherly likeness in the
two styles.

In the main Mr. Swinburne's review is quotation and
what is not text is not very remarkable. I should say
however that, as a *selling* critique, his must, for ever, rank
among the bonanzas—the bonanzas that most writers of
books must do without. And that, possibly, is because
(though most writers work much harder than Kenneth
Grahame worked) a book, in the best sense of the word, is
seldom born to them. And *The Golden Age* was a book in
every sense of the word ' best '. It was good on the counter
and good on the knee. And after nearly forty years, it
continues to possess these two goodnesses.

I have told of its most famous review—that of Mr.
Swinburne. And I have mentioned its worst—not a very
bad worst—at the hands of the *Saturday Review*. Its best
I will not attempt to name, for what (as the maidens of the
Stepney literature class, it may be remembered, once said to
the author) ' is one among so many ' ?

But I think that the pleasantest review of all received
came from New York. The reviewer mentions his finding
of *The Golden Age* in conjunction with his seeing, shortly
before that, of a White Admiral butterfly, the first that he
had seen for many years. He treats both events as one and
says of them, ' In the second half of a man's century he may
be thankful for anything that, for the time being, lifts two
score of years off his back.' His thanks therefore go both
to the butterfly and to Mr. Grahame. I think that ' Mr.
Grahame ' must have enjoyed these thanks and rejoiced
greatly in his co-recipient of them.

I have been struck, in my reading of these old press

notices, with the multitude of famous authors to which
Kenneth Grahame is compared by his critics—generally to
his advantage. I tried to keep count of the names but,
after making a list of seventeen, I recalled that comparisons
were odious, and I stopped counting. But Shakespeare,
Dickens and Thackeray are among that seventeen.

And again and again does some obvious person hail
Kenneth Grahame wearer of the cloak of Carroll. But the
two men are alike in no whit save that each made his reputation in mighty few words. Carroll was, though mathe-
matical, impractical and, though logical, absurd. Kenneth,
when he came to build Mole End and Toad Hall, was
sound, solid and illogical. Kenneth Grahame was a
philosopher. Carroll was a Don.

Lewis Carroll writing to a friend says, ' The favour I
would ask is that you do not tell me any more stories, such
as you did on Friday, of remarks which children are said
to have made on sacred subjects—remarks which most
people would recognize as irreverent, if made by *grown-up
people* but which are assumed to be innocent when made
by children.' The story which gave cause for the complaint,
' only made after changing my mind several times ', was
quoted from a recently published review of *The Golden Age*
in which was repeated the innocent alteration, by a little
girl, of a well-known text : ' Many are cold but few are
frozen.' And I dare say that Kenneth Grahame, reading
his review, smiled. Though, at the same time, I am sure
that he would not himself have committed the *bêtise* of
passing on the burlesque, blameless though it was, to a
prince of the Church.

Kenneth Grahame and Lewis Carroll were both ' Great
Lovers ' of all things, great and small. Kenneth has been
seen concerned over the fate of a fictional camel. And
' during the first public dramatic representation of *Alice in
Wonderland* at the Polytechnic, the entertainment took the
form of a series of *tableaux*, interspersed with appropriate
readings and songs. Mr. Dodgson (Lewis Carroll was, of

course, The Rev. Mr. Dodgson) exercised a rigid censorship over all the extraneous matter introduced into the performance, and put his veto upon a verse in one of the songs in which the drowning of kittens was treated from a humorous point of view.'

For my own part I do not know any author to whom I could liken Kenneth Grahame. Unless indeed it were to ' Syr Thomas Maleore Knyght, of Newbold Revell (the last a name Kenneth would have delighted in), Warwick '.

Sir Thomas, who died in 1470, gave to England the old Arthurian story, rescued for us *Lancelot* and *Guinevere* from the French. He gave us the Romance of Knight Errantry and he might almost have written ' The Reluctant Dragon '. His style was stately and dignified. He was soldier and romanticist, he was a scholar and a poet and, had Kenneth Grahame worn any mantle but his own, I imagine that he may have worn that of Sir Thomas Malory.

It was my own good fortune not to discover Kenneth Grahame piecemeal. The *National Observer* flourished on a day when I was little likely to be reading it, the *Yellow Book* cost five shillings a number at a time when my five shillingses were few. So I came on Kenneth Grahame in bulk on the counter of a book-shop in Bedford. I took up a little volume bound in yellow because I liked the name on the cover—*The Golden Age*. I hoped it was going to be something like *The Heroes*. I opened it at random and began to read. It was not quite as *The Heroes* and yet it might well have been made by one who had helped to wake ' the white-ash breeze ' on the benches of Argo. I didn't bother to look what that one's name might be, but I stood and read his book. Folk pushed me and trod on me and at last an assistant asked if he could ' show me anything '. I said, ' Eh? No—Yes, I mean, I'll take *this*.'

I did and walked home among the Saturday evening crowd in the High Street reading as I walked. I bumped into this one and that one bumped into me. Which is, perhaps, the right way to buy a book and read a book, but the book

has to be, of course, the right book that you have bought.
I did not look to see who had made *The Golden Age* until I
had finished it, even then, seeing that *some one* had, his name
seemed of no particular moment.

Three years later, in 1898, John Lane published a successor
and sequel to *The Golden Age* and proved conclusively that
a success can be repeated. Although to Mr. A. A. Milne
demanding a sequel to *The Wind in the Willows* (' a second
wind ' he calls it) Kenneth Grahame replied : ' Sequels are
often traps which the wise author does well to avoid, if he
wants to go, like Christian, on his way singing ! '

Dream Days, moreover, contained the top note of all
Kenneth Grahame's articles and short stories. For, to me,
the tale of ' The Reluctant Dragon ' marks the apogee of its
author's art.

It was natural that, as edition followed edition, both
books should begin to appear in illustrated form. Out-
standing among the illustrators is Mr. Maxfield Parrish, of
U.S.A., who, writing to the publishers, says of his pictures :
' It surprises me very much to hear that Mr. Grahame likes
the illustrations I made for his books ; such books, which so
thoroughly illustrate themselves, should not have pictures
in them ; the only reason for illustrating them is that they
sell better so—in Texas and Idaho ! '

In America Kenneth Grahame and his works boomed.
Elsewhere in this book I have shown to what extent they
appealed to the American Navy. And other seafarers than
American tars appreciated *The Golden Age*. Mr. Austen
Purves, writing to Kenneth Grahame in 1908, says, ' You
will be interested to hear that in the Kaiser's cabin, on the
royal yacht *Hohenzollern*, there are only two books in the
English language. One of them is the Bible and the other
is Kenneth Grahame's *Golden Age.*'

And had the author wished to make money by writing
for American publications, or by lecturing in the States,
he might have had it by the bushel.

Among a hundred unanswered letters and telegrams, the

senders of which literally clamour for the 'copy' which
never came, I pick one paragraph from one letter which
voices the united attitude of all American journalism. The
editor of the *Ladies' Home Journal*, of Philadelphia, finishes
an appeal for 'something reflective of the Christmas spirit',
an appeal of such poignancy that it surely *deserved* to succeed
(willing moreover as the Journal was to 'purchase this
material a year in advance'), thus : ' Will you simply think of
us as figuratively and literally standing with both arms ex-
tended in welcome to *any* Christmas material for next year ? '

Furthermore, a friend of President Theodore Roosevelt
writes : ' The President and Mrs. Roosevelt again alluded
to your book and Mrs. Roosevelt informed us that she was
now engaged in reading *The Golden Age* and *Dream Days*,
for about the tenth time, to her children. The President
requested me to write to you and say that he would esteem
it a great privilege and compliment if you would send him an
autographed copy of your books and that in return he would
be very proud to send you an autograph copy of works of
his own. He also requested me to say that if you ever
visit the United States during his term as President, he would
be delighted to have you spend a week-end with him at the
White House in Washington.'

Kenneth thereupon packed up the books asked for and in
each he wrote :

> ' To President Theodore Roosevelt
> with highest respect and in grateful
> recognition of his courtesy
> from
> Kenneth Grahame '

And on receipt of the parcel the President replied :

' The White House,   ' *Oyster Bay, N.Y.*
  ' Washington   *June* 20, 1907
  ' *Personal*

' MY DEAR MR. GRAHAME,—I am sure that no one to whom
you could have sent those two volumes would appreciate

them more than Mrs. Roosevelt and I. I think we could both pass competitive examinations in them—especially in the psychology of Harold !

'Now there are two people from Scotland whom we especially wish to see as guests in the White House while we are still there to be hosts. One is Oliver, who wrote the best life of Alexander Hamilton that has ever been written ; and the other is yourself. Isn't there some chance of your coming over here ?

' With renewed thanks, believe me,
' Sincerely yours,
' THEODORE ROOSEVELT

' Mr. Kenneth Grahame
   England.'

It is easy to understand, the Kaiser and the President of the United States to set the fashion, that Kenneth Grahame's ' fan-mail ' equalled that of a film star. From all over the world felicitations reached John Lane's. It is interesting to read from this profusion of letters and to note among it the mere handful that, obviously, come with difficulty and from the heart, that are something more than the multitude emotions of the glib. Here is a specimen of the former :

' Lindsay, California. Jan. 24/15.

' DEAR MR. GRAHAME,—I ought to say " Dear Sir " seeing that we are strangers perhaps but I feel too friendly for so chilly an expression. Whether this will find you I do not know. You are perhaps several inches deep in Flanders mud or at the bottom of the North Sea ? (not however directly resultant upon being an author). Not being an author my*self* I do not know how it feels ; or how one gets treated. And my present proceeding may strike you as a trifle peculiar. However, I can't help that, I am a queer guy I suppose and have led and am leading a queer life. It is Sunday morning and the deadly hideousness of the California scenery has been, as is often the case, much on my nerves—you see I come from the Wye Valley and from South Devon and from some years spent upon the high seas beneath the old red rag, and after that eleven years in the San Joaquin Valley are as a life in the Bastille. This morning I have happened upon your *Golden Age*—and the years have rolled away and I have been again a boy in England.—(I was an English public school boy once !) —and I lay in bed and laughed as I haven't laughed in years—And now, before I return to the existence that is at present my lot, I just want to drop you a line and thank you for having written *The Golden Age*. It has helped me out a lot.—I have small time for reading and small chance —Please don't think me impertinent—I am aware that it was not written for my especial benefit—But you have no idea how clearly I see the wind in the trees by the Wye— and one thousand things that are part of the life of a boy in England—May the blessings of the gods be yours ; and your princess exceeding fair—And now I'll lay my course again so so long.—

'Yrs. gratefully—'

This letter is one of the very few of its kind that is docketed as ' replied to '.

But to a little girl who, having read *Dream Days* from ' The Twenty-first of October ' down to ' A Departure ', writes, of the latter story, to ask ' could you please explain to me where the " res " is " an-gusta " and what are " weekly books "—i love your books ', Kenneth (a poor correspondent towards most people was punctilious towards Youth) has replied : ' *Res angusta* is Latin for a very small income. The " weekly books " are the tradesmen's account books which are supposed to be paid weekly, and when they aren't there's trouble, sooner or later. They are tiresome things and, when *you* reach that stage, I advise you to have nothing to do with them, but to pay cash. It may be troublesome, but it brings mental ease and peace ! ' A counsel of perfection indeed.

The success of *The Golden Age* and *Dream Days* caused a second blooming and booming in *Pagan Papers*. A lady reader of the last writes, concerning ' Marginalia ' : ' I have been puzzling over a certain passage and I have never met any one yet who seemed able to throw any light on the subject. On p. 78 you quote " By this single battle of Magnesia, Antiochus the Great lost all his conquests in Asia Minor " ; of course, as you say, battle can be changed into " bottle ", but *what* is the substitute for *conquests* ? In the ordinary way of things a small hitch like that would not worry me, but *Pagan Papers* is one of my much-beloved " bed-books " (as E. V. Lucas would say) and every time I come across that bit I wonder.'

She is probably wondering still, for the author, who might have made several answers to her query, preferred to make none.

But to a lady who sends him, in 1916, a book-plate of her designing the motto of which is taken from the ' Pagan Paper ' ' Non libri sed liberi ', he writes, ' Thank you for your beautiful book-plate, the Kelmscott wood-cut adapts itself admirably to its new purpose and—as for the motto—it might almost be classical ! Yes, Latin is passing fast away and many another thing with it, and a new world is being born wherein they will tell braver tales than those of tall Troy and Phæacia.'

' Non libri sed liberi ' [1] being set as the subject of an essay in an American literature class, a school-girl declares that, ' Kenneth Grahame advocates the purchase of old editions and yet this passion for first bindings often leads mothers to neglect their babies.' Bibliophiles indeed !

In the year that *Dream Days* went to press, its author, still under forty, was appointed Secretary to the Bank of England. A high place to have attained to. And one that only merit in Mammon could have enabled him to reach. Small wonder that admirers of his literary genius were

[1] ' Not books but children now and adopted within the circle.'— *Pagan Papers*.

confounded if they learnt as they did occasionally, that the creator of *Harold*, the writer of *The Golden Age*, was connected, and highly, with anything so near to the apotheosis of top-hatted respectability as The Bank of England. At the Bank the new Secretary was rumoured to be a writer on his afternoons off. A member of the Directorate, hearing of the Secretary's book, *The Golden Age*, ordered it under the impression that it dealt with bullion or bi-metalism, then a matter of financial moment. Or, at least, he says that he did in a letter of warm appreciation of the purer metal purchased, which he addresses to ' My dear Dark Horse '.

In the spring of 1899, recovering from an almost fatal attack of pneumonia (Kenneth and Mr. Kipling, his late colleague on the *National Observer*, were both at death's door of the same ailment at the same moment), he went to Cornwall to recuperate.

About this time he became engaged to marry Elspeth, the elder of the two gifted daughters of Mr. R. W. Thomson, of Edinburgh. Of Miss Thomson, a friend who knew her before and after marriage, writes : ' Elspeth had a happy indifference to the lesser conventions of the social world and her gift of imagination and intelligent sympathy enabled her to follow her husband's mind and give him, throughout his life, an ideal companionship.' And Kenneth, writing of his engagement to his old friend Miss Bradley, daughter of the celebrated Dean of Westminster, says :

' DEAR MISS BRADLEY,—Elsie refuses to have anything to do with an engagement ring of any sort. And I respect unconventionality of any kind too much to even protest. But I do feel strongly that there ought to be a ring in the business *somewhere*—to appease the gods—and circumstances seem to mark *you* out for it clearly. So I hope that you will not refuse to accept the one I send along with this. It is of no value, unless it will sometimes remind you of a friendly action—and if you do friendly things you must put up with being reminded of them.

'Yours most sincerely,
'KENNETH GRAHAME'

Miss Bradley says that her father was devoted to Kenneth ' and recognized in him a master of English prose. Not least did he appreciate his boyish mind. The regard was mutual. Together they would sit, old churchman and young banker, and quote their favourite passages from the classics or else the younger man would listen to reminiscences which went far back into the first half of the nineteenth century.'

Kenneth's uncle, the Reverend E. J. Hawkins (father of Sir Anthony Hope Hawkins), writing to Kenneth upon his engagement, adds to his congratulations this wisdom : '¡Marriage involves a constant exercise of the art of living well with an equal, living with superiors or inferiors is easy in comparison. I hope that it will be the happy gift of you both to perceive and do this.'

In July of the same year after (he writes), ' an operation, carbolic and a certain weary wallpaper ', the parties were married at Fowey where Kenneth was completing his convalescence.

The bachelor establishment at Kensington Crescent was taken over by Miss Sarah Bath—who preferred not to be at the call of one of her own sex—and Mr. and Mrs. Grahame went to live at 16 Durham Villas, Campden Hill.

There a boy was born to them in May 1900. And it was at this time that Kenneth became the friend of Graham Robertson, the playwright and artist, who writes of him thus :

' He was then in Durham Villas, Campden Hill and I in Argyll Road, just round the corner ; a two-minutes' walk lay between us and the path soon became well worn.

' His special room in No. 16 was most characteristic ; it looked like a nursery. Books there were certainly, but they were outnumbered by toys. Toys were everywhere

ELSPETH GRAHAME
From the Painting by Sir Frank Dicksee, P.R.A.

—intriguing, fascinating toys which could hardly have been conducive to study and may have accounted to some extent for their owner's very occasional literary output.

' As his house was full of toys so was mine full of dogs, and we each found the other's surroundings quite normal and satisfactory.

' Any one who wants to know Kenneth Grahame may still find him in *The Golden Age* and *Dream Days*, the eternal boy, keenly alive to the beauty and wonder of the world around him, yet shy of giving expression to the strange happiness that bubbles up within him. In those long ago days when we saw much of each other, I always felt that, with all the frankness and jollity of his boyishness, there was also the boy's reticence and half-unconscious withdrawal into himself ; and then again, beyond the boy, was a man known by few, remote, but very much to be reckoned with.

' I was but touching the fringe of a great personality. As we were such near neighbours, he would happen in casually to dinner or later in the evening, and though we often spoke hardly more than did the somnolent dogs couched at our feet, yet memory seems to give me back hours spent in long and intimate conversation. We never wrote to each other, but I always felt that I had his friendship and it was very precious to me.

' He had a marvellous gift of silence. We all know the old rustic who said, " Sometimes I sets and thinks and sometimes I just sets." Kenneth Grahame had reduced " just setting " to a fine art. He would slowly become part of the landscape and a word from him would come as unexpectedly as a sudden remark from an oak or a beech. He could not have been thinking, because a silent thinker is, socially speaking, quite as disturbing to serenity as a motor cyclist. No, he was " just setting " ; in other words he was on the threshold of Nirvana ; his brain was receptive but at rest, a great peace was with him and about him and his companion was drawn into it.

'Animals loved him. They felt safe with him, and indeed his presence ever brought a sense of security, like the shelter of a hill or the shadow of a great tree. His quiet strength soothed and sustained.

'My trio of Bobtail Sheepdogs accepted him at once as a friend and welcomed him with effusion whenever he appeared ; and on one of them, called Portly, he conferred immortality by giving his name to the lost baby otter in *The Wind in the Willows*. "I hope you don't mind," he said to me, "but I must call him Portly because—well, because it is his name. What else am I to call him?"

'Dogs were a great link between us and we shared other enthusiasms, chief among them, perhaps, a love for the work, pictorial and poetical, of William Blake ; and my rather comprehensive collection of Blake's drawings may have lured my neighbour into a neighbourliness that otherwise might have taken longer to develop.

'Another tie was our mutual interest in Fairyland, upon the manners and customs of which country we could both speak with authority ; and we would discuss the points of view, proclivities and antecedents of its inhabitants with all the passionate earnestness displayed by really sensible people when speaking of Latest Quotations, Lunch Scores or Cup Finals.

'For us the Folk of Fairy Tale were genuine historical characters and we always tried to enter sympathetically into their feelings, but I remember that we sometimes found the morals of the virtuous heroes and heroines, though much insisted upon, not a little complicated and perplexing. For example, in one well-known story, the Good Girl, having been extra good, received a visit from an angel who agreed to grant her three wishes.

'"I should like to become as beautiful as the day," said the Good Girl—and small blame to her. "Certainly," said the angel. "And," continued the Good Girl, warming to her work, "I should like my sister to become as ugly as the devil." The angel booked this order without com-

ment. " And I should like to go to Heaven when I die,"
added the Good Girl—just in time. Luckily the wishes
were limited to three, or the unpopular sister might have
been dispatched to quite a different address.

' But it was a little puzzling—the angel seemed perfectly
satisfied with the Good Girl. Perhaps angels were more
easily satisfied in those days, and certainly the sister had
been rather trying. Still—we were really quite worried
about it.

' Later, when a play of mine, *Pinkie and the Fairies*, was
put on at " His Majesty's " I induced Kenneth to bring
his little son to the dress rehearsal, which was, in reality,
a big children's party. We were both interested to note
the effect produced upon the child by Ellen Terry, who
was dutifully trying to play an elderly part ; and, on being
questioned, Mouse delivered himself thus, " I should have
liked her very much if she had been Cinderella or the Fairy
Queen, but she was only an Aunt." But so saying had
he not glimpsed the Fairy Lady under the dull disguise of
every day ?

' As the author of *The Golden Age* was the greatest living
authority upon Aunts, and as my play dealt somewhat
daringly with the same subject, I was naturally much
wrought up by his presence at the performance and enormously relieved when he expressed approbation. And I
really think he enjoyed himself—anyhow, he said less than
ever afterwards, which I knew to be a good sign.

' I had hardly ever, before then, met Kenneth Grahame
amongst a crowd, we had nearly always been alone together,
and I remember, as he came towards me through the press,
realizing how distinct he was from the people round him.
There was something not abnormal, but super-normal in
his presence—he was the slightest bit over life-size (any
painter will know what that means)—there was a splendour
about him that was both of the body and the spirit. He
was a being of a different race, or perhaps a throwback
to what our race may have been before it became stunted

and devitalized. It was the impression of a moment, but
I never forgot it. His good looks I had hitherto taken
as a matter of course—it seemed natural that the writer
of such books should look like that—but, as I then saw
him, towering above his fellows, his beauty took on a new
significance, showing him as the lost Arcadian, the wanderer
from the Country of the Young, one who had looked into
the eyes of Pan and listened to the Piper at the Gates of
Dawn.'

In May 1906, the Grahames left London and took, at
Cookham Dene, a furnished house beside the Thames.
Once again, was there,

> A living river at the door
> A nightingale in the sycamore.

FROM THE PORTRAIT BY JOHN SARGENT, R.A.

CHAPTER VII

' THE OLD LADY '

KENNETH GRAHAME entered the service of the Bank of England in 1878 on the nomination of Mr. William Lidderdale, a director, who later became Governor of the Bank.

The service of The Old Lady of Threadneedle Street is a good service and its fairly plentiful rewards are the safe and humdrum rewards of beaurocracy. That is to say they offer a moderate man security for himself and his family and allow him a financial peace of mind. And banking hours are easy when compared with those of other professions. So, on the whole, Kenneth Grahame, a man without the itch of personal ambition, found himself suited to his employment. Other spheres he might have preferred —grave scholarship and gay,—' the line of festal light in Christ Church hall '—but here he was and here he was content to be. Throughout his life he was a man who did the work his hand had to do with thoroughness and distinction. He passed the Bank's entrance examination with honours and, for the English essay set by the examiners, he obtained full marks—a thing without example before his day, or after it, in all the Old Lady's years. The essay had India for a thesis and though its success is still recalled the actual screed no longer exists.

In that ' private ledger ' (to which I have referred before now) I find this young philosophy of a virtuous apprentice towards his work and his play :

' A certain old clerk in one of the pay departments of the Bank of England used to spend his yearly holiday in relieving some turnpike man of his post and performing all the duties pertaining thereto till recalled to Threadneedle

Street. This was vulgarly supposed to be an instance of slavery to one's accustomed work—of " pay and receive " —and spoken of pityingly. But that man doubtless knew what he wanted, knew one way of seeing Life. And what better way? And if all he was good for was to pay and take payments at least he recognized the fact, accepted it, boldly built thereon and went for it in its best shape.'

Nevertheless, the first occupation of the young clerk's leisure hours was the mastery of shorthand. This achieved, he joined the volunteers and occupied himself further with social work in the East End. Miss Evelyn Lidderdale, at whose father's house on the Thames Kenneth and Roland Grahame were, as young men, frequent visitors, remembers going with a sister to see those fine London Scots drill in Hyde Park. The ladies went in a double perambulator with a dual chaperoning of nurses, whereof one, a Scotch woman of character, had formerly been nurse to the two tall warriors to-day the object of the excursion. Kenneth had become a sergeant and presently, recognizing his admirers, ordered a complimentary charge to be made upon the perambulator. His platoon, flourishing its muskets, therefore advanced with leaps, bounds and loud cheers. The two objectives in the perambulator were enchanted. Not so their guardian who thought that her Master Kenneth had ' gone gyte '. ' Mighty me,' she muttered, ' I must save the young leddies.' And she upset the perambulator, upset the whole ' rickmatick ', over the low railing. However, her particular soldiers picked up its contents who were more enchanted than ever.

Later Kenneth Grahame made, as we know, the acquaintance of Dr. Furnivall and, to his other off-time occupations, was added an interest in the conduct of the New Shakespeare and Browning Societies—Browning who had been, so nearly, a Bank of England clerk even as Kenneth was. And presently Kenneth Grahame began, as we know too, to dispatch those little ' literary meteorites ' to here and to there in the district of Fleet Street. Miss Lidderdale remembers him in those days. 'Very silent unless you got him to yourself and encouraged him to talk. Then he spoke most entertainingly and was a delightful and a witty companion. He never spoke of himself, but he was always so kind and so interested in what *you* were interested in. At that time I was interested in writing and Kenneth was most helpful and encouraging and, I do believe, happier even than I when an essay of mine gained a first prize.'

The young man himself, I imagine, while he enjoyed his Bank work and recognized that no fun can equal the fun of really High Finance and that Romance walks in Threadneedle Street as truly as she wanders by ' the stripling Thames at Bablock-Hythe ', yet carried another province, that of Saturn, in his heart of which he says :

' This is an over-surveyed age, and rarely now are atlases to be found containing those broad buff spaces so dear to our youth, unbroken by the blue of any lake, crawled upon by no caterpillar mountain ranges ; wherein you might rear a dozen clamorous cities of magic, and yet leave room for a prairie or two, a Sahara, and a brand-new set of Rockies. But there are kingdoms yet to discover, and golden realms that await their Marco Polo. Every one of these children, who are going about the business of life so absorbedly, with such small regard for us big fellows coming and going vaguely, out of focus, on the edge of their horizon, has got a particular one of his own, shimmering with barbaric pearl and gold, pleasantly elastic as to its boundaries. You may be quite sure of this ; and you may be equally sure of another thing—that you shall never enter in. Whatever the extent of his usual confidences, this gate is sternly shut.

' The reason why ? Well, perhaps mainly shamefacedness. The thing as seen by him would appear to you, he knows well, too incredibly fantastic. Possibly he would be laughed at—the sort of criminal dock in which a child most dreads to stand. In any case he lacks the language for the task. The expression of the commonest sentiments is

apt to gravel him ; how much more the voicing of these
nebulae—as impossible a business as if he were bidden to
sing in colour, or to paint in odours gathered from the
garden. But, above all, to reveal would be in some sort
to break the spell ; and this is his own treasure, his peculiar
possession—perhaps the only thing he has got which is
altogether and entirely his very own. Even with each
other, children do not usually share their kingdoms. To
be sure, a fellow-feeling in kingdoms is a rare fine thing—
the only thing, perhaps, really worthy the name of sympathy ; and kingdoms blossom and expand so splendidly
under a judicious dual control. But the risk is too great
—the risk of jeers, rebuffs, sheer incapacity to understand—
to make such confidences common.

' These kingdoms, it should be well understood, are no
casual resorts, but exist side by side with the other life
evident to the grosser visual rays, occupying at least a
fair half of actual existence. At regular periods, the child
steps deliberately out of the present tangibility into his
property over the border ; and again, when his time is up,
steps just as deliberately back. In continuity, in ordered
procession of facts, the thing goes on with just the same
regularity as that other routine of baths, bread-and-butter,
lessons and bed ; and is about as near a thing to a fourth
dimension as can be found in actual working order.

' Cases will vary, of course, with dispositions and tem-
peraments. Some wealthy and enviable mites run three
or four kingdoms at once, of differing qualities and capa-
bilities, keeping them all going together, as a juggler sus-
tains half a dozen oranges in mid-air. Others there are,
of more fickle nature, who periodically abandon their
kingdoms for fresh conquests in a newer Spain. The lion
and the lizard keep those forgotten courts, wherein they
were wont to disport themselves during church-service.
The owl hoots and the wind blows chill through those vast
buildings of yester-year, a short time since so full of song
and laughter. They themselves, forgetful ones, are up and

away across the virgin prairies of another land, unrepresented
in Europe by any ambassador.   But, as a general rule, the
kingdom is colonized in the earliest possible days of sub-
consciousness—undergoes alterations, of course, extensions,
re-peoplings, as time goes on and experience teaches lessons
—but remains practically the same kingdom, always there,
always handy to step into, up to a time when one would
blush to be suspected of such a possession.   At what specific
date indeed, dare one fix the terminus ?   Cataclysmal
periods arrive, and shake us, and pass, and the kingdom
endures.   There is the fateful moment, for instance, when
one " goes into tails ".   At school they nip for the first
coat-tail.   Nips are the direful penalty, and with nips comes
much besides.   Yet the kingdom often remains, surviv-
ing nips, dignities, and responsibilities.   Other portentous
changes succeed—I will not enumerate them ; with which
of them can one say the kingdom vanishes ?   One wakes
up some day and finds it gone.   Yet who can name the
date of the eclipse ?

'As for the population : your regular relations, whose
mistaken adherence to an indefensible scheme of life brings
them so frequently into collision with you,—they are rarely
seen there, and then only in distressingly menial positions.
Hewers of wood and drawers of water, all of them, if so
be as they have even the luck to get a ticket of admission
at all.   On the other hand, the casual people who have
been kind to you and passed, or have won your heart by
athletic or other similar gifts—here they walk as princes
and familiars, doing wondrous things, sharing with you
the ungrudged sweets of empire.   And yet, while the kingdom's chief charm lies in its constancy, in its abiding presence
there at your elbow, the smiling gate wide open, whether
fortune favour or frown, its inhabitants are sadly apt to
vary.   Other folk come on the scene, who tip you, and
take you to treats, and have to be recognized and considered accordingly ; so from time to time, as you revisit
the familiar land, fresh guests travel down with you, and

fresh heroes make up your house-party. Then there is the
Princess—well, honestly I think princesses are more permanent. They change at times, of course, they drop out,
they disappear ; but it is usually more their fault than
yours. They cease to be kind, perhaps they take up with
another fellow, or leave your part of the country ; and
under such circumstances only a novelist would expect
you to remain true. Absolute inconstancy, a settled habit
of fickleness, belongs, I am sure, to a later period. The
Princess, then, often sees out many a guest of real distinction ;
nay, she is frequently your sole comrade, through storied
cities, on desert isles, or helping to handle your cutter where
the Southern Cross is reflected in fairy seas. Then it is
that you say at your leisure all those fine things that you
never can get off through the garden-hedge ; while she,
for her part, is sympathetic, appreciative, and companionable, to a degree you never would guess from the shy awk-
wardness that masters her in this narrow little world down
here. And yet—an embarrassing person somewhat at times.
One has often a surmise that she is not being done full
justice—in spite of her capacities for pulling an oar or
loading a musket, she is meant for better things.

' These kingdoms, I have said, are always close at hand,
always attainable in case of need. But, of course, there
are special periods of vacation, when one resorts thither so
habitually that schemes and arrangements can be settled
beforehand, to be worked out in detail when the regular
hour arrives. The reading aloud of improving matter—
something without any story in it—at stated times, may
even come to be looked forward to, if you happen to possess
a fine, healthy kingdom, in good working order, that requires
your attention for a more protracted spell than just between
courses at table. A duty-walk with an uninteresting person
is simply a return ticket to cloudland. As bed-time arrives
you promptly book for the same terminus ; hence it comes
that you never properly fall asleep in this tangible world,
but pass through the stage of your own peculiar country

to that droll continent which mixes up your two existences
for you with a humour you could never achieve unaided.
But the services of the Church afford the most fixed and
certain periods of all ; for nothing short of a sick bed saves
you from the grim compulsion, while, on the other hand,
once there, little is asked of you but quiet and conformity
to a certain muscular routine. Parents, therefore, should
be very modest, when inclined to flatter themselves that
the passing thoughts and reflections of their children are
quite clear to them, and that they can follow the ripple of
every mood on those ingenuous countenances. The mother
who notes with delight the rapt, absorbed air of her little
son, during the course of a sermon that is stirring her own
very vitals, and builds high hopes thereon, is probably
egregiously mistaken. Ten to one he is a thousand miles
away, safe in his own kingdom ; and what is more, he
has shut the door behind him. *She* is left outside, with
the parson and the clerk.

' In the same way, a child who is distraught during the
conversational hour of meals, answering at random or not
at all ; who fails to catch the salient points of an arithmetic
or geography lesson—seeming, indeed, to regard these statistics and weary columns from very far off—is not necessarily a fool, nor half-baked as to mental equipment. He
has probably got a severer task cut out for him, and has
need of all his wits and all his energies. The expedition he
is leading, the palace he is exploring, the friends he is entertaining with that abandonment so characteristic of a land
without a currency—all these undertakings evoke commend-
able qualities. Indeed, who shall say he is not educating
himself all the time ? In his own way, of course, not yours.

' It should always be remembered that whenever a child
is set down in a situation that is distasteful, out of harmony,
jarring—and he is very easily jarred—that very moment
he begins, without conscious effort, to throw out and to
build up an environment really suitable to his soul, and to
transport himself thereto. And there he will stay, of a

certainty, until you choose to make things pleasanter. Life is so rough to him, so full of pricks and jogs and smartings, that without this blessed faculty of projecting a water-tight skin—nay, an armour-plating—his little vessel's seams would gape and its timbers crack too early. That which flows in his veins is ichor, closing the very wounds through which it issues ; and of the herb called self-heal he has always a shred or two in his wallet.

' This mental aloofness of the child,—this habit of withdrawal into a secret chamber, of which he sternly guards the key,—may have been often a cause of disappointment, of some disheartenment even, to the parent who thinks there can be no point, no path, no situation, where he cannot be an aid and an exposition, a guide, philosopher, and friend ; more especially to the one who, by easy but fatal degrees, reaches the point of desiring to walk in the child's garden as very God, both in the heat and the cool of his day. Let it be some consolation to them that they are the less likely to father a prig. This Bird of Paradise that he carries encaged within him, this Host that he guards within his robe through the jostling mart of shouting commonplaces, may be both germ and nutriment of an individuality which shall at least never suffer him to be a tame replica. The child to despair of is more rightly the one who shall be too receptive, too responsive, too easily a waxy phonograph.

' Meantime these kingdoms continue, happily, to flourish and abound. Space is filled with their iridescences, and every fresh day bubbles spring up towards the light. We know it—we know it : and yet we get no nearer them. Perhaps we are, unwittingly, even invited and honoured guests ; this is not the sort of invitation we would be likely to refuse. Possibly we may be walking, even now, arm-in-arm with some small comrade of real affinity of spirit, sharing in just those particular absurdities we would most like to commit. And all the time we are trundling about here dully in hansom cabs, while the other one of us, the lucky half, is having *such* a magnificent time! For the current is not yet switched on, the circuit is not yet made complete, by which we shall some day (I trust) have power to respond to these delightful biddings out of town, and get a real change of air. For the present we are helpless. Surely the shouts, the laughter, the banging of guns and the music, make noise enough to reach our ears? Ineffectually we strain and listen : we have lost our key, and are left kicking our heels in the dark and chilly street. And only just the other side of that wall—that wall which we shall never climb—what fun, what revels are going on!'

But for all these fine doings, these secret Saturnalia, Kenneth Grahame, the man built in compartments, was the perfect official. He had a noble presence, he dressed immaculately, he was immaculately groomed and, in his official existence, he seems to have shed some of the reserve which cloaked him in his private life. Sir Gordon Nairne, late a director of the Bank, first remembers him, 'fifty-one years ago. A winter evening and K.G. just about to leave the Bank in the London Scottish dress into which he had changed after hours. I did not know him at all then nor do I think we ever exchanged more than a word until he came some years later to work in the Chief Cashier's office where I also was engaged. He did not stay there very long but went to the Secretary's office where, so far as I can remember, he was at first occupied in cataloguing the books in the Directors' Library. As these were mainly on dry-as-dust subjects, I doubt if the task proved very interesting to him. Later he took part in the ordinary work of the Secretary's office and quickly rose, as his chiefs retired, to the position of Secretary.

'Although under the same roof our work was entirely different and many a day passed on which we only met at the luncheon table, where I occupied the seat next to him. I well remember an incident in connexion with which he had to write a very brief memorandum concerning the affairs of a pensioner of the Bank who had been under me.

He asked whether I thought the facts were clearly stated and I remember being much struck by the touch of romance with which he had invested the official life of a very ordinary man. I replied that it correctly described the case and that, had I laboured at it for a week, I could not have produced a description half so graphic.

' You ask about his gift of public speaking. He certainly possessed this in a remarkable degree and in a style peculiarly his own. He was slow and deliberate and seemed to pause frequently for the word which would most accurately describe his meaning, but this was only a prelude to the utterance of some dry and whimsical expression.'

When Sir Gordon Nairne was Chief Cashier Kenneth Grahame was Secretary and Mr. Wallace Governor of the Bank. The Bank's butler was Tolmie from beyond the Tweed. To him a visitor referred laughingly to the success of the Scot in London. Tolmie replied with all seriousness, ' Yes, Sir, and the Bank's an example. The Governor's Scotch, the Chief Cashier's Scotch, the Secretary's Scotch and *so am I* '.

Mr. Sidney Ward, of Baring Bros., once colleague of Kenneth's at The Old Lady's and a fellow toiler in Whitechapel, tells of his friend : ' He was older than I, and my senior by a few years at the Bank of England. I knew him well by sight some time before we actually met. This must have been in the latter part of the 'eighties and it was about this time that Kenneth was transferred to the Secretary's office where I was then working. It was there that I really got to know him. At that time he lived in a tiny little flat at the top of a building near the Chelsea Embankment. I well remember those interminable dingy stairs leading up to the charming little rooms where he lived. I don't suppose he ever suspected that I stood rather in awe of him in those days and it was only very occasionally that I plucked up the courage, of an evening, to go and call uninvited. Memorable evenings those were. I think the value of Kenneth's work in the Bank of England

lay rather on the literary and advisory side than on the
administrative and constructive. He left to others the
carrying out of big schemes. He preferred to keep existing
customs running smoothly rather than to launch out into
new schemes. He will not go down to history as a great
reformer, though many reforms were carried out during his
régime. He was always helpful and never obstructive,
conservative though he was. I can't imagine any one
who, at that time, was better suited for the position which
he held as Secretary of the Bank of England. In all the
push and bustle of a great institution, the conflicting
interests of different departments, and the personal jealous-
ies, sometimes, of their chiefs, Kenneth was just the man
to hold the balance—always there, always wise, never too
busy to see any one, a sound adviser of the Governor,
never rattled and universally respected—he was a far
greater force than most men imagined at the time. And,
as all those who have lived the best part of our lives know,
it is the silent forces, not the noisy ones, which guide the
world. Kenneth played a great part in the affairs of the
Bank of England and played it well. A delightful memory
is a week-end which I once spent with him at Streatley,
during a cold, sunny spring. A friend had lent him a
fourteenth-century cottage in the main street, and we had
a grand twenty-mile walk along the Ridgeway, the subject
of his " Romance of the Road ". If we either of us said
clever things that day they are forgotten, but we came
home happy and tired, bought some chops and fetched a
huge jug of beer from the pub. We cooked our dinner
over the open wood fire, and how good the chops were !
Then great chunks of cheese, new bread, great swills of beer,
pipes, bed, and heavenly sleep ! On the door of the cottage,
done in rusty nails, was the motto, " *Nisi dominus frustra.*"
An inquisitive American who was passing asked the old
woman who looked after the cottage what the motto might
mean. " I don't know what language it is," she said, " but
it means it's no good calling when the master's out ! " ' '

9

The duties of a Secretary of the Bank of England seem
to differ a little from those of a secretary to any other great
bank. At the Bank of England the Secretary acts as
the ambassador of the Governor and his directorate, and
is the Old Lady's official head of affairs which are not
purely financial. He opens negotiations in the first instance
and he closes them in the last. He must be a diplomat
and a courtier. He must be a man of infinite tact and
infinite charm. Of infinite firmness too. He must be
accessible and sympathetic to every one in his kingdom
from the Governor's self to the youngest member of his
staff. He must have all the threads in Threadneedle Street
within his hands and when he pulls the one or the other
none must know that it is he who is the compeller. And
the Bank, a great public institution, has its clubs, its
Literary Association (of which Kenneth was president), its
Libraries, its Debating Society and a score of similar
activities. And, at the last, the responsibilities of all must
lie, *ex-officio*, on the Secretary of the Bank. But Kenneth
Grahame was well fitted for the high post of a multitude of
duties that he occupied for ten years. The man who sits
in his chair to-day adds to the qualities I have outlined
that Kenneth had the knack of ' making men love him '.
He says that he personally owes his own position to the
sympathy and encouragement he received from his beloved
chief, ' a kind friend and a wise counsellor '. He says that
Kenneth's then growing fame in the world of letters was
recognized, and valued by many in the Old Lady's house.
He says that in all her stately story no visitor, whom
she desires to honour, has been received so worthily as in
the magnificent reign of Kenneth Grahame. But though
many at the Bank of England were proud of their ' literary
gent ', some shook their heads. Kenneth's old friend Dr.
Kingdon, the Bank's official M.D., wrote of the young
Secretary thus : ' Kenneth's a dear boy, a *very* dear boy,
but he doesn't think half enough of his position in the
Bank and in the City. They tell me that *he writes tales.*

So did Charles Lamb—but what of that ? Maybe Charles Lamb didn't think much of his position at East India House, but what after all *was* his position in the City to Kenneth's ? Kenneth should think *less* of books and *more* of being what he has come to be in the City.'

Of the many interesting visitors who came sight-seeing to Threadneedle Street when Kenneth was consul came the four young children of King George.[1] They were entertained royally, they were shown all the treasure of their grand-father's realm. They signed bank-notes, valued at £1,000 each, ' Edward of Wales, Albert of Wales, Mary of Wales and Henry '. And, surprise visit though it was, they had a tea which only Kenneth Grahame could have ordered and only his Old Lady could have supplied. And the guests went home happy and wrote the joint ' hospitable roofer ' which appears on the next page.

But not all visitors were so amiable as these. On the 4th of November 1903 a ' gentlemanly stranger ' (as the old romances say) called at the Bank and said that he wished to see the then Governor (Sir Augustus Prevost) with whom he was acquainted. The visitor was shown into a waiting-room and his name, Mr. George F. Robinson, was taken to the Governor's apartments. But Sir Augustus was not in the building. Mr. Robinson was so advised, but would he, in the Governor's absence, care to see the Secretary, Mr. Kenneth Grahame ? Mr. Robinson accepted the alterna-tive with every polite anticipation of enjoyment. Presently therefore Kenneth Grahame strode along the corridor to number one waiting-room. He entered with a compliment on his lips, but the visitor, without reply, thrust forth a roll of manuscript and bade the Secretary, ' Read this.' ' But,' said Kenneth, ' it is, I see, a very lengthy document—please state, briefly, what it amounts to ? ' ' Certainly,' said the obliging Mr. Robinson, and, as he spoke, he whipped out a heavy Service revolver, ' it amounts to——' *Bang ! bang !* Twice he let drive and no Harlequin ever jumped quicker

[1] Then the Prince of Wales.

April 23rd, 1907.

Dear Mr Grahame,

We thank you very much for your kindness to us to-day.

Edward.

Albert.

Mary.

Henry

FACSIMILE OF LETTER FROM ROYAL CHILDREN, 1907

through a door than did Kenneth Grahame. He returned
to the Secretarial Department and he summoned the
police. Mr. Robinson, finding himself alone, presently
stepped into the corridor where he fired yet a third shot,
just for fun. He then wandered down the Directors'
Corridor, followed, but with a very natural discretion, by
the Head Doorkeeper who, presently, marking his man to
ground in the Directors' Library, slammed the door on him
and locked it, without stopping to inquire if a stray director
or so were even then improving their minds within.

A council of war was forthwith held by the leading
athletes of the Bank and a certain middle-weight, as well
known at the Pelican Club as he was in the City, volunteered
to head an attack upon the strange occupant of the Library.
Now the Library was a long, narrow room—its sole entrance
being in the corridor. The volunteers entered on tip-toe.
At the extreme end of the long room sat Mr. Robinson and
his ever-ready revolver covered, in a discouraging manner,
the only approach to him. Thereupon the volunteers with-
drawing, listened to the saner views of their elders who said
that a frontal attack was certain to result in entirely
uncalled-for casualties.

At this juncture a Ulysses suggested that the Bank Fire
Brigade be called out. He said that the nozzle of the hose
could be levelled at Mr. Robinson, around the door's angle,
by an invisible hand. He said that a powerful jet, or stream,
of cold water would knock Mr. Robinson off his legs and,
this done, that then the main attack could at once be
delivered. The idea was put into successful operation
immediately. Mr. Robinson, on receiving the full force of
the hose, fell, as it had been said that he would fall, though
still he repeatedly fired his revolver, eventually hurling the
empty weapon at his invisible enemies. He was then,
but only after an epic resistance, secured. And he was, in
due course, found to be insane and sent to Broadmoor. But
when it was discovered that the only ' live ' cartridges in
Mr. Robinson's possession had been fired at Kenneth

Grahame in the waiting-room and that, since then, he had
been banging away with ' blank ' only, those who forbore
to attack prior to the inspiration of the fire-hose were full,
so I am told, of a manly chagrin. ' *Si jeunesse savait,*' they
said and sighed for a lost opportunity and laurels simply
thrown away.

At the Old Bailey the prisoner pleaded that his rolled
documents had been tied at one end with a black ribbon, at
the other with a white. These documents had been presented to Mr. Grahame lengthwise. It had therefore been
open to Mr. Grahame to grasp either one of the two ends.
Instead of the innocuous white end Mr. Grahame had preferred to take the end bound by the black ribbon, thus
proving that Fate demanded his immediate demise. Mr.
Robinson looked upon himself as a mere instrument in the
matter and quite without prejudice or guile.

Sir Augustus Prevost, the Governor of the Bank, for whom
Mr. Robinson had inquired in the first instance, was of Swiss
descent. A wag in the Discount Office, prominent in the
last stages of the scuffle, said, wiping his brows, that the
Governor's caller was obviously a compatriot—a Robinson
of the well-known Swiss family.

And Mr. *Punch*, next Tuesday, stated that : ' Mr. Kenneth
Grahame is wondering what is the meaning of the expression,
" As safe as the Bank of England ".'

But it had been a disagreeable affair and one that its
principal victim did not easily or lightly forget. And I
have no doubt that high banking officialdom was, for quite
a time, not a little chary about representing its chairmen
at chance interviews with gentlemanly strangers. The
Secretary of the London Joint Stock Bank, Mr. Edward
Clodd, voices the general feeling, rather humorously :

' *Prince's Street, E.C.* 25/11/03

' MY DEAR GRAHAME,—You will be flooded with congratulations on your happy escape but, when you can
retreat to a dry spot, please take mine, offered in all sin-

cerity and, perchance, touched with a fellow feeling.
"*Hodie mihi, cras tibi.*" If one, outside Arcady, could
have named an ideal spot, immune from risks, even were
the whole world running amok, it would have been such a
sanctum as yours !

'Sincerely yours,

'E. CLODD'

The Secretary of the Bank of England was, of course, as
Mr. Clodd said, overwhelmed with the congratulations of
those who, as one lady wrote, 'were horrified to hear of
his escape'. Yet no felicitations were more sincere than
those of his friend the head waiter at Littlehampton where,
on the ensuing Sunday, he stayed. 'But,' concluded the
former, 'to have missed *you* at *that* range, sir, well, 'e ought
never to be trusted with a gun in 'is 'and again, sir.' And,
when next Kenneth went to his barber, 'I saw your picture
in the paper the other day, sir,' said the 'scissor-man'.
'What did you think of it ? ' said the customer, anticipating
a compliment. 'I thought you wanted a hair-cut pretty
badly, sir,' answered the other professionally. On the
next page is the Press drawing referred to, displaying the
unruly lock which doubtless gave rise to the criticism.

In 1908 an intermittent and virulent form of influenza
at last sent Kenneth Grahame to Harley Street. There he
was told that a City and a sedentary life were undermining
him. He was advised that, could he afford to do so, he
should retire from the Bank of England. He determined
to act upon the advice given to him. And, though the
Bank's Directorate, that he had served so well, begged him
to take, for further consideration, a year's holiday on full
pay, he refused. His mind, he said, was made up and the
full pay would therefore be an emolument for which no
future return could be expected by the Old Lady.

So, one evening, he went home to Cookham Dene and
there he stayed by Father Thames and finished *The Wind in
the Willows* and made a fortune out of it which he did not

THE SECRETARY OF THE BANK OF ENGLAND
(From a newspaper sketch)

particularly want, although it was a much smaller fortune than might have been his had he, caring for fortunes, remained in Threadneedle Street where fortunes are.

When Kenneth Grahame, in July 1932, went further still from Threadneedle Street, *The Old Lady*, the Bank of England's well-known Quarterly, in a delightful memoir of her departed servant says :

' As more than twenty-four years have passed since Mr. Grahame retired from the position of Secretary of the Bank of England, only the more senior members of the Staff will have memories of him as a Bank Official, but all who are lovers of literature will share in the general feeling of regret that so brilliant a man has passed from the world, and will be proud to recognize that Mr. Grahame has, by his writings, conferred a distinction on the institution of which he was a member comparable to that with which Charles Lamb honoured the East India House.

' It was my privilege, when a junior in the service of the Bank, to come into personal contact with Mr. Grahame both before and after his appointment as Secretary, and I have pleasant recollections of many small kindnesses he showed to me and of the considerate manner in which he criticized my early efforts to adapt the Queen's English to the purposes of official letters. My impression of Mr. Grahame was of a shy, reserved man, with a fine presence and charm of manner, who did not fit in with my preconceived notions of a Bank Official ; but I had no idea that he was then engaged in writing the books which would gain for him a world-wide reputation, although I listened carefully to some advice he once gave me on the subject of punctuation and the construction of sentences.

' Amongst those who have served the Bank there have not been wanting men with definite literary gifts, but it was left for the nineteenth century to produce the man who was to be both an official of the Bank and a literary artist of the first rank, and the name of Kenneth Grahame will always be held in high honour by the Old Lady of Threadneedle Street and those who serve her.'

CHAPTER VIII

THE WIND IN THE WILLOWS

IF a man is Secretary to the Bank of England he must sit
for ever in the Governor's pocket where, naturally, there
is neither time nor place for literature. So the making of
books by Mr. Grahame came to an end. And, for a year
or so, life was lived at Durham Villas as in any other mag-
nate's home. There was early breakfast to be taken frock-
coated among cut flowers, silver and the floating fragrance
of very hot coffee. There was *The Times* to be crisply
turned over and glanced at. There was the rolled silk
umbrella and the newly brushed silk hat on the hall table.
There was the striking of a match followed by the sudden
morning scent of tobacco—and, *cloop*, the hall door closed
behind the master of the house, just as though he was any
clean-collared, well-dressed and upright City man who had
never heard of either Henley or Harland or even of a book
about children called *The Golden Age*. It was all very
unromantic.

But Kenneth Grahame was one of the exceptional men.
He was built in compartments. He was breathed on by
the ' rural Pan ' in the one and in the other—well, a man
does not attain to ultimate office in the Old Lady's service
without *some* ability to see also, the romance of Impersonal
Money. Which is a different thing entirely to personal
fortune. The former is Politics and the Poetry of Power,
the latter, though desirable indeed to most of us, is not
lyrical. Or few of us admit that it is.

Kenneth Grahame never in his life desired personal
fortune. Had he done so fortune was his for the asking
either in the City or among the morocco bindings of the

story-books. In the evening he left Threadneedle Street and came home, striding among the flower-beds of Kensington Gardens as good an Arcadian as Daphnis or as ' dear divine ' Comatas himself. And at home the baby was getting a big boy. Alastair Grahame (known, to his parents and his intimates, as Mouse) was four years old and the axis round which the world, at Durham Villas, revolved. Like many other little boys he was tyrannical about a bed-time story to go to sleep on. And his father was just the one to tell it. He would, when dressed for dinner, step into the night-nursery, quietly as only a big man can and, seating himself by the cot-side, slip a long black arm about a small white-night-gowned audience and begin.

For two years the nursery classics served his indolent purpose. But now Alastair was a four-year-old and the classics, which are strictly limited, were becoming exhausted. And one May evening in 1904 the lady of the house, anxious that she and her husband should not be *too* late in arriving at Lancaster Gate and the dinner engagement which even now waited them, said rather impatiently to her maid, attentive in the hall with cloak and fan and gloves, ' Where *is* Mr. Grahame, Louise ? '

Louise, a Wiltshire woman who still, even in the shadow of the Albert Memorial, used the archaic idiom of the Downs, replied with a sniff, ' He's with Master Mouse, Madam ; he's telling him some ditty or other about a Toad.'

Now ' ditty ', when used by a Downswoman, signifies, not Song but Story. And so was *The Wind in the Willows* born and Louise was its herald.

But as a tale it developed slowly, for there is much to interrupt bedtime stories when the teller must compose them as he tells. He pauses groping for an idea and, while he gropes, he attempts to interest the impatient listener with the extraneous affairs of workaday. And he succeeds in the attempt and, the listener cross-examining, the story-teller loses the thread of his discourse and Inspiration forthwith flies up the chimney.

And so the Saga of the Toad dillied and dallied and indeed might have died. But the weather turned warm and it was decided that London was no place for a little boy who was not, like his parents, bound to the Bank of England. Alastair, therefore, and his governess, went to Littlehampton and at that place of broad sands and blue water his father addressed him, frequently, by post.

Alastair was at Littlehampton for seven weeks and he received fifteen letters. Four of those letters are written to ' My darling Mouse ' and signed ' your loving Daddy '. Subsequent to the fourth letter the vocative becomes ' Dear Robinson ', and signature there is none, or none more intimate than a formal ' to be continued '. Alastair had taken the whim that Michael Robinson was a far finer name than Alastair Grahame and his father, while falling in with the fancy, found himself (so he said) incapable of affectionate familiarity towards an entire stranger.

But, to Mouse, or to Michael Robinson, each letter contains an instalment of the Adventures of Toad. And Michael Robinson's governess, reading, preserved the letters and, when she restored Alastair Grahame to his parents, she handed over his correspondence, and that of Michael Robinson, along with him. This is the first letter of the series, a continuation, no doubt, in holograph, of the latest bed-time romance :

' 11 *Durham Villas, London,*
' 10 *May* 1907

' MY DARLING MOUSE,—This is a birthday letter to wish you very many happy returns of the day. I wish we could have been all together, but we shall meet again soon and then we will have *treats*. I have sent you two picture-books, one about Brer Rabbit, from Daddy, and one about some other animals, from Mummy. And we have sent you a boat, painted red, with mast and sails to sail in the round pond by the windmill—and Mummy has sent you a boat-hook to catch it when it comes ashore. Also Mummy has sent you some sand-toys to play in the sand with, and a card game. Have you heard about the Toad ? He was never taken prisoner by brigands at all. It was all a horrid low trick of h s. He wrote that letter himself—the letter saying that a hundred pounds must be put in the hollow tree. And he got out of the window early one morning and went off to a town called Buggleton and went to the Red Lion Hotel and there he found a party that had just motored down from London and while they were having breakfast he went into the stable-yard and found their motor-car and went off in it without even saying Poop-poop ! And now he has vanished and every one is looking for him, including the police. I fear he is a bad low animal.

' Good-bye, from
' Your loving DADDY '

From this genesis the famous fantasy grew, told in disjoint to a little boy under the trees in Kensington Gardens, when caterpillars fall, or among the tea-baskets, when Thames water gurgled under the cushioned punt that dropped downstream to Cookham through the green shadows of Quarry Woods.

For in 1906 the Grahames had gone from London, as we know, to live at Cookham Dene, where Kenneth, long years ago, had first come under the ægis of old Thames. There ' the ditty about a Toad ' was finally finished, down to the ' base libel on Badger ', and committed to foolscap in the author's own distinct write-of-hand. It is a masterpiece of a manuscript for a hand-written one, there is hardly an alteration throughout it and never a blot at all. It is, of course, an elaboration of the letters written to Michael Robinson and ' My darling Mouse '. And a collector of such things, turning the pages, said enviously (his mind's eye on a day when conceivably these should come under the hammer) : ' It looks as if it had been written to *sell* ! '

It has been seen how firmly *The Golden Age* and *Dream Days* established their author's reputation in America. So

Have you heard about the Toad? He was never taken prisoner by brigands at all. It was all a horrid low trick of his. He wrote that letter himself — the letter saying that a hundred pounds must be put in the hollow tree. And he got out of the window early one morning, & went off to a town called Buggleton & went to the Red Lion Hotel & there he found a party that had just motored down from London, & while they were having breakfast he went into the stable-yard & found their motor-car & went off in it without even saying Poop-poop! And now he has vanished & every one is looking for him, including the police. I fear he is a bad low animal.

Goodbye, from

Your loving Daddy.

THE GENESIS OF TOAD
(Facsimile of part of a letter from Kenneth Grahame to 'Mouse')

firmly indeed was that fame established that, even after
ten years' silence, Kenneth Grahame was unforgotten and
always, in the publishing seasons, editor and publisher vied
(but vainly) for his further works.

Now it happened that the European representative of an
American magazine, *Everybody's* (Miss Constance Smedley),
was in 1907 living at Bray. She had been instructed to
coax Achilles from his tent at all costs, in other words to
pursuade the so obdurate Kenneth to write something for
her employers, he who had for ten years put his name to
nothing more worthy than the correspondence of the Bank
of England.

She met Mr. and Mrs. Grahame and commending herself
to them, I am told, by declaring herself to be related to
the very Miss Smedley, who, fifteen years ago, had been
governess to *Harold*, was invited to their house and soon
became a friend of the family. Speaking from her brief,
most eloquently, of *Everybody's*, she was presently given
the manuscript of a story called *The Wind in the Reeds* to
do with what she would.

It must have been a proud moment, a good moment, when
the successful ambassadress cabled to her principals that
she was posting to them a Kenneth Grahame manuscript.

Ulysses returning home from his travels was unrecognized
by all except his faithful hound. Charles Hawtrey turned
down *Charley's Aunt*. I could multiply similar missed
opportunities tenfold, but I will be content to say that
Everybody's turned down *The Wind in the Reeds*. The form
of the story, to those who had looked to get another *Golden
Age*, was, of course, wildly unexpected. So one more ' little
meteorite ' came home again.

But I like to think that the Editor of *Everybody's* lived
to call his country house in the Adirondacks (or somewhere)
' Toad Hall '. For when the book was published (in London
by Methuen & Co. and in New York by Scribner) it became,
after a slow beginning, world-renowned. It is now in its
fortieth edition and it continues to sell. Mr. Graham

Robertson who made its frontispiece, a lovely inspiration
illustrating the phrase, ' And a River went out from Eden '
(reproduced on page 316), suggested that the book should
be called, not *The Wind in the Reeds* (*The Wind among the
Reeds* being the title of a collection of Mr. Yeats's poems)
but something similar. However, under the former name
Messrs. Methuen advertised it and as *The Wind in the
Willows* (the author's own second string was *Mr. Mole and
His Mates*) it appeared in October 1908. Mr. Graham
Robertson wrote some of his suggestions thus :

' *Down Stream, With the Stream, The Lapping of the
Stream, The Babble of the Stream, " By Pleasant Streams "*
(Blake). *" By Waters Fair "* (Blake), *The Whispering Reeds,
In the Sedges, Under the Alders, Reeds and Rushes, Reeds
of the River, River Folk, The Children of Pan.* That's as
far as I've got at present but—to be continued in our
next—— Yes, I had an uncomfortable certainty that I
was right about Yeats.

' And, as far as I remember, *The Wind among the Reeds* is
one of his best collections of poems. I like some of his fairy
pieces a good deal, though I wish he would get rid of his
tiresome Irish love of genealogies. I never think of inquiring
who a Fairy *was*, do you ? And he insists upon supplying
his or her whole family-tree whenever he mentions one.'

To-day the artist-playwright says : ' I well remember
my joyful enthusiasm when I first read the MSS. It was
wonderful to be allowed to witness and even, in a tiny way,
to assist at so happy a birth. There was then some talk
of my providing illustrations, but time was lacking and,
moreover, I mistrusted my powers, for I could not number
an otter or a water-rat among my acquaintances though I
had once known a mole almost intimately and had several
toad friends. Yet I could not altogether forgo the honour
of lending a hand, so I drew, hastily and very badly——'
And Mr. Graham Robertson goes on to depreciate the frontispiece, the title-page design, which I have mentioned.

I have lately read the press notices that *The Wind in the*

Willows received on publication. These were respectful, the author of *The Golden Age* was entitled to respect, but on the whole guarded. Those reviewers who had looked for another child *Harold* were frankly disappointed—' A bread-and-butter *Jungle Book*,' says one of the disappointed ones—absurdly enough. Another turns round and girds at Messrs. Methuen : ' Our chief complaint is that our review copy is defiled with a mark like a dairyman's egg-stamp. No reviewer in his senses would want to sell so nice a little book as this. All the same we cannot help thinking it a false, as it is an undoubtedly ugly, economy on the part of the publishers.' *The Times* says : ' Grown-up readers will find it monstrous and elusive, children will hope, in vain, for more fun. Beneath the allegory ordinary life is depicted more or less closely, but certainly not very amusingly or searchingly. As a contribution to natural history the work is negligible. For ourselves we lay *The Wind in the Willows* reverently aside and again, for the hundredth time, take up *The Golden Age*.'

Years later, in 1930, *The Times* was to make a palinode. A leader, on the decline in the price and in the modishness of moleskin, entitled ' The Gentleman in Velvet ', mentions that the mole furnishes Hamlet with a title for his father's ghost and goes on to say, ' but, if moles could read, they would think William Shakespeare no great shakes compared with another English author. That other is Mr. Kenneth Grahame. There may, of course, be sparkish youngsters down below there ready to assert that moles are higher in the social scale and in intellectual attainments than Mr. Kenneth Grahame makes them out (at least they would know the modern and arbitrary distinction between " learn " and " teach "). But of the absolute molishness, of the drollness and fussiness and dearness of molehood, *The Wind in the Willows* is for all time the statement.'

But Richard Middleton, in *Vanity Fair*, winds up a two-column review thus : ' But the book for me is notable for its intimate sympathy with Nature and for its delicate expression of emotions which I, probably in common with

10

most people, had previously believed to be my exclusive property. When all is said the boastful, unstable Toad, the hospitable Water Rat, the shy, wise, childlike Badger, and the Mole with his pleasant habit of brave boyish impulse, are neither animals nor men, but are types of that deeper humanity which sways us all. To be wise, an allegory must admit of a wide application, and the man has read his *Pilgrim's Progress* in vain who does not realize that not merely Christian but Ignorance, Talkative and Justice Hategood himself, are crying for mastery in the hearts of us all. And if I may venture to describe as an allegory a work which critics, who ought to have known better, have dismissed as a fairy story, it is certain that *The Wind in the Willows* is a wise book. It is wise, moreover, with that simplicity which has its appeal to children as well as to grown-up folk. Just as young people read *The Pilgrim's Progress* and *Gulliver's Travels* for the story, so I fancy they will find Mr. Grahame's book a history of exciting adventures, and value it in this aspect no less than we, who find it a storehouse of glowing prose, gracious observation, delicate fantasy, and life-like and even humorous dialogue.

' It will be apparent to the reader, accustomed to the tepid outpouring of anonymous reviewers, that in writing this notice of Mr. Grahame's book I have been appreciative rather than critical. It may or may not occur to him that it is rarely possible to be both when the love is new. Time will often show us blemishes in the objects of our admiration, whether they be books or women, but I confess, though it is some ten years since I first read them, that I still find Mr. Grahame's *Dream Days* and *The Golden Age* as perfect as when they first taught me what my boyhood meant. *The Wind in the Willows* is a wider, fuller book than these, and yet I believe that Mr. Grahame has accomplished the harder task with no less sureness of touch, with no less qualified a success. And I think it will be time to lay down my pen, when I shall be able to review soberly a book that gives me such unalloyed pleasure at the first reading.'

And, writing a year later on children's books, Mr. Middleton sticks to his early opinion as follows : ' I should like again to register my opinion that the best book ever written for children and one of the best books ever written for grown-up people is *The Wind in the Willows* by Mr. Kenneth Grahame.'

Among the countless notices, British and American, the most-quoted-from chapter seems to be ' Wayfarers All '— the wander-lust of the swallows and later, of the Sea Rat. That chapter and also its antithesis, ' Dulce Domum ', the Mole's tearful *heimweh* for his own ' shabby, dingy little place, not like—your cosy quarters—or Toad's beautiful hall—or Badger's great house—but it was my own little home—'.

And reading these extracts, I am reminded of an essay that the author wrote thirteen years earlier in which he combines a Mole End, where he himself plays Mole, and an Odyssey in which the part of Sea Rat (or Ulysses) is taken by a respectable member of the Baltic Exchange who wore ' drab spats all the year round '.   It is a beautiful story and it is called ' The Iniquity of Oblivion ', and since it mixes the essential salts of ' Dulce Domum ' and ' Wanderers All ' much as a chemist, or the ' Red Gods ', mix a medicine, it seems apropos here :

' A man I know is fond of asking the irritating question —and in putting it he regards neither age nor sex, neither ancient friendship nor the rawest nodding acquaintance— " Did you ever forget an invitation to dinner ? "

' Of course the denial is prompt, passionate, and invariable. There are few crimes of which one would not rather be accused than this.   He who cannot summon up the faintest blush at the recollection of having once said " Season ", when no money had passed between him and the Railway Company whose guest he was for the moment, of having under-stated his income for purposes of taxation, or of having told his wife he was going to church, and then furtively picked up a fishing-rod as he passed through the hall, will colour angrily at the most innocent suggestion of a single possible lapse of memory regarding an invitation to dinner. But, none the less, every one finds it a little difficult to meet the natural rejoinder : " How do you know ? "

' Indeed, no other reply than painful silence is possible. To say, " Because I do ", is natural enough, and frequently quite conclusive of further argument ; still, it can hardly be called a reasoned refutation. The fact is, you *don't* know, and you cannot know. Your conviction that you do is based, first, on some sort of idea that you are bound to recollect, sooner or later, anything that you may have forgotten : an argument that only requires to be stated to display its fallacy ; secondly, on a vague belief that a deflection of so flagrant a character must inevitably be brought home to you by an incensed host or hostess—a theory that makes no allowance for the blissful sense of injury and offended pride, the joy of brooding over a wrong, which is one of the chief pleasures left to humanity. No, one doesn't know, and one can't know : and the past career of the most self-satisfied of us is doubtless littered with the debris of forgotten invitations.

' Of course invitations, being but a small part of life, and not—as some would imply with their practice—its chief end, must be taken to stand here for much besides. One has only to think of the appalling amount of book-lore one has " crammed " in days gone by, and of the pitiful fragments that survive, to realize that facts, deeds, achievements, experiences numberless, may just as well have been hurried along the dusty track to oblivion. And once it has been fairly brought home to us that we have entirely forgotten any one thing—why, the gate is open. It is clear we may just as easily have forgotten hundreds.

' This lamentable position of things was specially forced upon me, some time ago, by a certain persistent dream that used to wing its way to my bedside, not once or twice, but coming a dozen times, and always (I felt sure at the time) from out the Ivory Portal. First, there would be a sense of snugness, of cushioned comfort, of home-coming. Next, a gradual awakening to consciousness in a certain little room, very dear and familiar, sequestered in some corner of the more populous and roaring part of London : solitary, the world walled out, but full of a brooding sense of peace and of possession. At times I would make my way there, unerringly, through the wet and windy streets, climb the well-known staircase, open the ever-welcoming door. More often I was there already, ensconced in the most comfortable chair in the world, the lamp lit, the fire glowing ruddily. But always the same feeling of a home-coming, of the world shut out, of the ideal encasement. On the shelves were a few books—a very few—but just the editions I had sighed for, the editions which refuse to turn up, or which poverty glowers at on alien shelves. On the walls were a print or two, a woodcut, an etching—not many. Old loves, all of them, apparitions that had flashed across the field of view in sale-rooms and vanished again in a blaze of three figures ; but never possessed—until now. All was modest—O, so very modest ! But all was my very own, and, what was more, everything in that room was exactly right.

' After three or four visits, the uncanniness of the repetition set me thinking. Could it possibly be, that this was no dream at all ? Had this chamber, perhaps, a real existence, and was I all the time leading, somewhere, another life—a life within a life—a life that I constantly forgot, within the life that I happened to remember ? I tried my best to bring the thing to absolute proof. First, there was that frequent sense of extreme physical weariness with which I was wont to confront the inevitable up-rising of the morning—might not that afford a clue ? Alas, no : I traced my mornings back, far behind the beginnings of the dream. I could not remember a day, since those rare white ones at school when it was a whole holiday, and summer was boon and young, when I had faced the problem of getting up with anything but a full sense of disgust. Next I thought, I will consult my accounts. Rooms must be paid for in London,

however modest they may be ; and the blessed figures can't
lie. Then I recollected that I did not keep any accounts
—never *had* kept any accounts—never intended to keep
any beastly accounts—and, on the whole, I confess I was
rather glad. Statistics would have been a mean prosaic
way of plucking out the heart of this mystery. My only
chance seemed to lie in coming across the place by accident.
Then perhaps the extinguished torch would rekindle, the
darkened garret of memory would be re-illumined, and it
would be in my power at last to handle those rare editions,
not capriciously as now, but at any hour I pleased. So
I hunted Gray's Inn, Staple Inn, Clifford's Inn ; hung about
by-streets in Bloomsbury, even backwaters in Chelsea ; but
all to no result. It waits, that sequestered chamber, it
waits for the serene moment when the brain is in just the
apt condition, and ready to switch on the other memory
even as one switches on the electric light with a turn of the
wrist. Fantasy ? well—perhaps. But the worst of it is,
one never can feel quite sure. Only a dream, of course.
And yet—the enchanting possibility !

' And this possibility, which (one feels convinced) the
wilful brain could make reality in a moment if it were only
in the right humour, might be easily brought about by some
accidental physical cause, some touch, scent, sound, gifted
with the magic power of recall. Could my fingers but pass
over the smooth surface of those oak balustrades so familiar
to me, in a trice I would stand at the enchanted door. Could
I even see in some casual shop-window one of those prints
my other existence hoards so safe and sure—but that is
unlikely indeed. Those prints of the dim land of dreams,
" they never are sold in the merchant's mart ! " Still, if
one were only to turn up, in twopenny box or dusty portfolio,
down in Southwark, off the roaring Strand, or somewhere
along the quaint unclassified Brompton Road, in a flash the
darkness would be day, the crooked would be made straight,
and no policeman would be called upon to point out the
joyous way.

' If I have special faith in this sort of divining-rod, it
is because of a certain strange case I once encountered and
never quite elucidated. There was a certain man, respectable enough in every particular ; wore drab spats all the year
round, lived in a suburb, and did daily business on the
" Baltic ". When the weather was fine, and a halcyon calm
brooded o'er the surface of the Baltic, instead of taking his
suburban train at Cannon Street, he used to walk as far as
Charing Cross : and before departing, if time allowed, he
would turn into the National Gallery. Of a catholic mind,
for he had never strayed down the tortuous byways of Art,
he only went in to be amused, and was prepared to take
his entertainment from all schools alike, without any of the
narrow preferences of the cultured. From the very first,
however, the Early Tuscans gripped him with a strange
fascination, so that he rarely penetrated any further. What
it was precisely that so detained him could never be ascer-
tained. The man was not apt in the expression of subtle
emotion, and never succeeded in defining the strong " possession "—for such it seemed to be—by which he was caught
and held. The next phase in the case was, that he took to
disappearing. He disappeared literally and absolutely—
sometimes for a few days, sometimes for a fortnight or more ;
and on his return could tell nothing, explain nothing.
Indeed, he did not seem to be really conscious of any absence.
It was noted in time that his disappearances always coincided
with his visits to the National Gallery. Thither he could
be tracked ; there all trace of him would cease. His female
relations—an unimaginative, uneducated crew—surmised
the unkindest things in their narrow way. Still, even they
found it difficult to fling a stone at the Early Tuscans. For
myself, I like to think that there was some bit of another
life hidden away in him—some tranced memory of another
far-away existence on Apennine slopes—which some quality
in these pictures, and in these alone, had power to evoke.
And I love to think that, transformed by this magic touch
back into the other man of him, he passed, dream-possessed,

forth from the portico, through Trafalgar Square, and into Charing Cross Station. That there, oblivious of all suburbs, he purchased one of those little books of coupons so much more romantic than your vulgar inland slip of pasteboard, and in due course sped Southwards—irresistibly drawn— took the Alps in a series of whorls, burrowings, and breathless flights o'er torrent and fall—till he basked at last, still speeding South, in the full sunlight that steeps the Lombard plain. Arrived in time, where his destiny (which was also his past) awaited him, I could see him, avoiding clamour of piazza, shunning prim airlessness of Galleria and Accademia, climbing the white road to where, in some little village or red-tiled convent, lurked the creation, madonna or saint, that held the other end of the subtle thread. The boy-lover, had he been, of this prim-tressed model? Or the St. George or homely St. Roch who guarded her? Or himself the very painter? Whatever the bond, here I could imagine him to linger, steeping his soul in the picture and in the surroundings so native both to it and to the man whose life for a brief minute he lived again, till such time as that sullen devil within him—the later memory of the man he also was— began to stir drowsily and to urge him homewards, even as the other had urged him out. Once back, old sights and sounds would develop the later man into full being and consciousness, and as before he would tread the floor of the Baltic, while oblivion swallowed the Tuscan existence—until the next time!

' These instances, it is true, are but " sports " in oblivion-lore. But, putting aside such puzzle-fragments of memory, it is impossible not to realize, in sad seriousness, that of all our recollection has once held, by far the larger part must be by this time in the realm of the forgotten ; and that every day some fresh delightful little entity pales, sickens, and passes over to the majority. Sir Thomas Browne has quaintly written concerning the first days of the young world, " when the living might exceed the dead, and to depart this world could not be properly said, to go unto the greater number " ; but in these days of crowded thought, of the mind cultured and sensitized to receive such a swarm of impressions, no memory that sighs its life out but joins a host far exceeding what it leaves behind.   'Tis but a scanty wallet that each of us carries at his back.   Few, indeed, and of a sorry mintage, the thin coins that jingle therein.   Our gold, lightly won, has been as lightly scattered, along way-sides left far behind.   Oblivion, slowly but surely stalking us, gathers it with a full arm, and on the floor of his vast treasure-house stacks it in shining piles.

' And if it is the larger part that has passed from us, why not also the better part ?   Indeed, logic almost requires it ; for to select and eliminate, to hold fast and let go at will, is not given to us.   As we jog along life's highroad, the knowledge of this inability dogs each conscious enjoyment, till with every pleasant experience comes also the annoying reflection, that it is a sheer toss-up whether this is going to be a gain, a solid profit to carry along with us, or fairy gold that shall turn to dust and nothingness in a few short mornings at best.   As we realize our helplessness in the matter, we are almost ready to stamp and to swear.   Will no one discover the chemical which shall fix the fleeting hue ?   That other recollection, now—that humiliating, that disgust-ing experience of ten years ago—*that* is safe enough, per-manent, indestructible, warranted not to fade.   If in this rag-fair we were only allowed to exchange and barter, to pick and choose !   Oblivion, looking on, smiles grimly.   It is he that shall select, not we ; our part is but to look on helplessly, while—though he may condescend to leave us a pearl or two—the bulk of our jewels is swept into his pocket.

' One hope alone remains to us, by way of consolation. These memories whose passing we lament, they are torpid only, not dead.   They lie in a charmed sleep, whence a chance may awaken them, a touch make the dry bones live ; though at present we know not the waking spell.   Like Arthur, they have not perished, but only passed, and like him they may come again from the Avalon where they slumber. The chance is small, indeed. But the Merlin who controls these particular brain-cells, fitful and capricious though he be, after the manner of magicians, has powers to which we dare not assign limits. At any moment the stop may be pulled out, the switch pressed, the key turned, the Princess kissed. Then shall the spell-bound spring to life, the floodgates rise, the baked arid canals gleam with the silver tide ; and once more we shall be fulfilled of the old joys, the old thrills, the old tears and laughter.

' Better still—perhaps best of all—as those joyous old memories, hale and fresh once more, troop out of the catacombs into the light, these insistent ones of the present, this sullen host that beleaguers us day and night with such threatening obsession, may vanish, may pass, may flee away utterly, gone in their turn to lodge with Oblivion—and a good riddance ! '

And, again and again, reviewers of *The Wind in the Willows* claim that Mr. Kenneth Grahame is the discoverer of the mole as a character in nursery, or any other, fiction. And yet I remember a nursery book of fifty years ago. Its characters were animals and insects and its name was, I think, *The Butterfly's Ball*.

But it was not the famous poem of Mr. Roscoe, published in 1808. It was a very little book of about five thousand words, not more. I cannot remember the author's name. But among its principals were a butterfly, a bee, a fox— and a rather lachrymose old Mrs. Mole. She was sadly short-sighted and spoke, as a rule, although the book was prose, in rhymed couplets, such as :

> ' It is so sad I cannot see
> To drink my tea.'

She was a poor old thing and no sort of rival, no rival at all, to the tenant of Mole End. And yet I have a soft place in my heart for her and therefore I mention her here in famous company.

Now, whether the reviewers praised Mr. Grahame's new book or regretted it, they were united in naming it an allegory and almost united in prophesying that, to be successful, *The Wind in the Willows* wanted an illustrator. In both opinions they were wrong. The new book was already a classic, and in its eighth edition, when it was illustrated, in 1913, for the first time. The artist was Paul Bransom. Later it was decorated, both in its thirteenth and sixteenth printings, by Nancy Barnhart. And again, in twenty-fifth and thirty-third editions, by Wyndham Payne. And, in 1931, Mr. Ernest H. Shepard illustrated, charmingly, the thirty-eighth blooming. Truly ' the ditty about a toad ' had travelled far. But it was no allegory—Rat was not ' Nature ' nor was Mole ' Love of Home '. It was, and is, but a bedtime story, a fairy-tale, for a very little boy. And the wisest way to read it, and regard it, is the way recommended by Mr. A. A. Milne in the introduction to his play, *Toad of Toad Hall*, which he has adapted, of course, from *The Wind in the Willows*.

' Perhaps it has happened to you, as it has certainly happened to me, that you have tried to explain a fantastic idea to an entirely matter-of-fact person. " But they *don't*," he says, and " You *can't*," and " I don't see *why*, just because—" and ' Even if you assume that—" and " I thought you said just now that he *hadn't* ". By this time you have thrown the ink-pot at him, with enough of accuracy, let us hope, to save you from his ultimatum, which is this : " However fantastic your assumption, you *must* work it out logically "—that is to say, realistically.

' To such a mind *The Wind in the Willows* makes no appeal, for it is not worked out logically. In reading the book, it is necessary to think of Mole, for instance, sometimes as an actual mole, sometimes as such a mole in human clothes, sometimes as a mole grown to human size, sometimes as walking on two legs, sometimes on four. He is a mole, he isn't a mole. What is he ? I don't know. And, not being a matter-of-fact person, I don't mind.'

And, even as it was with *The Golden Age* and *Dream Days*, Kenneth Grahame's ' fan ' mails filled his letter-box to overflowing and fairly broke the back of the Cookham Dene postman. From a very few of these letters, from literally the one or two that ask for specified information—and get it—I will quote. I have already been able to tell how Mole End was swept and garnished and how its goldfishes were cared for in the absence of Mole. But before I go on to give similar detail, I will dispose of the allegory idea for good and all. I suppose that never man perpetrated a delightful bit of sheer nonsense without suspicious folk hunting through it for allegories as he of a similar kidney hunts through a fresh green salad for slugs and caterpillars instead of just enjoying the ' herbaceous treat ' trusting in Sydney Smith and in his own good appetite. Folk sought allegories in Foote's *Great Panjandrum* and in *The Hunting of the Snark*. So it was natural enough that *The Wind in the Willows* should, in its time, be turned over and over by the discontented and the ungrateful. But its author, who must know best, in sending a presentation copy of his new book to Mr. Theodore Roosevelt writes :

' DEAR MR. PRESIDENT,—You expressed yourself with such great kindness last year on the subject of my books that I think it possible you may care to have a copy of the English Edition of one that has just been published, so I am venturing to send you one. Its qualities, if any, are mostly negative—i.e.—no problems, no sex, no second meaning—it is only an expression of the very simplest joys of life as lived by the simplest beings of a class that you are specially familiar with and will not misunderstand.

' Believe me, sir,
' Yours very faithfully
' KENNETH GRAHAME

' To President Theodore Roosevelt,
  ' The White House,
    ' Washington,
' *October* 10*th* 1908 '

To which the President replied :

> ' *The White House,*
> ' *Washington,*
> ' *October* 22, 1908

' *Personal*

' MY DEAR MR. GRAHAME,—The book hasn't come, but
as I have never read anything of yours yet that I haven't
enjoyed to the full, I am safe in thanking you heartily in
advance. Of course it won't have " any problems, any
sex, any second meaning "—that is why I shall like it.
By the way, we have just been finishing *The Further Experiences of an Irish R.M.* I hope you know them, and are as
fond of them as we are.

' Again heartily thanking you, and with real regret that
you are not to come to this side while we are in the White
House, believe me,

> ' Sincerely yours,
> ' THEODORE ROOSEVELT

Mr. Kenneth Grahame,
  ' Mayfield,
    ' Cookham Dene,
      ' Berkshire, England '

And once again, some months later, the presidential pen
says :

> ' *The White House,*
> ' *Washington,*
> ' *January* 17, 1909

' *Personal*

' MY DEAR MR. GRAHAME,—My mind moves in ruts, as
I suppose most minds do, and at first I could not reconcile
myself to the change from the ever-delightful Harold and
his associates, and so for some time I could not accept the
toad, the mole, the water-rat and the badger as substitutes.
But after a while Mrs. Roosevelt and two of the boys, Kermit
and Ted, all quite independently, got hold of *The Wind
Among the Willows* and took such a delight in it that I

began to feel that I might have to revise my judgement. Then Mrs. Roosevelt read it aloud to the younger children, and I listened now and then.   Now I have read it and re-read it, and have come to accept the characters as old friends ; and I am almost more fond of it than of your previous books. Indeed, I feel about going to Africa very much as the sea-faring rat did when he almost made the water-rat wish to forsake everything and start wandering !

' I felt I must give myself the pleasure of telling you how much we had all enjoyed your book.

' With all good wishes,
' Sincerely yours,
' THEODORE ROOSEVELT

' Mr. Kenneth Grahame,
   ' 16 Durham Villas,
      ' Kensington W., London, England

This letter is to me an interesting one inasmuch as I have always held that no adult can get the full bouquet of *The Wind in the Willows* except at second hand, except through the heart of the child to whom it is read.   I am happy to have my humble opinion endorsed from Washing-ton and The White House.

And, apropos of Presidents, here is a letter from the Hon. Alfred Deakin, Prime Minister of the Commonwealth of Australia in 1903/4, 1905/8, and 1909/10.

' *Commonwealth of Australia,*
' *House of Representatives,*
' *January* 28, 1909

' DEAR MR. GRAHAME,—I have never been able to forgive myself for having neglected the opportunity afforded me by my only visit to the Bank of England (in 1907) of at all events acknowledging my debt and that of my family to you for *The Golden Age* and *Dream Days*, which I read to them years ago.   But after *The Wind in the Willows* I can no longer deny myself the pleasure of congratulating

you upon an even higher and still more original achievement—a prose poem perfect within its scope in style and
sentiment, rising to its climax in the vision of Pan—a
piece of imaginative insight to which it would be hard
to find a parallel anywhere. Certainly one would only
look for it among the rarest flowers of literature in that
vein.

' If this language appears to you strained, let me assure
you that it is not by intention. I have read the book as a
whole twice ; once out loud, and passages such as that
mentioned, " Mole's Xmas Eve ", and the " Sailor Rat's
Reminiscences ", &c., several times.

' It is now three or four weeks since I was under the
glamour, so that my verdict represents what lawyers call a
considered opinion, and, so far as I am concerned, is binding.
Nor am I the only beneficiary ; my wife and daughters were
equally fascinated, as were several friends upon whose
judgements I am accustomed to rely.

' Please therefore accept this spontaneous and informal
note of hand, just for what it is—an expression of gratitude and admiration from some of the many Australians
who find in your book a delicate and delicious insight into
nature and human nature, enriched and inspired by that
" natural magic " which touches the deepest chords of
poetry and of the soul with the simplest and most artless
sincerity.

' As, after all, I am writing this off-hand—merely a line
of thanks—I will only ask you to accept it, not as an attempt
to discharge, but a recognition of, a continuing debt. When
with your Governors at the Bank, my mind, alas, was full
of other debts in other spheres more material and yet perhaps
more evanescent than this.

' Yours sincerely,
' ALFRED DEAKIN

' To Kenneth Grahame, Esq.,
' The Bank of England, London '

Few letters of this sort arrive at The Bank of England, I imagine. And to it the addressee answered:

'*Mayfield*,
'*Cookham Dene*,
'*Berkshire, England*,
'*April 23rd*, 1909

'DEAR MR. DEAKIN,—It was most kind of you to write me such a welcome and more than generously worded letter about *The Wind in the Willows*. If I have ever received a pleasanter or more encouraging appreciation, I do not remember it.

'It is not exactly logical, but somehow to have given pleasure to readers very far away seems to bring a special satisfaction which one cannot feel about the opinion of the man round the corner. And as for the animals, though they might well look for recognition down here, with their native Thames a few hundred yards away, yet they are aliens in Australia and would have no right to grumble at prompt deportation; but your friendly greeting will make them feel adopted and at home among relations; and I hope they will stay.

'I am just back from a Continental wandering of nearly three months, which has delayed my reply. With many thanks again, and all good wishes.

'Yours very sincerely,
'KENNETH GRAHAME

'The Hon. Alfred Deakin, M.P.'

And now to name the one or two letters whereby Kenneth Grahame has been drawn into explanations. To Master Thomas Goodman of Wing, Leighton Buzzard, who wisely demands details of 'that good story about Toad and the lock-keeper' which the Otter began to tell and never finished, Kenneth Grahame answers:

'*Rome*,
'10 *July* 1923

'DEAR THOMAS GOODMAN,—Thank you very much for

your nice letter of 27th June—I was very glad to hear you liked reading about Mr. Toad.

' I am afraid I must not tell you the story about Toad and the Lock-keeper.   The fact is, they both lost their tempers, and said things they much regretted afterwards.   They are now friends again, so we have all agreed to let the matter drop.

' Yours very truly,
' KENNETH GRAHAME '

And Joyce of Whitchurch, Oxon, inquiring jealously for the fair fame of her own Oxfordshire bank, gets this reply from the one man able to answer a question and enable her to hold her head up proudly when she crosses the toll bridge at Pangbourne and stands on Berkshire soil :

' Church Cottage,
' Pangbourne, Berks,
22nd December 1930

' MY DEAR JOYCE,—Thank you very much for your nice letter about The Wind in the Willows.   It is very pleasant to think that you and your friends at Whitchurch like the book, because there is just as much of Oxfordshire as Berkshire in it, isn't there ?   And some of the animals must have lived on one side of the river and some on the other ; but I have always felt sure that Toad Hall was on the Oxfordshire side.

' Wishing you all a very happy Christmas,

' I am yours affectionately,
' KENNETH GRAHAME '

And to a spiering Perthshire grandmama who writes of the thirty-eighth edition (which, as we know, is illustrated by Mr. Shepard) and, after compliments, says :

' And now I want a little advice from the Author.   It concerns the illustrations.   They are perhaps quite all right for Grown Ups.   But I am going to my grandchildren and the Book goes too, and they will criticize, and what am I to say ?   For thus,—I read on page 29 " the Mole . . . took

11

the sculls, while the Rat settled himself comfortably in the stern " : I turn over the leaf, and what has the Ernest Shepard done ? *He has transposed our*, by now, *friends, in the boat*, *Rat* has the sculls, the *Mole* is settled comfortably in the stern—Oh wae's me ! Since my earliest childhood I have wondered why artists do not read the books they illustrate. Mr. Shepard by this inaccuracy proves he has missed Rat's beautiful gesture on page 24 " I'll teach you to row ", and the success of his lessons. I repeat, what am I to say to my grandchildren ?—Yours distractedly, MARGARET STEWART SOMERVILLE.'

Ably indeed does K. G. play out of the bunker into which his partner has landed him. He writes, after a moment's hesitation :

> *' Church Cottage,*
> *' Pangbourne, Berks,*
> 20*th December* 1931

' DEAR LADY,—Yes—it is exasperating. These artists are very tiresome fellows—and they all do it ![1] I hardly know what to suggest that you should tell the children. You might perhaps say that the animals had evidently " changed over " for just a minute while in full view of the windows of Toad Hall, in case Toad, looking out, should say afterwards to Rat, " Who's your crab-catching friend ? " For poor Mole couldn't row *very* well yet. But I admit it sounds lame. Let us hope that they may not notice it. (But they will !)

> ' Yours very truly,
> ' KENNETH GRAHAME '

But no precisian has written, so far as I can find, to ask if the Water-Rat was really a water-vole and if so, why not say so ?

In July 1908, the author, in reply to a request for a ' descriptive paragraph ' of his forthcoming book, writes :

' I will jot down on the fly-leaf of this some material for

---

[1] The drawing was subsequently altered by Mr. Shepard.

a descriptive paragraph for the announcement list, though probably any one else would do it better.

' " A book of Youth—and so perhaps chiefly *for* Youth, and those who still keep the spirit of youth alive in them : of life, sunshine, running water, woodlands, dusty roads, winter firesides ; free of problems, clean of the clash of sex ; of life as it might fairly be supposed to be regarded by some of the wise small things

' " That glide in grasses and rubble of woody wreck ".'

Kenneth Grahame, possibly because it was his last born, seems more interested in *The Wind in the Willows* than in his other works. In 1921 he writes to his literary agents regarding a request from his publishers that a chapter of the *Wind* should be included in a school ' Reader ' :

' I am so very anxious that Sir A. Methuen should not think me unreasonable in objecting to the course proposed that I will give my views at some length, in the hope that even if he does not agree with me he may admit that I have " made out a case " as the saying is.

' And first, as to the (complete) chapter proposed to be taken. Hear the Parable of the Small Holder. In our part of the country when the County Council endeavour to grab somebody's land to meet the ambitions of some would-be " small holder ", the objection of the former always is not that he has to part with land but that the small holder is trying to " pick the eye out of his farm " (which is usually true). Is not some one playing the part of the small holder here ?

' But there is the graver objection, the harm done both to the children themselves and to literature by the practice of giving them a dozen snippets from as many books when with a little trouble and arrangement the books might be read through. In the March No. of the *Atlantic Monthly* there is an article on this subject called " Literature in the Grades ". After dealing with the American fondness for " Readers ", the writer says : " In the English classes of

this school *what do they do* ? Why, they do what any one
would do who loved English literature and proposed to
spread that feeling to children. They tell stories and they
read books *through*. Will you substitute for this the
indifferent hash of the grade ' Reader ' . . . will you take
a chapter out of *The Wind in the Willows* . . . *Robinson
Crusoe* . . . and miss the opportunity to give your children
the whole experience ? Why ? "

' Now this is pretty straight talk. And if we feel that
there is anything in the argument at all—how, well, incon-
sistent is it not for us to be planning to put the book on the
school market as a whole, and at the same moment to be
offering to the same market snippets of it to the " Reader " ? '

And then years later he writes in reference to a proposed
abridged edition for use in elementary schools :

' Now as to the new proposal. I have taken a day or two
to think over the matter, and frankly, I do not care about
it, as it stands. The suggestion is, to issue the book in an
elementary-school edition as a complete story, though con-
siderably abridged for trade reasons. The book consists of
twelve chapters, much the same length, and it would be
necessary for me either (1) to cut out four complete chapters,
or (2) to " blue-pencil " liberally and by whole paragraphs
till I have reduced the whole contents by over one-third.
I have had another look at the book again, from this Pro-
crustean point of view, and I do not think that either course
of treatment could be satisfactorily carried out. I quite
appreciate the remark that the very heaviness of the " cuts "
would render the abridgement less likely to interfere with
the ordinary edition, but that is not quite my present point,
which is that I do not care about having a form or version
of the story in print, which has been cut down, not for any
literary reason, such as redundancy, or verbosity, or parts
being not quite suited for children, or too much over their
heads, and so on and so on, but the purely arbitrary and
" trade " reason of getting it within 192 pages—though I
fully understand, and sympathize with, the hard necessities

of trade. I can't abridge satisfactorily without loss of quality, and that's the long and short of it. I know that School Committees will only have books on their own terms, more or less, but that's not my fault.'

And once more, in 1929, he discusses those ' Foreign Rights ', so negligible to most authors but which, to Kenneth Grahame, had become and were continuing to be, such very practical matters :

' Before I received your kind letter of the 18th, I had frankly suspected—and no doubt you suspected—that the account that had so shocked me had been a piece of quite laudable if mistaken departmental over-zeal, which had somehow escaped the eye of the Capitoline Jove. But when I read your classic periods, so firm yet so tender, I wilted, I sagged, I crumpled. I shed bitter tears. I finally collapsed on the floor, a sodden heap of misery. As I lay there, however, I found myself murmuring something, but very soft and low, so that it should not reach your ears. Something like this : " Alas, yes, how true it is, and how well I know it, that there are publishers who claim 50% on Foreign rights, and others who ask 100, and many who will demand 150, and then ask for a little bit more for ' all their trouble ',

' " but—

' " but—

' " (here I became almost inaudible)

' " Since when—(I was now only whispering)—

' " Since when have —— Ltd., based their practice on the tenets of Messrs. B-r-bb-s & Co ? "

' Then I shed a few more tears.

' Then I rose to my feet and washed and had some light refreshment—the first for days.

' So now that is all over, and I will try and be good, and I will try and not do it any more. And I am ever so glad that you couldn't have heard a word of those awful sentiments I murmured to myself as I lay crying on the floor. But——

' (No, I won't begin again.   I have sworn it.)
' All the same——

' No, the end of the page is in sight, and I am not going
to get on to a new one.   At least, I *will* turn over a new
leaf, of course, for I have said so already.   But not a new
leaf of this letter.

' ~~BECAUSE~~-~~IF~~--~~I~~-~~DID~~· O this unruly typerwriter!   It
all comes of using a Blick.   Common little beasts, Blicks.   I
ought to get something high-class and toney and expensive.
"~~BUT~~--~~HOW~~--~~CAN~~--~~YOU~~--~~IF~~"------ There he goes
again!   He must be stopped.

' Yours finally and very truly,
' KENNETH GRAHAME '

The Wind in the Willows was the final comer of Kenneth
Grahame's four books.   By the majority of his readers it
is the best beloved of all.   I believe that it will live when
The Golden Age, already dated, is dead.   For children to-day
do not of necessity see their elders as The Opposition.   But
The Wind is artless and nursery-ageless and it, probably, is
the work by which its author would best wish to be remembered.   For since that long ago day when the Kings of the
East came to the manger, bringing with them their gold and
frankincense and myrrh, surely all men, Kenneth Grahame
among them, give of their heart's best only when they give
to a child.

CHAPTER IX

ALASTAIR

ALASTAIR GRAHAME was born at 16 Durham Villas, Campden Hill, on the 12th of May 1900. He was a big baby and, curly-haired as Hyacinthus, a hair-brush was the first gift that came to him from a friend. He sat up, took notice and developed rapidly. He was christened Alastair and no more because his father held that one name was enough for any man. He was the only child of his parents. And though it is easy to think of the one adored child of a gifted father as a little creature of somewhat different clay to the rough-and-tumble members of a nursery tea-table-for-six, there can be small doubt that Alastair Grahame was of that rare infancy who come, we cannot know why though we humbly presume that it is for some high purpose, and who, that purpose achieved, the experience perhaps gained, must go again to the work that, elsewhere in the scheme of things, doubtless awaits them. Marjorie Fleming, the lovely little familiar of Sir Walter Scott, was of this elfin-celestial sort. And, in fiction, Du Maurier's *Martia*, the young daughter in whom a father's rare genius became an actual living thing, is another of the same short-lived, belovéd leaven.

In a chapter of this book I have told how Alastair, a little night-gowned boy, was the inspiration of *A Wind in the Willows*, a happy birth that has since taken its happiness with it into a million night nurseries. Perhaps this alone was sufficient to have compelled Mouse (for so his friends named him) to come to Campden Hill? Who shall say? Not I anyhow.

And of him and of his short life I, who never knew him, must borrow the words of others to tell.

149

Of his personal appearance when, I suppose, he was about five years old, Miss Smedley says, in her *Crusaders* : ' He was an unusually attractive child, beautiful and gallant, with thick dark hair cut straight across his forehead and bright calm eyes.' And Sir Arthur Quiller-Couch exclaimed, on being introduced to the baby Alastair, ' Never be afraid for a boy with a head shaped like his.'

His governess, Miss Naomi Stott, writes of her first meeting with Alastair when he was about the age at which Miss Smedley has described him : ' We were to meet for the first occasion and it was near bedtime. He was not yet six. He had had a devoted nurse, but she had gone. Would he resent the change ? However he had been prepared and, when he saw that his bath was being got ready as usual by the fire and that his mother's own maid, a special friend of his, was collecting the towels, the stranger greeted him, took off her hat and began reading a Pink Book (one of Stead's penny treats). Alastair approached. He was at once eager to listen and to look and seemed unaware that he was being undressed and that it was time for his bath. I was often to notice afterwards how reasonable he was and, in sickness and health, how entirely fearless under all circumstances. He never shirked anything however disagreeable it might be to a child of his imaginative and highly strung nature. He was entirely unselfish. He was entirely straightforward. He was a gay and a happy little boy, always laughing and playing. He loved to put his hand against a running tap and see the water squirt. For this on one occasion I had to punish him. A few moments later his mother asked him to choose a birthday present for me. He said, at once, " a brooch, no, *two* brooches so as she can have one for Sunday ". He was like that, there was never a petty spirit in him. He lived a great deal in an imaginary land of his own making. He called it " Puppyland where it is never silly to be silly ". In that land lived his band of brigands and his dog Kaa who (to shock *me* I fancy !) drank only blood and, " what do you think he likes best

MOUSE

AND HIS MOTHER

From the Miniatures by Winifred Hope Thomson

to *eat* ? " Mouse asked me. I said that I did not know.
" An *angel*," said Mouse in a voice that was half a whisper.
For all his love of fun he respected the dignity of others
and once, at Littlehampton, left his seat because the funny
man in a beach-troupe was knocking another about. He
loved animals and would never want to catch crabs, shrimps
or butterflies. He loved flowers but did not want to pick
them. He was quick of repartee. For instance once, (we
were in a hurry to get out between showers) I noticed
that he required a new bootlace. " Quick," said I, " take
out the old one." " I suppose, like the Devil, you have
but a short time," said Mouse. He was a bit of a mystic
too, a strange thing in so young a child. On one of my
early days with him he saw a picture of Our Lord in a
Holland Street shop. Mouse pointed it out to me. " That
is my Friend," he said, " the Carpenter. When I was ill
(he had had appendicitis) He came to see me and sometimes
I go and talk to Him." On another day he said to me,
" Death is promotion." I told his father what Mouse had
said for I thought it possible that the child (Mouse could
not then read) might have heard him say something of the
kind. But Mr. Grahame assured me that neither he nor
Mrs. Grahame had ever spoken to Mouse about death.
Mouse was a most considerate host and once when a little
girl of two stayed with us for a night he showed her Caldecott
books and invited her to sit up for supper. Though to
me he pretended, " Why should a bachelor have a babe
thrust on him ? Take care that I do not hear it in the
night." He was a most generous child and I still have a
copy of *The Old Wives Tale* which he bought for me because
he heard me say that I should enjoy a story " about sisters ".
I knew Mouse all his short life. Once, as a big Etonian,
he said to me : " Scratch us, we are all barbarians but it
happens that I prefer curios and they prefer cricket bats."
Nevertheless, he was always interested in cricket, he was a
horseman and an excellent boy in a boat. The first time
he went hunting he was " blooded " and so proud was he

that he would not wash his face till bedtime came. He had, as a child, a vocabulary beyond his years and his speaking voice was one of noticeable beauty. Of the former a girl, much older than he, said to him once, " You are only a baby who has swallowed a dictionary." When we went to Cookham Dene Mouse edited (the literary instinct was strongly alive in him) a magazine of his own called *The Merry Thought*. He was never at a loss for a story or a rhyme. Sometimes his parents contributed to *The Merry Thought*, sometimes literary friends of Mr. Grahame would send a poem or an article.

' You ask me how I best remember Mouse. I have so many memories. But perhaps as clearly as any I see him as a young schoolboy. It is after the Grahames went to Blewbury on the Berkshire downs. It was Christmas eve and there was a party for the village in the big barn at Boham's. Mouse had been put up to sing and he stood on a table, under a storm-lantern from the lambing-fold, swung to a rafter. He was a tall young thing and if I say that he was beautiful you won't misunderstand me ? He stood in the light, round him in the shadow sat the party, Newgate fringes and gaiters, shepherds, gamekeepers and carters, men and women of the down country. Mouse piped as sweetly as a thrush :

> " Like silver lamps in a distant shrine
>   The stars are sparkling well
> Now a new Power has come to the Earth
>   A match for the armies of Hell ;
> A Child is born who shall conquer the foe
>   And the armies of wickedness quell."

' I think I remember *that* best of all.'

Alastair had, from the earliest age, a certain delicate sarcasm. And a dislike of being kissed. I am told that, at the age of three and on a railway journey, he was continually urged by his nurse to ' see the pretty lambs ' or other objects of the flying landscape. Presently the travellers caught sight of the sea and Nannie made haste to call attention to the ' pretty ships '. Alastair said, ' Oh, Nannie, *do* leave the boats in the water, they look very well there.'

An example of the latter prejudice is given by Mr. Anstey Guthrie in his appreciation of Alastair. Yet later, on the west coast of Scotland, when his parents asked three Highland fisher girls (who had never seen the inside of an hotel) to take tea with them at ' The Duke's Arms ', Alastair, on his own initiative, kissed with ceremony each departing guest and handed her a sprig of white heather. The spokeswoman of the party, the lass who ' had the English ', (the other two had not) assured her host later that ' to be kissed by so fine a gentleman and the son of so fine a gentleman was just the honour of our lives and of all our lives to come '.

Alastair was, as Miss Stott says, entirely straightforward. As a four-year-old, some treat depending on his having ' been good ' all day, he was asked whether or no this had been the case. He made the qualified reply : ' Yes, but there was a good deal of vulgar eating and arms on the table.'

' Why is there trouble in the world ? ' he asked one day. He was a *very* small boy then.

He was no respecter of ancient lineage. To enjoin the virtue of perseverance upon him in some particular task he was reminded that he was by descent, connected with Robert the Bruce. ' I am interested but not impressed,' he said.

At Eton he was reproached by his ' Dame ' because he did not talk to his neighbours at table. Alastair inquired, ' How can I talk to people whose powers of conversation lie only in their elbows ? '

Among this brilliant little child's letters to his parents I find his earliest letter of all. It reads thus :

' DEAR MUM,—I have been thinking.—A. GRAHAME '

And to his father, at about the same time, he writes :

' DEAR DADDY,—We received the toad letter. *I* will send *you* a story. The ship, the Dragon, started at 10

from Portsmouth on a Friday and it was such a fine day
that every body forgot that it was unlucky.—From your
affectionate MOUSE

The magazine to which Miss Stott refers seems to have
appeared at no stated dates but as and when the editor-
proprietor thought to make an issue. It was published in
holograph and its circulation seems to have been limited
to one copy at a time and that copy for the family circle
at Mayfield, Cookham Dene. *The Merry Thought* continued
to appear at intervals until Alastair went to a private
school. I quote, from its entertaining pages, a contribution
by Kenneth Grahame, wherein, I am told, none of the
characters are fictitious :

BERTIE'S ESCAPADE

I

IT was eleven o'clock on a winter's night. The fields, the
hedges, the trees, were white with snow. From over Quarry
Woods floated the sound of Marlow bells, practising for
Christmas. In the paddock the only black spot visible
was Bertie's sty, and the only thing blacker than the sty
was Bertie himself, sitting in the front courtyard and yawn-
ing. In Mayfield windows the lights were out, and the whole
house was sunk in slumber.

' This is very slow,' yawned Bertie. ' Why shouldn't I
do something ? '

Bertie was a pig of action. ' Deeds, not grunts ' was his
motto. Retreating as far back as he could, he took a sharp
run, gave a mighty jump and cleared his palings.

' The rabbits shall come too,' he said. ' Do them good.'

He went to the rabbit-hutch, and unfastened the door.
' Peter ! Benjie ! ' he called. ' Wake up ! '

' Whatever are you up to, Bertie ? ' said Peter sleepily.

' Come on ! ' said Bertie. ' We're going carol-singing.
Bring Benjie too, and hurry up ! '

Peter hopped out at once, in great delight. But Benjie

ALASTAIR
THE EDITOR OF *THE MERRYTHOUGHT*

grumbled, and burrowed down in his straw. So they hauled him out by his ears.

Cautiously they crept down the paddock, past the house, and out at the front gate. Down the hill they went, took the turning by the pillar-box, and arrived at the foot of Chalkpit Hill. Then Benjie struck.

'Hang it all,' he said, 'I'm not going to fag up that hill to-night for any one!'

'Then I'll bite you,' said Bertie. 'Choose which you please.'

'It's all right, Bertie,' said Peter. 'We're none of us going to fag up that hill. I know an easier way. You follow me.'

He led them into the chalk-pit, till they stood at the very foot. Looking up it was like the cliffs at Broadstairs, only there was no band at the top and no bathing-machines at the bottom.

Peter pulled out a large lump of chalk and disclosed the entrance to a long dark little tunnel. 'Come on!' he said, and dived in; the others followed.

II

They groped along the tunnel for a considerable way in darkness and silence, till at last they saw a glimmer of light; and presently the tunnel ended suddenly in a neat little lift, lit up with electric light, with a seat running round three sides of it. A mole was standing by the door.

'Come along there, please, if you're going up!' called the mole sharply.

They hurried in and sat down. 'Just in time!' said Peter.

'Any more for the lift?' cried the mole, looking down the tunnel. Then he stepped inside smartly, slammed the door, pulled the rope, and they shot upwards.

'Well I never!' gasped Bertie. 'Peter, you do know a thing or two, you do! Where—what—how——'

The lift stopped with a jerk. The mole flung the door

open, saying ' Pass out quickly, please ! ', and slammed it
behind them.   They found themselves standing on the fresh
snow, under the open starlit sky.

They turned round to ask the mole where they were, but
the lift had vanished.   Where it had been there was a square
patch of grass free from snow, and in the middle of the patch
was a buttony white mushroom.

' Why, we're in Spring Lane ! ' cried Bertie.   ' There's the
well ! '

' And here's Mr. Stone's lodge, just in front of us ! ' cried
Peter.

' Splendid ! ' said Bertie.   ' Now, we'll go right up to the
⅃ouse, and sing our bewitching carols under the drawing-
room windows.   And presently Mr. Stone will come out,
and praise us, and pat our heads, and say we're dear
clever animals, and ask us in.   And that will mean supper
in the dining-room, and champagne with it, and grand
times ! '

They hurried up the drive, and planted themselves under
the windows.   Then Bertie said, ' First we'll give 'em " Good
King Wenceslas ".   Now then, all together ! '

' But I don't know " Good King Wenceslas ",' said
Peter.

' And I can't sing ! ' said Benjie.

' Well, you must both do the best you can,' said Bertie.
' Try and follow me.   I'll sing very slow.'   And he struck
up.

Peter followed him, as best he could, about two bars
behind ; and Benjie, who could not sing, imitated various
musical instruments, not very successfully.

Presently they heard a voice, inside the house.   It was
Mrs. Stone's, and she was saying ' What—on—earth—is—
that—horrible caterwauling ? '

Then they heard another voice—Mr. Stone's—replying :
' It sounds like animals—horrid little animals—under the
windows, squealing and grunting.   I will go out with a big
stick, and drive them away.'

' Stick ! O my ! ' said Bertie.
' Stick ! Ow, ow ! ' said Benjie.
Then they heard Mrs. Stone again, saying, ' O no, don't
trouble to go out, dear. Go through the stable yard to
the kennels, and
LET—LOOSE—ALL—THE—DOGS.'

III

' Dogs, O my ! ' said Bertie.
' Dogs, ow, ow ! ' said Benjie.
They turned tail and ran for their lives. Peter had already
started, some ten seconds previously ; they saw him sprint-
ing down the carriage-drive ahead of them, a streak of
rabbit-skin. Bertie ran and ran, and Benjie ran and ran ;
while behind them, and coming nearer and nearer, they could
hear plainly
Wow—wow—wow—wow—wow—WOW !
Peter was the first to reach the mushroom. He flung
himself on it and pressed it, and, click ! the little lift was
there. The door was flung open, and the mole, stepping out,
said sharply : ' Now then ! hurry up, please, if you're going
down ! Any more for the lift ? '
Hurry up indeed ! There was no need to say that. They
flung themselves on the seat, breathless and exhausted ;
the mole slammed the door and pulled the rope, and they
sank downwards.
Then the mole looked them over and grinned. ' Had a
pleasant evening ? ' he inquired.
Bertie would not answer, he was too sulky ; but Peter
replied sarcastically : ' O yes, first rate. My friend here's
a popular carol singer. They make him welcome wherever
he goes, and give him the best of everything.'
' Now don't you start pulling my leg, Peter,' said Bertie,
' for I won't stand it. I've been a failure to-night, and I
admit it ; and I'll tell you what I will do to make up for
it. You two come back to my sty, and I'll give you a
first-rate supper, the best you ever had ! '

'O ah, first-rate cabbage-stalks,' said Benjie. '*We* know your suppers!'

'Not at all,' said Bertie earnestly. 'On the contrary, there's a window in Mayfield that I can get into the house by, at any time. And I know where Mr. Grahame keeps his keys—very careless man, Mr. Grahame. Put your trust in me, and you shall have cold chicken, tongue, pressed beef, jellies, trifle, *and* champagne—at least; perhaps more, but that's the least you'll have.'

Here the lift stopped with a jerk. 'Tumble out, all of you,' said the mole, flinging the door open. 'And look sharp, for it's closing-time, and I'm going home.'

'No, you're not, old man,' said Bertie affectionately. 'You're coming along to have supper with us.'

The mole protested it was much too late; but in the end they persuaded him.

IV

When they got back to Mayfield, the rabbits took the mole off to wash his hands and brush his hair; while Bertie disappeared cautiously round a corner of the house. In about ten minutes he appeared at the pig-sty, staggering under the weight of two large baskets. One of them contained all the eatables he had already mentioned, as well as apples, oranges, chocolates, ginger, and crackers. The other contained ginger-beer, soda-water and champagne.

The supper was laid in the inner pig-sty. They were all very hungry, naturally; and when everything was ready they sat down, and stuffed, and drank, and told stories, and all talked at once; and when they had stuffed enough, they proposed toasts, and drank healths—'The King'—'Our Host Bertie'—'Mr. Grahame'—'The Visitors, coupled with the name of Mole'—'Absent friends, coupled with the name of Mr. Stone'—and many others. Then there were speeches, and songs, and then more speeches, and more songs; and it was three o'clock in the morning before the

mole slipped through the palings and made his way back
to his own home, where Mrs. Mole was sitting up for him,
in some uneasiness of mind.

* * * * *

Mr. Grahame's night was a very disturbed one, owing
to agitating dreams. He dreamt that the house was broken
into by burglars, and he wanted to get up and go down
and catch them, but he could not move hand or foot. He
heard them ransacking his pantry, stealing his cold chicken
and things, and plundering his wine-cellar, and still he could
not move a muscle. Then he dreamt that he was at one
of the great City Banquets that he used to go to, and he
heard the Chairman propose the health of ' The King ! '
and there was great cheering. And he thought of a most
excellent speech to make in reply—a really clever speech.
And he tried to make it, but they held him down in his
chair and wouldn't let him. And then he dreamt that the
Chairman actually proposed his own health—' the health
of Mr. Grahame ! ' and he got up to reply, and he couldn't
think of anything to say ! And so he stood there, for hours
and hours it seemed, in a dead silence, the glittering eyes
of the guests—there were hundreds and hundreds of guests
—all fixed on him, and still he couldn't think of anything
to say ! Till at last the Chairman rose, and said, ' He
can't think of anything to say ! *Turn him out !* ' Then
the waiters fell upon him, and dragged him from the
room, and threw him into the street, and flung his hat
and coat after him ; and as he was shot out he heard
the whole company singing wildly, ' For he's a jolly good
fellow—— ! '

He woke up in a cold perspiration. And then a strange
thing happened. Although he was awake—he knew he was
awake—he could distinctly hear shrill little voices, still
singing ' For he's a jolly good fe-e-llow, and so say all of us ! '
He puzzled over it for a few minutes, and then, fortunately,
he fell asleep.

* * * * *

Next morning, when Miss S. and A. G. went to call on the rabbits, they found a disgraceful state of things. The hutch in a most untidy mess, clothes flung about anyhow, and Peter and Benjie sprawling on the floor, fast asleep and snoring frightfully. They tried to wake them, but the rabbits only murmured something about ' jolly good fellows ', and fell asleep again.

' Well, we never ! ' said Miss S. and A. G.

When Albert King went to take Bertie his dinner, you cannot imagine the state he found the pig-sty in. Such a litter of things of every sort, and Bertie in the midst of it all, fast asleep. King poked him with a stick, and said ' Dinner, Bertie ! ' But even then he didn't wake. He only grunted something that sounded like ' —God—save—King —Wenceslas ! '

' Well ! ' said King, ' Of all the animals ! '

And here is a ' Hunting Song ', written, I imagine (from the topical allusion to Women's Suffrage) when Alastair, the author, was nine years old :

> ' Ye Huntsman winds ye clarion horn,
>   Ye dappled hound doth yap,
> Ye poacher plods his weary way,
>   To set ye rabbit trap.
>
> ' Ye rabbits leap o'er thorn and bryre,
>   Ye poacher to avoid,
> Ye wrathful keeper seezes him,
>   Ye poacher is annoyed.
>
> ' Ye angler waiteth patiently,
>   To catch ye bonny trout,
> His patience is rewarded,
>   And he hooks him by the snout.
>
> ' Ye Scottish Laird to pot ye grouse,
>   His neighbours all doth ask,
> Ye canny Scottish gillie
>   Doth drain ye whiskey flask.

' Ye fat red-faced policemen,
    Ye suffragette pursue,
Ye magistrate says " fourteen days ",
    Ye suffragette says " Booh ! "

' Ye huntsman Cupid shooteth
    At lovers with his dart,
It never pierceth through the head,
    But always through the heart.

' I pause, for now ye angry mob
    Disturbs ye poet's peace,
" Ye stocks, ye horse pond," is the cry,
    And I perforce must cease.'

And, also by Alastair, I find a play of which the title and characters are :

BEAUTY BORN

Characters

JOHN CHIFFIELDS	. .	A labourer.
GEORGE LEE	. . .	King of the Gypsies.
MR. MARSDEN	. . .	The Vicar.
MR. JONES	. . .	The Undertaker.
BEAUTY BORN	. . .	Daughter of John Chiffields.
MARY CHIFFIELDS	. .	Mother of Beauty Born.

GYPSIES, neighbours, &c. &c.

The prologue, or short first act, goes thus :

ACT I

Scene. Inside the Chiffields' cottage. Mrs. Chiffields is making tea. Enter John Chiffields.

Mary Chiffields :   Why, John, how late you are to-day
               And only guess who's come to stay ?

John :   I hope it's not my uncle Jim
               I simply hate the sight of him,
               I hope it's not your fat Aunt Prout
               You know she always put me out ;
               I want no visitors, not me,
               Now do make haste and get my tea.

Mary (drawing a curtain and showing a cradle with a baby
    in it) :

> *This* visitor's a different thing
> And fit enough for any king.

John :   A baby boy ? That's not so bad
> He looks a pretty little lad.

Mary :   But it's a *girl* !

John :   Dash !

Mary :   Do not mourn
> I tell you she's a Beauty Born ;
> She'll do to sew your buttons on
> And cook when I am dead and gone
> So look upon the brighter side.

John (beginning his tea) :

> Well, since she's here she'd better bide.

The play proceeds to relate how Beauty Born, growing up,
is beloved by Lee—the Gypsy King. Beauty does not
reciprocate his affection so Lee attempts to kidnap her.
John Chiffields comes to his daughter's aid and fights with
Lee who, finding himself worsted, falls down and pretends
to be dead. Lulled into a false security Beauty Born thereupon goes for a walk alone. Lee, following her, now succeeds in his design. John Chiffields traces Lee and Beauty
to the gypsy encampment. John is taken prisoner. But
Beauty helps him and they both escape. On arriving home
they find that Mrs. Chiffields has died of a very natural
alarm. They give her a handsome funeral which is largely
attended, and there we meet Mr. Jones, the undertaker, who
comforts Beauty thus :

Mr. Jones :   Young lady, kindly do not cry
> But take my arm and wipe your eye.

And *Mr. Marsden*, a clergyman, who says, helpfully :

> This is indeed a doleful day
> For better times we all must pray.

And presently we find Beauty Born and John Chiffields at
home again. (Lee has apparently resigned himself to the
loss of Beauty) and we reach the final curtain thus :

Beauty Born (setting John's tea before him) :
          There, Father, isn't it a joy
          That I'm a girl and not a boy ?

John Chiffields (eating bread and jam) :
          Yes, Beauty Born, I'm very glad
          That you're a lass and not a lad.

It seems that a little boy who, barely out of the nursery,
could perpetrate such a plot and action might have gone
far. *Beauty Born* remains for me as remarkable a piece
of ' child literature ' as ever I read.

Mr. F. Anstey Guthrie (F. Anstey) writes to Mrs. Grahame
of her son as follows :

' He must have been about seven, when, on calling one
day at Durham Villas, I was first introduced to him. I
have never never met a boy with such natural distinction,
or a more fascinating personality. It was rather like being
presented to a young prince. He was a handsome little boy,
tall for his age, with rather long brown hair, a singularly
clear and beautiful voice, a subtle smile and an air of
complete self-possession.

' He did not suffer visitors at all gladly. One afternoon
when some people were calling he was observed to run about
the drawing-room with extraordinary activity during the
whole of their visit, his explanation being : " I thought if
I kept moving I might escape being kissed." It is not
likely, however, that they had any suspicion of the reason,
for his manner towards all visitors had an invariable grace
and charm.

' From our first meeting I had been struck by a certain
maturity, not in the least priggish, in his choice of words,
and a delicate sense of humour which was far beyond his
years.

' I like to think that I was admitted to his friendship.
We had some interests in common at all events ; toys being
one of them, and just then Mouse had a passion for any
kind of mechanical toy.   I remember a clockwork pianist
who, on being wound up, elicited a faint and tiny sound
from his instrument.   He was no Paderewski, but Mouse
was quite well satisfied by his performance.

' It is so many years ago now that I have few recollections
of anything that Mouse said at our meetings.   The circus
was, however, one of our subjects, for he fully shared his
father's love for it.   Once about this time a telegram arrived,
which Mouse eyed with eager expectation, only to be told
that it was on some business matter.   " Oh," he said in a
crestfallen voice, " I thought perhaps it was to invite us
all up to a Circus ! "

' We also compared notes on Kensington Gardens, which
I had known at a much earlier age than his.   But he did
not divulge to me the private opinion of that pleasure ground
which he expressed later on going to live in the country.
" Kensington *Gardens* ! " he said disdainfully, " simply
starchy with perambulators ! "

' Even then I realized that, in addition to a charming
and lovable nature, Mouse had ability and originality that
in all probability would develop into genius.   I know now
that as he grew up, he never lost his charm, and as a boy
and a young man, was fearless, generous, kindly and gracious
to all he met, while there were already indications that he
would eventually be among those who leave Literature the
richer for their existence.   I myself believe that he would
have been a very great writer.'

Alastair was, as the son of his father, a true lover of
Christmas and of Christmas trees and, when a few Christ-
mases had made him connoisseur, his parent took thought
and decorated for him the finest Christmas tree in Christen-
dom.

He chose first a bulgy bay-window in the hall at Cookham
Dene so that the tree, when lighted up, might be seen, by

those who approached the house, at all its gorgeously pink-candled angles. He chose his tree (a spruce fir, of course) and stood it within the window upon a carpet, thick, orderly and square, of red beech leaves, dusted on with a hoar-frost of ' diamond-dust '. Above the tree he hung a shepherd's star to sparkle. On the top of the tree he caused, gold-crowned, an angel to stand. Within the angel was a mechanism that made it revolve whilst it emitted a tinkling carol in praise of Christmas. There were icicles of glass upon the dark and symmetrical branches, there were pink candles, there were guns and pop-guns in the old classic colours—magenta and scarlet and crude yellow. There was Father Noah and his Ark. There were horses and riders in red, there were sabres and monkeys and fruits of wax whose cheeks were the one of scarlet and the other of yellow. There were gilded walnuts and silver boats, small boats rigged in cobweb of silver. There was even, without, a slight snowfall to be seen through the window. It was the perfect tree and when lighted up it looked like the Queen of Sheba in a ball dress of peacock tails, only far finer.

And the poet who had made it for the little boy made this poem to go with it :

> ' The time is drawing nigh when Trees
> Shall rustle in the parlour breeze ;
> And Pines and Firs shall wave indoors,
> Scattering their needles on the floors.
> Then we shall wander 'neath the boughs
> That whisper in the scented house ;
> And, looking up for Stars, shall see
> Pink candles twinkle bashfully !
>
> ' O noble steed, with Rider red !
> O Ark, that sailest overhead !
> Dolls, in the branches blossoming,
> Whence Trumpet, Drums, and Sabres swing !
> Strewn on the carpet's sward so green
> Strange gold and silver fruits are seen ;
> While from a Box sweet tinklings flow,
> Like Robin fluting in the snow !

' And then—the Story-Teller comes !
—Let fall the Trumpets, hush the Drums !
Wolves in the street may howl and wait—
The Camp-Fire glows within the Grate !
Round it we Pirates, Scouts and Trappers
(Hugging our Presents in their wrappers)
Spell-bound, in semi-circle snug,
Drink the enchantment, on the rug ! '

And when the stories were told the carol-singers came (very like the carol-singers, ' villagers all ', in *The Wind in the Willows*) and the Mummers came too, just as they came in *The Golden Age*, stamping and crossing and declaiming, ' till all was whirl and riot and shout '. And altogether it was the merriest Christmas that ever was. And here I should like to leave little Alastair Grahame, a happy day behind him and heir-apparent, one would have said, to many happy days.

Yet I will add that his bigger boyhood (though the latter part of it was lived in the War years) seems to have been a happy time too although the literary promise, so marked in nursery and schoolroom days, is now only to be noticed in his letters. There develops, however, a passion for acting and for swimming. And a character for kindness, courtesy and courage in all things. His letters are full of a gay and spritely humour—occasionally expressed in Latin verse or in English Limericks—such as

' There was a young Frenchman called Jules
Who jobbed as a waiter at Buol's
        The customers said That his Welsh Rabbit's head
Was as hard as an Indian Mule's.'

In a letter from his private school he writes : ' I and Jennings discovered a ripping cave in the quarry. We are having a ripping game there. The cave is on a desert island and there is buried treasure (doubloons, Louis d'ors, pieces of eight). Also cannibals and a pirate ship. Need I say that Jennings is Rupert of Hentzau and that I am Dick Lawless, the Bloody Buccaneer ? On Tuesday I swam over

the ledge and into the open sea. On Wednesday we played
Durlston Court and won by about 100. On Friday was
The Parents' Match. The Parents were as numerous, as
arogant (*sic*) and as over-dressed as they always are. On
Saturday we went down to the ledge and had a look at the
sea. The waves were magnificent. Even on the cliff-top
we could feel the spray in our faces. I think a stormy sea
is one of the finest sights one can see anywhere. Afterwards
we went down to Swanage and I bought a sixpenny edition
of George Borrow's *Bible in Spain*. Borrow seems to have
been a tireless traveller and as a linguist he was simply
extraordinary. . . . Daddy's verses move me to break into
song too :

> ' Once I met a fellow
>   Tramping down the road
> A truss of straw, bright yellow,
>   Was all that bumpkin's load.'
>   *The Impressions of a Clodhopper.*

> ' Yours affectionately,
>   ' A. GRAHAME (Titwillow) '

' *P.S.*—I am glad to hear that Uncle Harold has been
made Mayor of Westminster. May his period of office be
as prolonged as that of Sir R. Whittington of feline fame.'

After leaving Eton, Alastair (he had been too young to
undertake personal war service) went to Oxford. About
then his father writing of him to a friend says, ' It was most
awfully good of you to give the boy such a splendid time.
He seems to have enjoyed every minute of it. Owing to
the War he has been simply starved on the social side of
him and this visit was just what he wanted and what was
best for him. For he is a " social animal " really. I dare
say you discovered what a passion he has for abstract dis-
cussion and first principles as opposed to anything concrete.
He would, for instance, sit up all night discussing the
principles that went to the drawing up of the American
Constitution, while being languidly indifferent to personal
details concerning any President.'

In Alastair's second year at Christ Church, in May 1920, in the days when Death and Sudden Death began once more to be exceptional in Youth and forgotten in the land, an accident at a level-crossing near Oxford Station took him instantly.

Of the many hundreds of letters arising out of the tragedy, letters from every sort and condition of sympathizer, I will quote from three. I make my brief choices for representative reasons. I quote a letter of the Dean of Christ Church, dated July 1920, because I think that its restrained allusion to a terrible meeting and moment leaves no more to be said as to what was tragic and final in the cruel matter. Dr. Strong writes from Christ Church :

' DEAR MRS. GRAHAME,—I thank you for your letter. I am leaving this house to-morrow. And a great part of my possessions have been already removed. But I am still working in my study, which has many memories—none sadder than that here I had to tell you and his father of your dear son's death.

' Yours very sincerely,
' THOMAS B. STRONG '

I quote from a letter of Miss Anna Gregory, ' boys' maid ' at Alastair's House at Eton, because it is well, above all things, to be remembered for kindness and courtesy and in the friendly terms of workaday. Miss Gregory writes : . . . ' I shall never forget his memory. He was always so kind and courteous. He was the only boy in his tutor's house that I ever even *thought* of cutting the bread-and-butter thin for. I trust you may be comforted.'

And a fellow undergraduate writes of Sir Arthur Quiller-Couch's appreciation of Alastair : ' I think you must be glad that somebody has written down so well what we all felt instinctively but could not express.'

I quote these words because they speak for every one who was sorry and also because they serve to introduce what Sir Arthur said, in the *Oxford Magazine* of 18th June 1920.

' It is a pious office (and the *Magazine* has, from the first, faithfully performed it) to print some record of any son of Oxford whose end rounds off an honourable tale of accomplished work. We pay, so far as their numbers allow, a like tribute to those who fell in the late War ; equalling them with their seniors. We owe that much at least to *them*, and we can go on pretending to ourselves—for without the soothing lie life would be unendurable—that they were not betrayed to early death. But, the War ended, there begins again the old quarrel with Fate over those whom *abstulit atra dies*, whom it is snatching just as before, without any shade of a plea that they died to save us, or to save England, or to save any other mortal thing the preservation of which would compensate for murder of youth and promise. Whatever our date at Oxford, we have all known one or two contemporaries " perished in their prime " over whom we have had to dismiss the professional mourner to the street ; over whom in the strength of indignation we really are able to browbeat Fate and demand whether or not it knows its business.

' Alastair Grahame was an undergraduate of Christ Church. He went out for a solitary walk after Hall on the night of May 7th, and on his way home, crossing the intricate railway lines by Port Meadow, was cut down by a train and instantly killed. No, after all, there is nothing to accuse, if a boy— with, as he had, some defect of eyesight—choses to stray, at night, across the complicated metals of two railway lines. Aware of it or no, he has run the risk, and there's an end. And this will do, if we as sternly cancel out humbug on the other side—all talk about Guardian Angels, " it is not growing like a tree ", &c., or " Death's self being sorry ".

' I knew Alastair Grahame from his infancy. He was always an " unusual " boy : not merely one of the boys (far more usual than is commonly supposed) who are unable to view Rugby or Eton save as prisons and look forward to Oxford or Cambridge for the gaol delivery of their souls ; but one who, coming to adore Oxford, still

saw it as a preparative. School games afflicted his soul,
because it was impatient. It could not wait to play with
taken-for-granted amusements ; it was (I think) a trifle too
contemptuous of his fellows so easily accepting themselves
as, at the best, " noble playthings of the gods ". But he
found delight and gaiety and wisdom in the simplest happen-
ings of animals and people. Above all he was gentle : to
animals quite instinctively a young image of St. Francis
(yet I must not say instinctively, remembering that one
of the loveliest books of our time and the least appreciated
commensurately with its worth, *The Wind in the Willows*,
is based all on letters written to amuse him as a child).
To all his elders and to the poor, he bore himself with the
sweetest of courtesy. On whatever else he might have
improved, his high manners were his own and absolute.
As for patriotism, he was too young to serve ; but this did
not prevent his offering himself more than once. He was
turned back twice ; and he took these reverses seriously,
envying the luckier ones so far as his nature allowed him
to envy.

' He fell back, as I know, on a dream of sacrifice to make
the world better when this turmoil should be over. He
was consciously fitting himself ; and I do not doubt that
he was wandering, occupied with these dreams, when brute
force hurled itself upon them and annihilated them all.

' A few, I dare say, who look back upon this Summer
Term of riotous renewal will remember a small tragedy
which opened it. But I wish that all who are building up
hopes, just now for their country, might realize what a
paragraph in *The Times*—" Undergraduate's Death : killed
on the line at Oxford "—meant to one who, himself bound
for Cambridge, and the avid young life there renewing itself,
actually repeating, as his eyes withdrew from the English
landscape of Spring,

" I turned from all she brought to those she could not bring,"

found himself staring stupidly at the announcement and

the name of the victim, Alastair Grahame. Above all
private sorrow and sympathy I knew the quenching, suddenly, brutally, of a high hope, not selfish. It was as if,
among the few stars left in an elderly man's heaven, one
had suddenly dropped to extinction. Well enough I see
Oxford indifferent to the fate of any particular son ; but
sorely must we lament one who never began to live until
he had found her and would, we believe, have lived to reward
her with honourable achievement.'

Above the dust which young Alastair was done with,
his father caused these words to be written : ' Here was
laid to rest on his twentieth birthday, 12th of May 1920,
Alastair, only child of Kenneth and Elspeth Grahame, of
whose noble ideals, steadfast purposes and rare promise
remains only a loved and honoured memory.'

Well did the child Alastair ask, years ago, concerning a
world whose acquaintance he had so lately made, ' *Why*
is there trouble ? ' Now, mayhappen (since ' Death is
Promotion '), he has been answered.

CHAPTER X

THE LIZARD LIGHTS

In a man's working life there must be holidays, if his work is to be the best work, if it is to be good work even. Kenneth Grahame's ' spiritual homes ' were ' the two sea-boots '— Italy and the Duchy of Cornwall. To the one or the other he went, when young, on vacation. And when, in his later years, the fogs of November sent him to seek the sun, it was in the Duchy or in Italy that he sought it. Kenneth, Edinburgh born though he was, rarely visited Scotland, a ' gangrel Scot ' he preferred the South—the ' uncovenanted lands '. But when he did go North he was content there and he writes of his last visit to Scotland that ' it was really an immense success. The weather was magnificent and we were, even for the Highlands, in the most beautiful country. The boy [1] was simply drunk with it all and grieved sorely to leave it. There was a joy of colour everywhere. But of course (there's aye something) travelling in August is always infernal and we had to couch like the beasts of the field, in temperance inns and such '.

But though the blue Adriatic summoned him periodically, as likewise did the haunted groves and Sicilian beaches, Kenneth Grahame was a Cornishman, if not by birth at least by inclination. He went to the West for the first time in 1884. Then he and his sister, Kenneth being on holiday from the Bank of England, visited The Lizard in idle August and there Kenneth gazed into the sea pools (as other young men gaze into the eyes of a girl) and was captivated. And back in Bloomsbury, he remembered and he wrote of Triton and Mermaid and the ' dragon-haunted ' sea :

[1] His son, Alastair, then about 14 years old.

'From each generation certain are chosen whom Nature, in those rathe years when she imprints our plastic wax with that wonderful signet-ring of hers, leads by the hand one fated day within sight and sound of the sea. There —howbeit scarce in years enough to distinguish between vision and fact—the elect is made aware, or dreams, of a marvellous emergence and dazedly hears the very Triton blow on his wreathed horn. And in the blare that issues from out the crooks of the sea-thing's shell are mingled many elements—wind-shaken water, whip and creak and rattle of shrouds, flap of idle sails in halcyon spells, cry of gulls at pasture on the pale acres that know no plough ; but run through them all, making the chord perfect, is a something that suggests the dazzling laughter of Oceanus in a crinkling calm, with a certain haunting smell of weed and tar. Henceforth, that adept is possessed. Desk-bound, pent in between city walls—a fellow, say, fast held in the tangle of Christ Church bells ; a solicitor behind wire-blinds in some inland market-town—henceforth the insistent echo will awake and take him betimes, claiming him as one with the trident brand on him. For the Triton knows his man, and whom he has once chosen he never again lets go.

'This thing may befall him, indeed, who has never even sniffed salt in the air, nor watched the solan, a rocket reversed, spirt high the spray in his joyous huntings. On him it will come suddenly out of some musty book of magic : wherein the sulphur clouds roll tremendous round the tall masts of fighting ships topped by the meteor flag, or the boats, with muffled oars, steal forth to the cutting out of the French brig. He will hear the lap and gurgle of waves he has never seen, along the sides of a craft whose streaks no man has laid : wherefore it has come to pass that many a stout mariner of England has known nothing more nauti-cal than the brown sails of barges sliding by his farmstead, through pasturage dotted with browsing kine. If the con-ditions be reversed, and Nature, as first known to him, was

ever one half of it the shifting sea, then the Triton will
have certainly hailed him one day or other, and thenceforward the call sounds ever in his ear. Or, it may be,
having thrilled to the Triton's note ere he knew right from
wrong, the vision it evokes for him shall be circumscribed
and homely as the writer's own : which is of big black-
sided fishing-boats, drawn high and dry on a wondrous
beach. These were his daily food, though once a week
the mysterious steamer from the outer world crawled by
with clockwork singularity. Fishing-boats and the weekly
steamer—these he had endlessly limned and dislimned,
though the slate was given (sure) for better ends, ere the
white day when the little plump of yachts cast anchor off
the tiny town. The first reading of the *Arabian Nights*—
they were something like that to him, these slim Sultanas
of the sea ! Had not the rural policeman been courting
his nursemaid, the vision had lacked completeness ; to the
young god he owes it, that he was rowed out, enraptured,
himself and the maiden in the stern, the man of order at
the oars, while the unseen Eros balanced it in the bows.
The writhing golden sea-weed shimmered fathoms deep
below. Above were these fairy galleys, and you could
spy their dainty fitments, and spell out the names on their
gilded bows. And when at last they spread white wings
and vanished, the slate for long would record no meaner
portraiture. It is small wonder that to this boy the trains,
whose acquaintance he was soon to make, should seem
ungainly rattletraps. True it is that they held one piece
of fascination ; for the arms of an ancient city were painted
on the carriage-doors, and these were made additionally
mysterious by the rhyme communicated by a good-natured
porter, which told how " This is the tree that never
grew, this is the bird that never flew ; this is the fish
that never swam, this is the bell that never rang." But
for all that, the train was damned, in that it took you
away, out of earshot of the Triton's bugling ; so that
only once you might get a certain small effect of grace

when suddenly, as it rattled past some dingy town, over the reeking house-tops there appeared a tangled tracery of masts, while a delicate waft of tar and harbour-mud breathed of the authentic, unsuspected Paradise at hand.

' Isled in far-reaching downs, the inland farmstead knows no harsh Atlantic : the sole murmur that surges and breaks about its doors commingles the cackle and grunt and lot of its dependants. Two china dogs of seductive aspect adorn the mantelshelf in a kitchen recking not of nets nor crab-pots, with certain fruits in wax, cunningly fashioned, fairer far than Nature's own, and with two great smooth shells, wherein the sea's secret lingers, in shadow as it were, and eternized. Once, long years ago, they were filled with the Triton's music, and ever since, the natural phonographs of the god, they have faithfully retained its echoes till the understanding one shall come. And as he listens at the lips of them, farm and farmstead melt away ; the solid miles break up and disappear ; and once again he is walking the wind-blown sands, while at his side his ancient mistress, malicious, serpentine, beautiful, coils and fawns, and laughs and caresses, and calls to him, as of old.

' And what of the Triton's point of view ? He, too, is doubtless drawn to an alien element by some subtle attraction not in the unstable glancing world wherein he abides. Is there far down in him a sympathetic string responding to the voice of the wind in the pine tops, the flow of gorse and heather, the hum of wandering bees ? Hath he an affection for the warm-skinned beasts that stray by the shores, which the cold flocks and herds of Proteus fail to satisfy ? Or doth he turn, perchance, from the chill caresses of green-haired mermaidens, to dream of some rich-blooded minion of the dairy ? Whatever the reason, who doubts that there are discontents down in the sea as well as high on his banks ? And neither of us can change places, which is possibly just as well. No : we can but hail each other fraternally, on those rare occasions when recognition is

13

permitted, and the last tripper has left the beach one moment free.'

Year after year Kenneth returned to that remote West. There he spoke as an equal to the dark men of the sea who sat on the settle at the inn and smoked and lied and drunk a glass and put to sea again their lives in their own strong hands.

He learnt to ' whiff ' for pollock (a matter of rowing) and to ' sail ' (a red mainsail and a little mizzen) for mackerel (a form of trailing with three plummet lines, one on each side and one astern, by which you may fill a boat with the bonny fish), he learnt to lay, and haul, a ' boulter '. And a ' boulter ' is a mile-long sea-line punctuated with corks and bristling with a system of ' dropper ' hooks baited with mussel or lug worm. When you haul the boulter it brings in-board eight glittering furlongs of fish.

Conger, too, he learnt to catch, putting out to a summer sea at 6 p.m. The pilchard fleets are shooting their nets beyond Fowey and the August dusk has come by 7.30. The lugger lamps glitter. In six fathoms of smooth water the anchor falls. The stout lines are baited with squid. The conger—but Kenneth Grahame held that the fun with a twenty-five-pound conger only really began after you got it into the boat. And it was fun rather appropriate (he said) to some rollicking old farce at the Vaudeville of other days. The conger usually knocked the lamp over and then went, full of fight, ' swingeing ' and slithering from stem to stern, Kenneth meanwhile, and the boatman, bludgeoning each other by moonlight in their attempts to subdue it. Great knockabout business it was.

And once, off Kynance Cove, trolling with rod and line, a spoon of great dimensions and a wire trace that would hold a narwhal, a fish, in the late afternoon, took the gargantuan bait and ' sounded ' with a prodigious dive of five fathoms. It then, still deep down, began to tow the boat out to sea. After a while the boatman, weather and tide being contrary, said that he would not be responsible for the safety of the ship's company unless the fish was cut adrift. The angler laid his rod down and took hold of the line and hauled upon it with all his mighty strength, and Kenneth was a big man and in the flower of his youth. He says that he saw, or ever the sea-line parted, a great and sinister shape, or shadow, in the water—'like the shape that followed Rorie's cobble in Aros'. And, with the night falling and the wind coming on to blow, he was well rid of whatever it was, I think.

So Kenneth became a Cornishman by adoption and learnt to love the Cornish fisherfolk and to enjoy their friendliness to him. He liked their Spanish looks, he liked the foreign names by which some called themselves, he liked the soft southern voices that addressed him (or any one else) by such affectionately-sounding utterances as 'my dear life' and 'my dear soul'.

And once, when he landed and stood among his fisher friends after a night with the pilchard fleet, he, sunburnt and covered with scales 'like Harlequin', this is what came of it. The late principal of Hertford College, Oxford, Dr. Boyd, was a visitor at The Lizard and out betimes. He was a benefactor of the fishermen who, as a class, he loved and with whom he was always anxious to converse. What wonder then that on this occasion Dr. Boyd singled out a splendid-looking young man in a blue jersey and a peaked cap as the subject for his friendly advances? In Kenneth Grahame's own words :

'He came up and asked had I had good luck with the fish? "The best, sir," said I and touched my cap. Presently, after a few more remarks, he went away. But, in a minute, he was back again and begging my pardon for his mistake. "Sir," said I, "I have never been more flattered in my life." '

Most of all he liked Cornish food—'Thunder-and-Lightning' (which is Cornish cream and treacle zig-zagged over warm, new bread, in the form of forked lightning and of sheet). ' Splits ' he liked also (fresh rolls opened, spread thickly with the thickest of cream and closed again) and ' Star-Gazy Pie ' which is made from fresh pilchards whose noses peer upwards through the lightest and most flaky of pie-crust.

> (Can ye tell me, fisher laddies,
> What's gotten into the heads o' the haddies ?)

' Licky Pasties ' too, of which one of the constituents is a leek, were the fine fare and one that the women would wrap in hot flannel and give to their men-folk to take to the fishing. Delicacies indeed.

And the westerly weather appealed to Kenneth, not only in its idylls of summer evenings and estuaries, the gorse yellow on the cliff-tops, the hunting-call of the swifts loud and low down about the boat that drew to her moorings, but the great gales also that praise the Lord. He loved the roar of the rain that rattles like small shot against an ' oily ', he loved the salt sting of the spume that flies over the cliff when the great, grey seas, swinging out of the mist, explode below and, recoiling like a mill-race, suck the gravel beaches after them in thunder—a moil of green water, a turmoil of white suds.

This Lizard that Kenneth took to his heart is the last of English land to be sighted by down-Channel shipping. Two lighthouses wink there when the dark falls. The peregrine nests on the sea cliffs and there the fulmar flies. Off shore that grim coast is fortressed with rocks, it is fringed and fanged with reefs where, even in the endless summer days, the blue-and-white fountains spout continually.

But, ruggéd and gigantic, a hard and scanty land is this and its people wring want from the sea which in turn takes her toll of them. And those who do not fish toil in serpentine, for so the colour-veined rock of Lizard is called. Kenneth Grahame, in his time, bought many a ' tourist article '—a candlestick here, an inkstand there, or, perhaps

a photograph frame, all in this heavy granite, and just to
' help-along ' a Cornishman.

Salvage occurred sometimes.   Kenneth has been remembered as he stood on the turf-covered cliff-top among an
acreage, and much more, of fleeces from Morocco.   A great
ship had driven, head on, into the black fangs of the reef
and there she had broken asunder.   Her cargo of valuable
sheepskins was to salve.   Throughout the parish every
occupation, from the boiling of an egg to the building of
a church, was suspended and, creeping child to nonogenarian,
all hands were to the salving, grabbing and drying and
cleaning the wool which, high in quality, promised a noble
dividend to those who could get it—a dividend greater than
any that pollock or pilchard could pay.

For a while Kenneth Grahame stood among the salvors.
Then he too went to the beaches—an amateur of might.
What the sea brought to him or what, waist-deep, he
wrested from her he gave to the oldest of the gleaners, or
to the brown-faced youngest who had, he said, ' much cry
and little wool '.   Anyhow it was a great harvest and, at
the end of the week, more watches were bought at The
Lizard than had been sold in the memory of man.

For in Cornwall the possession of a watch is a hall-mark
of a solid prosperity and the owner of a silver watch is a
man of luxury, even leisure, whom all must respect.   For
only the luxurious possess a silver watch.   At The Lizard,
and in sea-faring Cornwall generally, gold is unknown.
Silver is the only ware.   Watches are of silver and so are
wedding-rings.   In fact when Kenneth, about to be married
at Fowey, wanted a wedding-ring, the ' plain gold ring ' of
the ballad, it was to Plymouth that he must journey before
he could buy one.   But, as I have said, after the wreck of
the *Suevic*, silver watches were common at The Lizard—
' common as pilchards at Looe '.   Indeed one granddad,
the richer for the flotsam, the extra wool that Kenneth
had won for him, treated himself to *two* silver watches.
And lived twice as happy ever after.

Tom Roberts was Kenneth's friend who took him to the fishing. Tom was, for twenty-one years, coxswain of the lifeboat and, at seventy-four years of age (when he could still go aloft ' like a boy ') he had taken his boat out through the tumbling rock-staked tides to the sinking *Suevic*. He had climbed on board the wreck and calmed the crew with the tidings that ' she was so fast on the rocks that she couldn't sink—not yet awhile, anyway '.

Mary Ellen was the daughter of Tom Roberts, she was married to Mr. Squibb the signalman of the lifeboat. She has lately written a letter telling of these Cornish days. I quote a few lines of it, just as Mrs. Squibb has written them down : ' I remember young Mr. Kenneth, he was very fond of my father and was always very nice to us and to my family. He used to love going out fishing all night with father. They used to set a boulter and they would catch very big fish, cod-fish and ling, which people used to salt and dry for the winter. They don't seem to do that now. Father named his boat the *Mary Ellen* after me. Rather a funny name for a boat but he thought a lot of me. I think the first time I remember Mr. Kenneth was in 1887. He had been out with father fishing that day and he called in on his way back. I happened to be out getting something and when I came in he was sitting in his sea-boots with my two little girls in their night-gowns one on each knee. They had heard some one come in and come creeping down for to peep who it was and he had taken them up. I can see the three of them now.'

Mrs. Squibb still lives at Gue Graze, The Lizard. And she lets lodgings and one of ' the two little girls ' cooks most beautifully.

Another of Kenneth Grahame's Cornish friends was ' Captain James '. He was not really a captain but, after years of strenuous toil, he had (something like Mr. Kipling's *McPhee*) amassed a reasonable competence—and the two watches which confer the honorary rank of Captain. So he built himself a fine house and then Mrs. Captain James

invited her old acquaintance, Mr. Kenneth Grahame, to
take tea.

The new house had a ' slab ' which is Cornish for kitchen
range and marks the millionaire.   Kenneth arrived punctually.   The Captain was seated on one side of the ' slab '
(which, polished like a mirror, was ' too good to use '), on
the other side sat ' the girl ', an appendage of new-found
state, who shuffled her feet in agonies of shyness, crossing
and uncrossing them, and bending a flushed face above a
new duster which she made pretence to darn.

The two supported Mrs. James who stood between them
to receive the guest.   This done, Mrs. James, leaving her
husband to his new-found, and tedious, inaction, began the
' showing-over '.   The furniture was from Plymouth, the
parlour was ' Louis-quinsey ' and the dining-room ' Chewter '
(Tudor).   There were four upstairs rooms, two furnished
individually, in period styles, by the free-hand Plymouth
firm.   Both, sighed Mrs. James, were ' too good to use '.
But the Captain and she made the best of it by putting
' the girl ' to sleep in the box-room and sleeping themselves
in the latter's very modest bedroom which, being of no
particular period, seemed more homelike than the ' Queen
Annie ' and the ' George-g-i-an ' of the other two chambers.

As the viewing became more prolonged Mrs. James became
the more melancholy, until, exhibiting the labour-saving
contrivances of the larder, she, who had lived her happy
married life in a wooden shanty, broke down and broke
out—' I doubt whether we shall ever get our healths in
this close place (the gale-swept Lizard !) and besides I do
belong to work and there's naught to do here but polish
the " slab " and " the girl " does that.'   (To ' belong to '
means in Cornwall, to be accustomed to ; as, for instance,
if one asked for fish-hooks, one might be told by the vendors,
' we do belong to keep them but we're out of them this
day '.)

So Kenneth spoke kind words and the two returned to
the kitchen and the Captain, who ' belonging to work '

(just as did his old wife) had not even ' the girl's ' consolation
of darning a duster and might but sit and admire the
' slab '.

Kenneth was touched, he has told, by the pathos of a
dream of Kubla Khan so sadly fulfilled as to be, in the fact,
a nightmare. But the tea was excellent.

In his ' private ledger ' I have found these lines written
down. I like to imagine that they were composed on a
summer evening while the *Mary Ellen* beat out to the conger
grounds and, of a sudden, the orange beam stabbed the
blue dusk.

THE LIZARD LIGHTS

Lizard Lights, our eyes were dim
When we watched your beacon swim
Down the gloom and disappear,
Last of all we held most dear,
On that far distant night of nights
When last we saw you, Lizard Lights !

Now, what magic spell is shed,—
Like a dream the years have sped ;
Dream-like, gone the fears and frets,
Gone the longings and regrets ;
Your glad ray at last requites
All our sorrow, Lizard Lights !

The above verses sound so sadly that only a happy
young man, an after-tea pipe in his mouth and a night's
conger fishing before him, could have made them.

Kenneth Grahame first went to Fowey in 1899. It was
at St. Fimbarrus Church that he was married. St. Fimbarrus
of Cork (of all places) and *not* of Cornwall ! Fowey is
pronounced Foy. It lies on the west shore of the estuary
of the river Fowey. It has a deep sea harbour and the big
ships go in and out of it. It has a Fort and a Ferry—but
most people know Fowey best because it is ' the little grey
sea town that clings along one side of the harbour ' which
the Sea-Rat describes, so exactly, in *The Wind in the Willows*.
Therefore there is no need that I should describe Fowey.

Beyond saying (the Sea-Rat has omitted to say this) that
when elephants visit Fowey—sometimes elephants *do* and
a circus toward—they find the street of Fowey so perpendicular, such a toboggan-slide of a place, that they must
go down it philosophically, and in all their gilt trappings,
seated upon their poor tails. Which the boys of Fowey,
of which Kenneth was ever one, think is comical.

Fowey is also the ' Troy Town ' of Sir Arthur Quiller-
Couch. To whom Kenneth Grahame, writing to thank
Sir Arthur for the dedication of his book, *The Mayor of
Troy*, says, ' I feel now really officially connected with the
place, through its Mayor ; and some day I shall put in
for an almshouse, if you have any.' *The Mayor* is, of course,
dedicated to ' My friend Kenneth Grahame and the rest of
the crew of the *Richard and Emily* '. The *Richard and
Emily* was the rowing-boat used by Mr. and Mrs. Grahame
when on their honeymoon, which was spent at Fowey.

Mrs. Grahame writes of the two children of Sir Arthur
Quiller-Couch thus :

' The eight-year-old page at our wedding was Bevil
Quiller-Couch the only son of " Q "—a splendid little fellow
who, even at that age, was so clever and so sensible that
his opinion was weighed and gravely taken, as later it came
to be sought and valued, alike by towns-people and sailor-
men. He grew up to be what he then promised—a tower
of strength, ever to be relied on—cheerful, charming—with
a genius for friendship in every walk of life, and for those
of all ages. Always a great man in a boat, sailing, rowing
—and indeed as much at home in, or on, the water as on
land—full of courage, as when he scaled an all but unsur-
mountable cliff to get succour for an old friend whose small
yacht had filled and sunk in the bay below. As much
loved at Winchester, at Oxford and in the Army, as he was
in his native place, he lived to serve through the War,
from August 1914 to the end, taking all risks yet being
miraculously spared.

' He won the M.C. and later, the D.S.O. Going out as a

Subaltern he rose rapidly to his Majority, and then to command a Battery—his beloved " Royal Ninth " of the Second Division during the last two years of fighting in France. He died of pneumonia in the Army of Occupation, to which he had returned, when he could have been demobilized, in order to see the story of his Battery closed to perfection and provide that its horses were sent home to England, in the pride they had deserved. They and his men, so he had written home to his parents on Armistice Day, " were my children ".

'Who would have thought that the little laughing boy in his white sailor suit with the bunch of roses for a buttonhole would have played so brave and enduring a part in so terrible a war, from the start to the finish of it, only to die of illness on the eve of his marriage ? Some one at our long-ago wedding remarked to the little page, " Well, Bevil, it will be your turn next "—to which Bevil, with the common sense he shared with Dr. Johnson, replied calmly, " There are a good many in this town to be married before me."

'He was a boy who then, and as long as his short life lasted, held a great place in the hearts of those who knew him, and in leaving this world left a great sense of grief and permanent loss, because somehow that place which he held would for ever remain empty—as no other could fill it as he had, with his cheery kindness, his unfailing courage and his vivid individuality. His resourcefulness was remarkable, and he was always a character and a personage, counselling and ruling those far older and (presumably) wiser than himself. But Bevil was always wise even as a child.

'Fowey was the best place in the world. The skies so blue, the sun so golden, and the moon so silver. Picnics with the Q's, long sails in their yacht, the *Vida*, over the Bay to Penrice, the home of Admiral and Lady Graves Sawle, the latter, in her youth, an inspiration to Savage Landor. Rowing with the Q's in their red boat, the *Picotee*,

later to be " manned " by the golden-haired girl who at the
earliest age was put into a tiny boat of her very own to
be coached by her brother Bevil, who, eight years older
than she, carried her up and down the room as a long-
clothes baby, and cried exultingly, " See how good she is
with me, I believe she likes a man's step " (the man being
eight !).

'That long-clothes baby when arrived at the age of four,
came to spend an afternoon with us at the Fowey Hotel,
and on her nurse coming for her at bedtime said, " You
needn't *try* to fetch me, Nurse, but you can get my nightie,
for I am going to *live* with the Grahames."

In the summer of 1899, Kenneth, at Fowey and writing to
a lady, says : ' My sister said that she went along the cliffs
and climbed down to a little cove and as she sat there a big
rat came out and sat beside her and ate winkles ! Said I
to my sister, " Did he buy them off a barrow and drop them
into his hat ? " But she looked puzzled and said, " No, he
only scraped in the seaweed with his little paws and fetched
them out." Then I began again—" Was it a *black* pin
that he ate them with ? " And she thought I was raving
so I dropped the subject. But had *I* been there he'd have
given me winkles and I'd have lent him a pin out of my
tie. Another T.B. Destroyer has just come in. This looks
like war [1] and the chaffinch on the pea-stick is swearing
at it like anything because, I suppose, his motto is " Peas
at any Price ". Talking of peas there's a vegetable cart
here that goes around and the driver, instead of bellowing,
plays on a cornet, " Then you'll remember me " and " Come
to the Cook House Door ", while his missus sells taters
from the back of the cart. And talking of taters reminds
me of flowers. In the lanes, they are pink and yellow
and blue like the boats. There's valerian in masses of
pink which sets off the blue of the sky as the Judas trees
do in Italy—by the way I saw a Judas tree in blossom
just lately at Torquay—and there's pink campion and

[1] In Pretoria, at that time, Kruger was being obdurate.

cranesbill and blue speedwell and white stitchwort thrown in and yellow wild-mustard—and here and there a scarlet poppy, not many, but big ones. The *Dashing Wave* (brig) is loading up with china-clay. A beautiful schooner yacht is slowly passing out under my very nose. It's a fortnight now come Monday and I continue to " be a nigger ", which is to like the place and loaf around it and never want to leave it. The schooner *won't* let me alone, she's just tacked across—like a minx. The sea has all the blues in the world and a few over. And thank you for the book, I shall enjoy it and it shall be duly returned (even though there is no book-plate) which is rather a concession, since one has to acquire books *somehow* ! '

This letter, apart from being in itself a delightful letter, is instructive because it is, so far as I know, the earliest indication of the writer's interest in the Rat and his literary possibilities, an inspiration afterwards, of course, to come fully to flower in *The Wind in the Willows*. And as for the black pin, Kenneth Grahame, even in the eating of a winkle, was always gourmet.

It has been seen that Kenneth hankered for the simple Cornish fare he ate on the quays and in the country places. He was impatient, in the more fashionable hotels, of the fashionable menus served to him by waiters in black swallow-tails and reasonably white shirts. To one of such who (bringing *hors d'œuvres*, after a quarter of an hour's inactivity) volunteered the information that his great-grandfather had been a bishop, Kenneth made no direct reply. Though he said presently, to his companion, that he'd liefer the waiter had had a butler for an ancestor than a bishop for then he might have inherited a talent for his profession. ' Though even so,' he added, ' the fellow's a natural fool and would probably have hidden it in a napkin.'

He says, in a letter of much later years, ' I get down to Fowey occasionally where Time always seems to stand still at the same point as on that bright summer day when you and your mother touched at the quayside ; it is always holiday to me to catch a sight of the shipping there once more.'

But I best like to think of the Kenneth of the Cornish days as the jolly young giant in the dark-blue jersey, the brown face and the fish scales who stands at the top of the worn old water-steps after a night with the pilchard boats, stands and looks back at a blueness of sky and morning sea, a very blueness, the joy of which seems to him, even at that moment, better than breakfast.

CHAPTER XI

BOHAM'S (PART I)

MAYFIELD, Cookham Dene, whither the Grahames had gone when the Durham Villa days were done, was not meant to be a permanency. Mayfield had a carriage-sweep and educational advantages and Kenneth Grahame wanted neither. The neighbourhood too was a social one and he had no desire for society. Early in 1910 he heard of a farmhouse that sounded suitable. He went to see it and it was as suitable as it sounded. He had made a point of it having no billiard-room. He had wished it to be difficult of access. In both respects it met his views. The nearest billiard-table was ten miles away and folk who wanted to get to Boham's usually walked.

The disadvantages of carriage-sweeps had been illustrated when Mr. and Mrs. Grahame had gone to lunch with Mr. and Mrs. Thomas Hardy. The Grahames arrived at Dorchester early on a fine morning and, hiring a fly, they told the driver to drive to various places of interest in the neighbourhood. Towards one o'clock Kenneth, now ravenously hungry, told the cabman to go to Max Gate (the novelist's house). The latter said that to do so was as much as his licence was worth. He turned his horse and drove in the opposite direction. Indignantly told to obey orders, he stopped and, from his box, addressed his fares. He explained that Mr. Hardy had been so much annoyed by Americans and (pointedly) *others* driving up to his door and peeping through his windows that he had forbidden the public vehicles of Dorchester to accept a charter to his house. If his (the driver's) present passengers wished to go to Max Gate they must walk there. But he advised them

not to risk it and he took no responsibility.   In the end he
compromised by putting them down ' as near as he dared '
—about a mile's walk from the flesh-pots.

Thomas Hardy said that his sole compensation for his so
many uninvited visitors was to see their expressions of
deep disappointment if they did, by accident, meet him
face to face.   Kenneth said that he, for his personal part,
was by nature debarred from even this poor satisfaction and
therefore the new house must have no carriage entrance
at all.

Boham's, at Blewbury, was as old as Doomsday Book.
Blewbury is in the Berkshire Down country.   There are
other parts of England that give the visitor a feel of anti-
quity, but I know nothing so *timeless* as the country of the
White Horse.   It is a land of grey grasses, cloud shadows,
shepherds, sheep-bells and skylarks.   And if (as did the
boy who went to call on ' The Reluctant Dragon ') you will
go uphill on a quiet autumn day you will, as Kenneth
Grahame did, see Berkshire's best, from the bare and billowy
downs to the slow plough-teams in the vale, and think,
maybe, the thoughts that he thought, and was inspired to
write down, thus :

' Up there, on the windy top of the downs, the turf is
virgin still to the share ; the same turf that was trodden
by the hurrying feet of Saxon levies ere they clashed with
the Danish invader on yonder ridge.   But down in the
valley that they shelter, the conquering plough has sped
and swayed for centuries ; and here, where this great
shoulder merges into the fields with a gentler incline, it has
gone out and made conquest ; breasted the hill behind a
double team, and made this spur captive.   This year its
turn has come late, and the furrows still gleam unbroken,
touched each, on the side the share has polished, with warm
light from the low, red, winter's sun.   The stillness all
around, the absence of chirping and singing life, the slight
frost that holds the air, all seem silently to plead for a good
word on behalf of a season that rarely gets one.   After all,

these brief sunless days, this suspended action of the year, impose restful conditions which those whose minds are in proper harmony with Nature only too gladly accept. Like the earth beneath us, we silently renew our forces for the coming awakening of life in nature and action in men ; taking the while somewhat sad account of the past year's words and deeds, which, vital enough as they may have seemed at their doing and saying, none the less surely now strew our path with their withered leaves, rustling with recollections. We, who for our sins are town dwellers, when the summer sun lights up gloomy squares and dusty streets, chafe at every sunlit day that passes as worse than wasted. Are we equally quick to miss and to long for the enforced repose of a winter with nature ?

' Meanwhile, leaning on the gate, it is pleasant to look upon a piece of work as honestly done as it could be. No truer furrow could the divine herdsman himself have driven, when the fingers that had swept the lyre on Olympus were laid on the rude plough stilts, and the slow-plodding oxen, the very inanimate wood and iron, were stirred and thrilled by the virtue that went out of a god.

> When by Zeus relenting the mandate was revoked,
> Sentencing to exile the bright Sun-god,
> Mindful were the ploughmen of who the steer had yoked,
> Who ; and what a track showed the upturned sod !

This at least he was good to do, the god turned thrall : to make his " drudgery divine " by perfection ; to tend Admetus's sheep so that never should one be missed at folding-time, even as he herded the " broad-foreheaded oxen of the Sun " on the trackless asphodel meadows ; to drive his furrows straight and true, as when, with his huntress sister, he sent his silvery shafts, one after the other, clanging to the mark.

' But the Delian suggestion jars on us as with a sense of incongruity, and recalls us to ourselves and our chill surroundings. Under modern culture our minds have become cosmopolitan in the widest sense ; they range and possess not only the world that is, but that has been. Florentines we are perhaps, and encounter Beatrice with her salutation by the way ; or we ride with Tannhäuser to Rome, with burden of sweet, strange sin.   When the summer sun is high we know and hail the Pythian one, the far-darter ; and the old Pan still pipes to us at Mapledurham or in Hurley backwater.   Only when winter has us fast do we truly feel our kinship with the Scandinavian toilers of old time, who knew life to be a little space in which to do great deeds, a struggle with Nature and inclement seasons and the mightier unseen power of hostile fates.   Such were our fathers, fighting nature for eight months of the year, wresting a hard sustenance from her by force, seeing in the iron sky above only another force that had to be combated also ; and a tinge of this feeling in our minds is their heritage to us, and pricks us like a conscience when our imaginations would fain stray in Socratic myrtle groves or *gelidis in vallibus Haemi.*

' The warping influence of toil and stress of weather, common heritage of the north, shows itself so clearly in the pictures of the Northern or Flemish school as to give us a feeling towards them that we do not experience in inspecting other examples of early art.   Some of the tender pity we might feel for the toil-worn face of a poor relation smites across us at sight of some of their homely Madonnas, pallid and drawn in face, bowed and warped in figure, only very human :   the mothers and sisters of their painters. Most of all, their St. Christophers seem to epitomize their own history—the rude gigantic disproportioned figures, rough hewn as the staff that supports them, struggling to stem the torrent and bear the bright boy-Saviour to the shore.   They, too, carried their divine burden safe to land, but the struggle was sore, and its marks are imprinted on their work.

' Pain, and toil, and suffering, whether from fate or man's brutality, run like an under song through these pictures of the North ; and it is our fellowship with these pains, these common sorrows, small or great, that is the enduring tie, the touch that kins us.   A Flemish Massacre of the Innocents which I once saw in a Continental gallery has made a more enduring impression on me than any carefully composed apposition of naked men's and children's legs and arms could do.   It is a still dull frosty winter's afternoon, with a haze in the air and ice on the pond and puddles of the little village.   School is over, and the children are returning to their low-roofed houses in the little street ; and though the place is very poor, they are warmly clad in their mittens and gaiters and wraps.   Suddenly round the corner and down the street ride a group of gaunt and hard-faced spear-men, who fall on the children in a passionless businesslike way, clambering up water-butts and spouts, giving each other a shoulder, to get at those who escape into the houses. And the mothers—clumsy, awkward, loving women— amazedly run hither and thither, begging a little pity with grotesque extravagant gesticulations, the best they can command.   Day by day they have wrapped their little ones warmly for school : what hope or promise can they see now, in their blank dismay and crying appealing terror ?   For such as these remains no joyful vision of their innocents triumphing, as in Holman Hunt's great picture, hailed by the infant Saviour as his first-fruits, marching, a mystical priesthood.

' So, too, the many small domestic touches appeal especially to our home-loving natures : as when, in our own National Gallery, the Virgin sits alone, under no silken canopy, backed by no gracious enwreathment of olive or myrtle, but with homely oaken chest and cupboard about her ; while, seen through the small window, couples stroll home in the evening light—the evening that brings all home ; not knowing that for them a new hope has arisen, a new solace and comfort at the end of a weary day.

' But chiefest of all, to me—watching the tender evening light on these furrows, and thinking of the toil-worn bowed figure that drew them, and has done for many a year, he and his friendly companion beasts—appears, in its severe outline, Holbein's drawing of the gaunt ploughman, hardly better clad than his grim and terrible companion, who takes from him the guidance of the horses. " Of this other picture," says Ruskin, " the meaning is plainer, and far more beautiful. The husbandman is old and gaunt, and has passed his days, not in speaking, but in pressing the iron into the ground. And the payment for his life's work is that he is clothed in rags, and his feet are bare on the clods ; and he has no hat, but the brim of a hat only, and his long unkempt gray hair comes through. But all the air is full of warmth and peace ; and beyond his village church there is, at last, light indeed. His horses lag in the furrow, and his own limbs totter and fail ; but one comes to help him. ' It is a long field,' says Death ; ' but we'll get to the end of it to-day—you and I.' "

' Here pain and suffering are hardly felt. It is Death the serene and gracious, " Death the Friend." It is Tennyson's Death who

> ' Like a friend's voice in a distant field
> Approaching through the darkness, called.'

Or Whitman's—

> ' Undulate round the world, serenely arriving, arriving ;
> In a day or a night, to all, to each,
> Sooner or later, beautiful Death.'

But it is death none the less ; we must go to the southern Botticelli for the glad poetry of Birth—of the birth of Venus, and of Spring, with the air full of mysterious blossoms ; of Christ, with the angels encircling the lowly shed with enraptured, almost delirious dance of joy.

' To the northern artist, life is a no less precious possession : rather dearer from the more conscious presence of " the Shadow waiting with the keys ". As Mr. Pater has it, " it is with a rush of homesickness that the thought of death presents itself. He would remain at home for ever on the earth if he could ; as it loses its colour and the senses fail, he clings ever closer to it ; but since the mouldering of bones and flesh must go on to the end, he is careful of charms and talismans, that may chance to have some friendly power in them when the inevitable shipwreck comes."

' So, from no love of them, but rather with a shuddering fear, he must be busy with all emblems of mortality : often unconsciously, as children play at funerals ; or as the plough here, speeding on its fertilizing mission, turns up bones and skulls which have rested " under the drums and ramplings of three conquests ".'

It was to Boham's then that Kenneth Grahame came, and, in the words of his dragon who lived in the neighbour-hood, said, ' It seems a nice place enough—but it's rather a serious thing, settling down. Besides—now I'm going to tell you something ! Fact is I'm such a confounded lazy beggar. . . . I like to get my meals regular and then to prop my back against a bit of rock and snooze a bit, and wake up and think of things going on. . . .'

Boham's, with its other advantages, was just the place for regular meals and thought and Boham's was acquired. It consisted of a parlour, an office for paying the farm hands, two magnificent kitchens (always the best rooms in a farm-house) and, upstairs, a bedroom or so, a granary and an apple loft. At the back was running water—the little local trout stream. In no time the new tenant and the village carpenter transformed the old house—much as did the fairy godmother transform a pumpkin into Cinderella's coach.

The doors of the rooms (they wore eight coats of paint) were scraped and pickled and found to be of oak, ' linen-folded ', and three hundred years old. The parlour mantel-piece, painted in imitation of black and white marble, popped into a pig-trough, revealed itself as a William and Mary piece in carved chestnut with a central medallion of pear wood, exhibiting a profile—supposed to be a portrait.

Kenneth, congratulating Miss Smedley on her marriage and her choice of Gloucestershire as a home, writes of Blewbury :

' I wish I could show you this antic corner of Berkshire, in King Alfred's country, probably much as it was a thousand years ago. A little way off there is a farmer whose family has been here for a thousand years. They are real Saxons. They live in a lovely old farmhouse with a ghost in it. Indeed all the houses here are very old. They do not build the horrid little red houses that spring up round Cookham. Of course *you* will live in Gloucestershire—there is only one *more* possible county for you and that is Double-Gloucestershire—if you can find the way there.

' Of course you know that there are sort of " astral " counties, much nicer than the real ones. Cheshirecatshire is another delightful one : and Yorkshirepuddingshire and Devonshirecreamshire are first-rate to live in. Lie-in-bed-fordshire is warm and sheltered, an excellent county for a prolonged stay. Ten-to-Forfarshire is chiefly inhabited by retired government officials : you would not care for that. But Hunt-the-slipperingdonshire has lively society, and several packs meet in the neighbourhood.

' Still, you can't beat Gloucester, double or single, where you will build with the native stone,

> ' And the cottage will be. white,
>   As you say,
> And the napkins will be " peasant "
>   —very gay !
> (He who calls 'em " serviettes "
> Will deserve what e'er he gets),
> And the chintz will match the china
>   All the day ! '

Miss Smedley (Mrs. Maxwell Armfield) wrote recently of Kenneth Grahame's personality : ' There was the Banker, not so much alarming as austere, the Scholar, rather remote, the Author, approachable ; and then there was the man who was more exactly right than any one I have known about the world of Fairytale. There is a fairy world in which no one believes. It is entered with a full inward consciousness of unreality, glossed over with a pretence of being imaginative or young in heart. Kenneth Grahame hated this. In his fairyland, which was that of Grimm and Andersen, animals mingled with humans on equal terms of intelligence, but he was not curious about their habits, he respected their private lives. He lived and wrote simply and with dignity. He never seemed interested in himself or his writings. But he was passionately interested in the outdoor world ; in noble literature ; in " all things lovely and of good repute ". And he believed that beyond what he saw now lie wider revelations.'

The walls of Boham's were thick and ' what a kitchen it has—a room to fill Charles Dickens with delight ! ' But Kenneth does not say which ' astral ' shire corresponds to Berkshire—possibly Berks is well enough for him as it is.

But Boham's had no ghost, which was regrettable, since the ghost would surely have entwined his, or her, self round the new tenant's heart. Or so I think from what I have found concerning ghosts among his manuscripts :

' There be times of worry common to us all, when we cannot, howbeit not in the least misanthropical, help feeling that our daily round is passed among such gibbering simulacra that to foregather with a ghost would be a mild but very real and pleasant relief. The dear fellow would be so much more really akin to us in tact, experience, discretion, and repose ! He would so immeasurably surpass all these more solidly embodied annoyances that jostle about and round ! Who, indeed, if he come to look into the question, but has to traffic with beings in every way more objectionable than ghosts ? Who (for example) would not any day prefer a ghost to a broker's man or a Salvationist ? Who can honestly say that he has ever suffered a tithe of the annoyance from ghosts that he has had from organ-grinders ? Yet we endure the one sort of infliction at least in sullen acquiescence ; and we shriek at and menace the other, attacking it with that last weapon of civilization, a Society ; a refinement of brutality formerly reserved for criminals and poets !

'Of those happy in the ownership of authentic ghosts, it may be noted that some men are born to ghosts—these mostly sit in the House of Peers ; some achieve ghosts, by committing murder, sacrilege, robbery, or taking some such common piece of pains ; and some have ghosts thrust upon them. At the first of these three classes, we can but gaze, sighfully and admiring. Here is no competition, here none shall enter in and demand his part in the joy. These minions of Fortune have the real ghost-aristocracy ; theirs are the blue-blooded hidalgo-spooks of the Pre-Restoration times. Any one can be made a Peer, but it is satisfactory to think that he is not brought an inch nearer to accomplishing a family-ghost thereby. Beer buys no ghosts ; no, by'r lady, nor building churches neither ! A reflection that should make Tories of us all ; and would—if all of us were sweet on the ghost. Meanwhile it is to the second class, the achievers, that these should turn ; for it is obvious that almost any one, by bestirring himself and taking the necessary trouble, may by some murder (after all, not half so difficult as it looked) find himself the proud possessor of a very good working private ghost. The worst of it is that this method of production (ghost-forcing, we may term it) is not always infallible : and it is easy to conceive the annoyance of some decent, well-disposed amateur in psychical research—an Elder, say, or a Bank Director— who may have inconvenienced himself repeatedly, and become quite a nuisance to his friends, by a course of experiments which has proved persistently barren of good results.

'Those of the hapless third class—who have had ghosts thrust upon them—are usually the victims of house-agents. Indeed, these traders occupy a very interesting position with regard to the Invisible World. They know the whereabouts of almost every ghost in the country, and could, if they chose to take the pains, produce a ghost-map of England, dotted to show the favoured localities. Yet, as business must come first, and the ghost is the agent's natural

enemy, all this special knowledge is wasted. Seriously,
their yearly loss from this cause is said to amount to something considerable : so much so that a Ghost Insurance
Company is declared to exist (though it does not seem to
have been registered) for their peculiar protection. It would
be interesting if some statistician—laborious Dr. Giffen, say
—would compile a table showing the annual loss to the trade
of the United Kingdom due to ghosts. Of course there is
much to be said on the ghosts' side of the question ; and it
would be pretty to witness a stubborn set-to between a
somewhat pig-headed, conservative ghost and a strong-
willed house-agent, on a question of ownership. For once,
at least, how entirely our sympathies would be on the side
of the ghost ! If one ever felt inclined to take a ghost to
one's heart, it would be at that proud moment when he
wiped his honest brow, exhausted but victorious !

' That dogs can perceive the presence of spirits invisible
to the human eye has been counted unto those over-praised
animals for righteousness ; but really a dog who can detect
any peculiarly precious and lovable stink while it is still
three streets off and across a square and down a mews,
ought to make no bones (which, indeed, were hard for him
to do) about a healthy, full-sized ghost in the same room.
It would be more to the point to know if ghosts see dogs ;
and if they do, what do they think of them ? Also, if the
ghost of a certain distinguished General would flee at the
quiet entry of the parlour cat ? Be this as it may, it is a
fact that ghosts, if you let them, are apt to take credit to
themselves for qualities of which they have no monopoly.
Why are they entitled to plume themselves upon a dislike
to cock-crowing ? One need not be a ghost to curse the
day when the first cock strutted out of the Ark, and, letting
fly his war-whoop, set an eternal fashion of defiance to
humanity asleep. Their habit, again, of appearing unexpectedly when you are busy and themselves not wanted,
is shared by many of your dearest friends ; whose power
of sudden evanishment is not, alas ! so general a gift.

' 'Tis strange, considering how armorial bearings were
allotted for deeds of valour, and often chosen from the
object on which such valour had displayed itself, that
you never find the ghost in heraldry, either as original or
as augmentation. " Sable, three spectres gules, sheeted
argent " would be a chaste and pretty blazoning : but it
never occurs. Can it be that these famous men of old were
none too fond of tackling a ghost ? Something of the sort,
probably ; for courage is much a matter of fashion, and in
those days little credit attached to this sort of valiancy, at
least among laymen. On the contrary, it might even get
its possessor mixed up with stakes, tar-barrels, faggots,
and similar unpleasantnesses. Of course, exceptions will
at once occur to the reader—more especially in northern
legend. In the Sagas, indeed, it seemed usual to " qualify "
on a ghost before experimenting with your pals ; and when
the Widow Thorgud asks Howard the Halt to help her against
her dead husband, who has a most unwarrantable habit (for
a dead man) of coming home to bed, Howard says he is
getting too old for that sort of thing, but advises her to
ask his son, for " meet it is for young men to try their
manliness in such wise ". The Beowulf-and-Grendel con-
flict is only one of many such duellos ; but the weird and
magnificent ghosts of the Sagas (fit rivals to them of Japan)
belong less to the spectral order than to the class of
" haunts "—the actual dead body, spirit-possessed ; of
whom Thrawn Janet is a lineal descendant.

' In fine, the ghost may have his faults (as who has not ?) ;
but he has entwined himself securely round our affections,
and we should miss him sore if he were taken from us.
" And with a tale, forsooth, he cometh unto you," as Sidney
said of the poet, " with a tale which holdeth children
from play, and old men from the chimney-corner." Thrice
fortunate, then, this age of ours : which, having shaken
itself free of revealed religion, and that old bugbear of a
First Cause, has yet managed (Science aiding), to " go more
solid " for the ghost than any of its ancestors before it ! '

CHAPTER XII

BOHAM'S (PART II)

SOON the house was ready, the family in. One of its first
visitors was an American Naval Officer. He was taken to
see the Saxon farmhouse I have referred to. The sailor said
to the farmer's wife that, where he hailed from, a hundred
years was considered a ' long-way-back '. He was prompted
to say this by the date, 1600, upon the parlour mantelpiece.
His hostess said, ' Oh, if you're interested in old houses
you may like to see the rest of this one ; we are at present
in the new wing.'

Houses apart, Blewbury was full of interest. There were
the racing stables ; and the sheeted strings of thoroughbreds were to be seen in charge of the village choir (the lads
from Mr. Cannon's) on their way to or from the gallops
presided over by old White Horse himself. There were the
ancient Arcadians of the place, shepherds, cress-pickers and
others, to be cultivated. The shepherds were of the true
archaic type, old as the chalk itself, wise and slow as Time,
telling the tale of their sheep in notches notched upon crook
or staff. To one of them, Zephaniah Grace, husband of
Hephzibah, Kenneth Grahame refers naming him ' one of
the greatest gentlemen I ever knew '. He adds, of Zephaniah's bob-tail ' Jack ' : ' I always feel I have known him
longest of the three, because, when I first came to these
parts, and used to meet master and dog on the roads,
Zephaniah would slip by, silently, in his shy, shepherdy
way, but Jack would linger behind a moment, leap upon
me for a swift lick, and then scurry after his master,
for sheep dogs are very severely disciplined hereabouts.
Perhaps we all ought to serve a term of two years or so

as sheep dogs on the downs—we should be better men and women.'

In Blewbury, Christian names (as Zephaniah) were chosen from the Scriptures. The village was full of Lukes and Keziahs, Aarons and Dorcases. In one family of seventeen (the Bible exhausted), twin brothers were named (the mother had been in service and had had ' a real old book ' given her by ' the lady she lived with ')—Orson and Valentine. Orson was old when Kenneth knew him. His father had raised his seventeen children on a maximum income of nine shillings per week and on that he had reared them, each one, strong and tall. Orson had himself become a wage-earner when still ' horse-high '. That is to say, while he was still small enough to walk, without stooping, under a horse's belly. He earned sixpence a week and worked twelve hours a day for it (and an occasional raw turnip) ; and, at harvest-time, little Orson worked sixteen hours a day.

The Grahames were served, at one time, by Job and Deborah—or Debbie. Job was Debbie's third husband. He had waited for her since her girlhood and now, once more, he nearly missed her. For it was only on learning that her current fiancé's late wife had hanged herself that Debbie prudently gave a possible cause of suicide his congé and wedded Job. The girl who made Debbie's wedding-dress said to Debbie that she hoped the new husband would be kinder than the last. Debbie said, ' Abigail Barley, you ain't no call to say nothing about the one who's gone. I forgave him freely and never more shall you make wedding gown of mine.'

Another of Kenneth's village cronies was the nonogenarian known as Blewbury Jones's ' last baby '. Blewbury Jones was the miser parson of Blewbury (immortalized in *Our Mutual Friend* and noticed also in Miss Sitwell's, recent, *English Eccentrics*) and old Harry was the latest babe at font in his incumbency. This ' arid and joyless ' old cleric, on a stipend of eighty pounds, yet saved £18,000—a colossal fortune in his times.

War and Peace found the Grahames at Boham's Farm. In the war days Kenneth, ex-sergeant of the London Scottish, drilled the Blewbury boys, aged from fourteen years to ninety, in Mr. Caudwell's big barn. This was the barn whose door and its decorations had been, in happier days, motive to one of the infrequent essays of the ' Boham ' years :

' In the time of the waning year, a stroll through the woods may force one to own up to and acknowledge the season's conventional melancholy. The recognition is annoying : one so much prefers to find convention in the wrong. But on that particular morning the spirit of melancholy walked abroad, too potent to be denied. My only chance seemed to be resolutely to reject the application to my own condition, and, with a touch of joyance, to reflect instead, as I sauntered along, on the exceeding parlous state of my friends.

' I had mentally run through the sorry catalogue ('tis no long one), and damned them all most heartily, ere I quitted the wood, and sought the lee-side of the great barn, to kindle a fresh pipe in its shelter ; and it was as I raised my eyes from the expiring match that the mute, sad decoration of the barn-door struck me with some touch of remorse. The Tuscan poet, led by the Mantuan Shade, saw below many a friend of old time planted in fire, in mud, in burning marl, " ove i bolliti faceano alte strida " ; but to come across them nailed in rows on a barn-door, seems to have been specially reserved for me. I had handled them severely, perhaps, during my meditations in the wood : but certainly I neither expected nor desired to find them all thus transfixed, with plumage smirched and fur bedraggled, wasted by the sun and rain. You now, with the soft white throat and delicate paws, all sinuous grace and sleek beauty when alive —so it has come to this ? And yet, my fair lady, you were once the arrantest of blood-suckers, and drained the life out of many a one in your merry career. What ? They were only silly rabbits ! Well, perhaps they were a brainless lot, not greatly to be pitied ; but the wheel has gone round, and now it is the rabbits' turn to laugh. And your fine

neighbour of the tawny back, with the vivid glint of tur-
quoise-blue on either wing : the handsomest spark in our
English woods—I was thinking of him only just now. A
loud-voiced fellow rather ; fond of showing off and cutting
a dash ; with a weakness for a lord ; altogether not quite
the best form perhaps ;—and yet, what a good sort of chap
he was, after all ! now, his strident accents are hushed, his
gay feathers drop one by one. What strange fate has fixed
him cheek by jowl with our friend of the solemn face and
round eyes ? Of him we were wont to see little ; during
daylight hours ; but after dinner, when he flapped around
seeking his prey !—well, they are all now in the same silent
row, the bore as well as the chatterer. Yon dingy fellow
with the hooky beak and cruel claws—you knocked some
fur out of *my* back once, old boy, though I just managed to
wriggle down a friendly burrow in time ; I don't grudge *you*
to the barn-door—nor yet this half-dozen of rats, rodent
no longer. But in the ranks I still espy another friend or
two for whom this fate seems unduly hard.

' And yet one might come to a worse end. The merry
winds still sing in our plumage—what is left of it ; the kindly
sun still warms us through, sounds of the cheery farm-yard
are ever in our ears, light and life and song surround us
still, and nothing any longer has power to hurt. Was I a
churl, haply, in life ? a mean and grasping niggard ? No
more liberal fellow now decorates a barn-door. Does any
one want a lock of my hair, a gay feather from my plumage ?
'Tis at your service ; to weave into your nest, or enshrine
in a locket—all's one to me—help yourself. Proud was I,
perhaps—stand-offish, given to airs ? There's no pride
about me any longer. Your barn-door is a mighty leveller,
and clears the mind of cant and prejudice. Why was hanging in chains ever condemned as relic of barbarism ? It is
civility itself ! Let us swing and creak in the wind, and
brother call to brother across the barren moor, till the elements shred and take us piecemeal.

' Yet the human majority, by some such instinct as

that which drags the wounded rabbit to his hole, shrinks ever from uplifted exposure such as this. " Out of sight " is still their cry : " only let it be somewhere out of sight, once we are worn and old and dropping to pieces ! " The burden of Brer Rabbit's appeal to his tormentor was, whatever he did, not to fling him in " dat brier-patch " ; and humanity leaves to the fates an exceeding wide choice, so long as only they are not nailed up on that barndoor.

' Perhaps, then, my poor friends are not entirely happy in their unsought publicity. Might it not be a kindly act on my part to give their poor remains a decent burial ? To scatter just that gift of a little dust which shall bring to their unquiet shades release and repose ? I owe them some sort of reparation for my hard thoughts concerning them half an hour ago, when I never dreamt of finding them gibbeted here. And yet—a sudden suspicion chills the blood. Were it not wise to get away quietly, but swiftly, while time yet serves for retreat ? For the Grim Old Keeper who fixed them there—may he not be lurking somewhere hard by—with a mind, perhaps, to seize me and nail me up alongside the rest ? '

Much else than sergeant-majoring fell, in war-time, on Kenneth Grahame's shoulders. The successor of Blewbury Jones had gone to France ; Kenneth Grahame helped his locum. There was no squire in Blewbury and no doctor. Kenneth did, what he might, of the duties of both. He organized a local factory of surgical aids. He arranged, and presided at, the feast given to the soldiers of Blewbury who, after the Armistice, returned to their homes. And he wrote the memorial of those who did not return.

From 1914 to 1918 he spared himself not at all in the interests of the small community which looked up to him ; he was its stimulus, its example and its consoler. In the last rôle he once sympathized with an old villager who had lost a devoted wife. Kenneth summed up the virtues of the

deceased by saying, ' She did make you so comfortable
always.' The bereft husband replied, ' Why, drat the
'ooman, say I, if she couldn't do that.'

I cannot better describe Kenneth Grahame's attitude
towards his neighbours in this Arcady than by borrowing
his own words and asking a reader to imagine the author's
self in the garb of his Pan : ' Both iron road and level high-
way are shunned by the rural Pan, who chooses rather to
foot it along the sheep-track on the limitless downs or the
foot-path through copse and spinney not without pleasant
fellowship with feather and fur. Nor does it follow from
all this that the god is unsocial. Albeit shy of the company
of his more showy brother-deities, he loveth the more un-
pretentious human kind, especially them that are *adscripti
glebae*, addicted to the kindly soil and to the working thereof : perfect in no way, only simple, cheery sinners. For
he is only half a god after all, and the red earth in him is
strong. When the pelting storm drives the wayfarers to the
sheltering inn, among the little group upon the bench and
settle Pan has been known to appear at times, in homely
guise of hedger-and-ditcher or weather-beaten shepherd from
the downs. Strange lore and quaint fancy he will then
impart, in the musical Wessex or Mercian he has learned to
speak so naturally ; though it may not be till many a mile
away that you begin to suspect that you have unwittingly
talked with him who chased the flying Syrinx in Arcady
and turned the tide of fight at Marathon.'

And at harvest-homes (still, in the shadow of the downs,
the old-fashioned feasts were held when barns ' resounded
to flap of flail ') the social red earth was strong in him.
Kenneth was kindly welcome, beneath the flitch and ham-
hung rafters. There would he take one end of the long
oaken table and there the guests, weather-beaten and hob-
nailed, would come, and, knuckling their foreheads, sit down
and open out their coloured handkerchiefs wherein nested
plate and beer-mug, knife and fork. It was the mighty
platters then, heaped high with pork and crackling, with

roast beef and gravy, that Kenneth Grahame and the host, each at his respective end, would carve.

And when the plum-puddings and apple-tarts had succeeded the joints and when enough, enough to float a frigate, of the strong, brown, humming ale had been taken, followed song and recitation—to the mighty enjoyment of the burly ' half-god ' sitting ' vice ' to—Farmer Larkin (as likely as not). ' The White Rose in its Splendour ' was a favourite. So was ' Green Brooms to Buy ', the refrain of which, roared in thunderous, smock-frock melody, is, ' I'm a lady by nature, a lady by name, and all that I have is my own.'

There were ' Fly's on the Turmuts ' and ' The Proud Tailor ' (the tailor fell through the bed thimbles and all). And there would follow, ' Do not trust him, Gentle Lady ' and ' The Pilgrim of Love '. The mugs were filled and emptied and filled again, and it was time to go home. ' So they set off up the hill. The lights in the little village began to go out, but there were stars and a late moon, as they climbed the downs together. And, as they turned the last corner, snatches of an old song were borne back on the night breeze.'

And, sometimes to Blewbury, the painted caravans came, halted and again took the road. And who so pleased to welcome the Egyptians as Kenneth Grahame ? And who, in Blewbury or elsewhere, wrote better about them ?

' In a hedgeless country of high downland, on a road that came flowing down, a long white ribbon, straight as it were out of the eastern sky, we would watch, each succeeding spring, for the first appearance of these fairy cruisers of the road. But when at last we caught sight of a certain small yellow caravan, with pretty Mrs. S. and the latest baby sitting in front, her husband (who had charge of the dart-throwing department) walking at the horse's head, then we knew that our turn had come at last ! " Enter Autolycus singing ! " For close on the yellow caravan would surely come the larger one, with father and mother and the cooking utensils ; and then that other which held Mrs. S.'s three comely young sisters, whom we knew as the Princesses, each, though so young, already a specialist of some sort, and who all slept in one broad bed placed across the rear of their caravan, looking, I should imagine, like three little St. Ursulas by Carpaccio. Later the swing-boats and the wooden horses would straggle in, and all the paraphernalia of the stalls and booths, and the horses (not the wooden ones, of course) would be led away and picketed. Then perhaps, beside a late camp fire, time would be found to renew acquaintance and hear all the news of the past winter ; for the winters, to the women at least, were by no means a period of suspended animation.

' One does not, it seems, when autumn is over, desert one's caravan for humdrum bricks and mortar. One camps, by arrangement with some one or other, on some piece of waste land or only partly used builder's yard or undeveloped building site on the outskirts of London itself, or of the big new towns, but lately villages themselves, that have sprung up as dormitories to the great city ; and there, through all weathers, through rain and frost and snow, one sticks it out in one's little wooden caravan. This may sound very poor fun ; but the actual fact was far otherwise. These girls were at first quite strangely reluctant to enlarge upon the joys of a leisured winter life in the neighbourhood of a large city. The reason for this only transpired later, and showed a quite charming delicacy of feeling on their part. " We thought," they explained in effect, " that it would make you dissatisfied with your hard lot as compared with ours, and perhaps you would be feeling jealous and discontented. For you live in this poky remote little village all the year round, and see nothing and know nothing, and never even guess at all the glamour and excitement that more fortunately placed classes such as ours are free to enjoy." We meekly admitted our social disadvantages, but pressed to be allowed a peep at urban life and its glories ; and by degrees heard all about the jolly excursions to town, after the train with the black-coated city men had departed, and visits to Parks, Piccadillies, Regent Streets ; the studies

15

of shop-windows, and all the ladies' frocks ; then bun-shops, matinées, more bun-shops, and a first-class performance at some West End theatre ; finally the rush for the last train back, the sleepy journey down, the tramp along a muddy lane and across a field or two to the little caravan at last, making a blacker spot against the dull winter sky ; and then the cheerful dazzle of the reflector-lamp on the wall, the cup of cocoa and snack of supper, and laughter and sense of snugness ; and so to bed at last, St. Ursula-wise, in the little cabin that was all their very own.

' The Princesses told us they had another married sister, and that *she* lived in a house with a real doorstep, which she could whiten, twice a day if she liked ! " But," we protested, " look at the beautiful steps of your own caravan ! Real mahogany, with brass finishings, and hook off and on with a touch ! " " Yes, but you can't *whiten* them," sighed the Princesses wistfully. " And, besides," they added, " *she* has a permanent address ! " They went on to confess that when the time came for them to think of marriage too, they intended to aim high—to aim even at a permanent address and a doorstep that could be whitened ! Such are the rash dreams of youth ! But it is good to carry an ideal about with you, however unattainable it be ; and, as R. L. Stevenson has it, to travel hopefully (and in a caravan too !) is better than to arrive (even at a whiteable doorstep).

' Talking of caravan steps, which are really short ladders, almost perpendicular and without hand-rail, these have a special influence on the development of the caravan child. For the caravan-born infant, as soon as it can notice anything at all, is swift to detect the contrast between his own cabin'd, cribb'd, confined surroundings and the wonderful great world he catches a glimpse of through the little door —a world consisting of a mighty green common, dotted with white geese plucking at the grass of it, and horses and donkeys tethered here and there, and Daddy and other gods passing freely to and fro. But alas ! between you and it stretches a mighty cliff, down which a dizzy ladder crawls !

Well, what of it ?   Such things have got to be tackled sooner
or later.   So as soon as it can roll or wriggle, and certainly
before it can walk, the caravan-infant is down that ladder,
somehow, and in due course up it again, and no one knows
how it does it, because they are too busy to notice, and they
wouldn't interfere if they did in any case, and it never falls,
and wouldn't in the least mind if it did.'

It is a short step from a caravan to a conjurer and from
a conjurer to a music hall.   Among Kenneth Grahame's
papers are some notes and fragments upon which he had,
perhaps, intended to build (some day) an article.   I give
these odds and ends as I find them.

' Plate Smashing and The Conjurer

(' The sub-conscious ego explains the appeal)

' *Ego.*   " Are these japes to continue ? "
' *Sub-conscious Ego.*   " It would seem so."
' *Ego.*   " But if we won't laugh ? "
' *Sub-conscious Ego.*   " *You* don't laugh, it is we, the *S.C.E.*"
' One may make a beginning modestly setting up before
us and carefully examining the jokes that may have tickled
the childhood of humanity but are now no longer worthy
of us adolescents and may be allowed to expire peacefully.
But they won't and they still continue to work.

' Well, if you show to gain, you must be prepared to justify
yourself.   And it is not enough to say " It is funny " ; a
thing simply can't be funny for ever.   And you wouldn't say
definitely, " It amuses me."   That's not argument.

' I have always been able to laugh consumedly, and so
has everybody else if I may judge by my surroundings, at
the smashing of plates at a music hall.   Now there is nothing
inherently funny in breaking a plate.   If you break a plate
at breakfast you lose your temper ; if you break a plate,
maybe Worcester or Sèvres, in your rich uncle's collection you
probably lose something much more serious than your temper.

' It was borne in upon me gradually that while the smashing of *a* plate would leave one serious, even depressed, or of two plates, three plates, even four plates, it was the smashing of a quantity of plates that was irresistible. It must be an extravagant abuse of plates ; a cataclysm of plates ; a cataract of plates dancing from dresser or table ; an unimaginable holocaust of plates. Thus viewed, the thing explains itself. From a petty annoyance it passes instantly into the ranks of tragedy. It is akin to thunder and lightning ; to the bursting of dams ; to tidal waves and typhoons. It becomes, in fact, elemental and therefore demands the instant tribute of pent-up emotion. This, in our case, happens to be laughter since we have usually dined well and are sitting in a plush seat and expect to laugh anyhow ; but it might just as well be tears. Emotion is the thing, surging forth in unison with the nightmare enormity of this utter, stupendous destruction of silly, harmless plates.

' I have always been immensely amused at the sight of a rabbit easily produced out of a silk hat and long I wondered why. Of course I knew that there must be a trick somewhere, because silk hats do not naturally yield rabbits. If they did Jermyn Street would be, instead of the dull and respectable street it is, a rabbit warren and full of bracken and sand and popping things.

' It occurred to me suddenly the other day that what really amused me was that such a fellow as this conjurer should be able to possess a silk hat at all. How did he come by it ? It will be said that he borrowed it from some one in the audience. But who in his senses would lend his good silk hat to a mountebank ? An accomplice, you say ; but the drollery increases. If such a one as this cannot attain to a silk hat, how can his underling aspire ?

' Meantime, the rabbit lollops off the stage, the silk hat remains—a comedy unexplained.'

And I have found also some pencilled lines relating, obviously, to hay-harvest and honeysuckle weather when the canoe (Kenneth was fond of canoeing and Blewbury is

not far from the Berkshire bank of Thames) drifted downstream between haycocks and to the swish of scythes in
the summer grass : ' Problems such as present themselves
are here of the simplest and least complex form. As, for
instance, when I glided through the hay-fields, I lazily
envied one who stood on a graceful Wessex wagon knee-deep
in hay tossed up to him by moist helpers below. Catching
sight of my canoe, he was fain to observe cheerily, " Ah, if
I had lots o' money *that's* the way I'd travel." To which
I could not help answering the thought that was in me ere
he spoke—that there were worse ways of going about than
on a hay-cart. This prompt retort courteous seemed to take
my interlocutor aback. It was evident that he had passed
some thirty years of cheery existence and never once paused
to consider how exceptionally situated he was to spend such
a percentage of his life happily atop of a hay-cart. Rejoinder
he could possibly have supplied, but the stream bore me out
of hearing. That is one of the special charms of the Thames.
The River of Life has remorseless eddies and backwaters
which forbid escape from such disputes.'

But Blewbury life was not spent entirely with the *adscripti
glebae*. There were visits to Oxford, of one of which he
writes to Alastair : ' Last Tuesday I went to Oxford to meet
Mr. Roosevelt. He was giving a lecture there and after the
lecture he received his friends at Magdalen (you pronounce
it Maudlin) College where he was staying. I had a long talk
with him. Rudyard Kipling was there and Lord Curzon
and a lot of old gentlemen in scarlet gowns.'

And Mr. Roosevelt wrote, on his return to the States and
in the *Saturday Evening Post*, how he had met Kenneth
Grahame that day at Oxford and how he had proved to be
' simply charming '.

And sometimes a publisher, or a journalist, would come
visiting to Boham's and obtain copy—or not as the case
might be. From a New York magazine I'm able to quote
a word or two concerning one of these visits (the visitor was
Mr. Clayton Hamilton) and to say what host told guest

about things in general and the writing of books in particular : ' No other place on earth ' (says Mr. Hamilton) ' could be further in feeling from the English countryside than the Grand Canyon of the Colerado.

' Perched upon the edge of the great chasm, at the outset of Bright Angel Trail, I found a little bookshop. Its stock-in-trade consisted mainly of picture books descanting on the beauties of Arizona and New Mexico and the sort of fiction which celebrates the great open spaces where men are men. Yet in the very middle of the table, isolated in that place of honour, I saw a copy of *The Wind in the Willows*. I said to the proprietor, " What, in the name of Heaven, is this doing here ? "

' She was a quiet woman, with grey hair. Her answer, as I learned a little later, was completely logical. " I am very pleased to meet you," she remarked.

' She went on to tell me that in 1908, when *The Wind in the Willows* had just been given to the world, she had been a saleswoman in Chicago, and that she had registered a vow that if ever she had a bookshop of her own there must always be a copy of that classic in the place of honour.

' In the spring of 1910 I moved to London. I had hoped that one of Stevenson's [1] friends would, if still living, be able to introduce me to Kenneth Grahame. Each of them —particularly Andrew Lang—gave voice to an expression of regret that they never saw him any more. Thereupon I wrote to Kenneth Grahame. By return mail I received an invitation to come down to Berkshire for a week end.

' At Didcot, on the platform, Kenneth Grahame stood waiting me. He was very tall and very broad—a massive figure, but with no spare flesh. At that time he was fifty years of age. His hair was white, but his face was young, and he had the clear complexion of a healthy child. He was dressed in knickerbockers, a soft shirt, and a baggy coat of tweeds.'

[1] Mr. Hamilton was collecting material for his book *On the Trail of Stevenson*.

(At a Blewbury fair, Kenneth Grahame once won a
shoulder of mutton in a 'handsomest man' competition.
One of the local ladies, who loyally voted for him, declared
that, 'she *really* thought he was'.)

Mr. Hamilton goes on : ' Boham's was a brick farmhouse,
with a heavily thatched roof ; it dated from early Tudor
times. The proprietor said to me, " In England we may
choose from any of a dozen different centuries to live in ;
and who would select twentieth century when he might
live more simply in the spacious times of Elisabeth ? "

' Certainly life seemed spacious as we sat in the courtyard, surrounded by the rural erections of that ancient
Saxon whose name had happened to be Boham. By comparison, it seemed a little cramped when we went indoors
for meals.

' I had known, of course, for years, that all of Kenneth
Grahame's work had been posited upon the opening stanza
of that great ode of Wordsworth which is one of the saddest,
as it is one of the wisest, utterances of mankind. It was,
therefore, not merely for information that I asked him why
he had written mainly about children and about animals.
This is the gist of his reply.

' " The most priceless possession of the human race is
the wonder of the world. Yet, latterly, the utmost
endeavours of mankind have been directed toward the
dissipation of that wonder. Everybody seems to cry out
for a world in which there shan't be any Santa Claus.
Science analyses everything to its component parts, and
neglects to put them together again. A bare-foot boy
cannot go wading in a mountain stream without being
told that he must no longer spell the fluid that sings round
his feet by the age-old lettering of W-A-T-E-R, but must
substitute the symbol H_2O. Nobody, any longer, may
hope to entertain an angel unawares, or to meet Sir Lancelot
in shining armour on a moonlit road. You have quoted
Wordsworth—' It is not now as it hath been of yore '. But
the poet *began* by reminding us that, ' There *was* a time '

. . . It is that time which I have attempted to recapture and commemorate in *Dream Days* and *The Golden Age*.

' " Granted that the average man may live for seventy years, it is a fallacy to assume that his life from sixty to seventy is more important than his life from five to fifteen. Children are not merely people : they are the only really living people that have been left to us. Any child will agree with your American poet, Walt Whitman, when he says : ' To me every hour of the day and night is an unspeakably perfect miracle.'

' " In my tales about children, I have tried to show that their simple acceptance of the mood of wonderment, their readiness to welcome a perfect miracle at any hour of the day or night, is a thing more precious than any of the laboured acquisitions of adult mankind.

' " As for animals, I wrote about the most familiar in *The Wind in the Willows* because I felt a duty to them as a friend. Every animal, by instinct, lives according to his nature. Thereby he lives wisely, and betters the tradition of mankind. No animal is ever tempted to deny his nature. No animal knows how to tell a lie. Every animal is honest. Every animal is true—and is, therefore, according to his nature, both beautiful and good. I like most of my friends among the animals . . . come, and let me show you." '

(Kenneth Grahame enjoyed making friends with birds, robins especially. They would sit on his boot or on his shoulder and bullyrag him for a currant or a mealworm, much in the same way as a small boy might plague for a story—' with threats and curses and blows ', as the story-teller himself said of his very youthful, very exacting yet exact Alastair, who replied, ' I never threated or cursed him, I only blowed him.' But the robins did all three.)

' And, similarly, " I have come here," continues Mr. Hamilton to his host, " to pick a quarrel with you. *The Golden Age* was published in 1896, and *Dream Days* in 1898. Then *ten years* elapse before the publication of *The Wind in the Willows*. That ten years was too long. We were told, that you were busy at the Bank of England ; that excuse no longer holds. My quarrel with you is precisely this : I cannot wait another decade for another book from you." There was a silence and then Kenneth Grahame said, " What you say has touched me deeply, because I know it is sincere. And yet I doubt very much if I shall ever write another book. A certain amount of what a countryman of yours called *life* must go into the making of any page of prose.

' " A sentence that is easy to read may have been difficult to put together. Perhaps the greater the easiness in reading, the harder that task in composition. Writing is not easy. There is always a pleasure in the exercise ; but also there is always an agony in the endeavour. If we make a formula of these two motives, I think we may define the process. It is, at its best, a pleasurable agony.

' " I am not a professional writer. I never have been, and I never will be, by reason of the accident that I don't need any money. I do not care for notoriety : in fact, it is distasteful to me. If I should ever become a popular author, my privacy would be disrupted and I should no longer be allowed to live alone.

' " What, then, is the use of writing, for a person like myself ? The answer might seem cryptic to most. It is merely that a fellow entertains a sort of hope that, somehow, some time, he may build a noble sentence that might make Sir Thomas Browne sit up once again in that inhospitable grave of his in Norwich.

' " But language—before the world grew up and went astray—was intended to be spoken to the ear. We are living now in an eye-minded age, when he who runs may read and the average person glimpses his daily reading on the run. What is the use, any longer, of toying with the pleasurable agony of attempting stately sentences of English prose ? There are not more than six men in the United Kingdom who have inherited an ear for prose. I would set Austin Dobson at the top of the list ; he is endowed

with a delicate and dainty sense of rhythm. Rudyard
Kipling knows his King James Bible, and that means very
much—now that Ruskin has passed away. But, tell me,
in *your* country, is there still any one who entertains an
ear for English prose ? "

' I mentioned one. His name was Brian Hooker.

' " And all that agony, for half a dozen readers."

' " The lovers of *The Wind in the Willows* have been
counted by thousands," I objected. " All of them are
eagerly awaiting another book by the same author."

' " They liked the subject matter," he replied. " They
did not even notice the source of all the agony, and all
the joy. To toil at making sentences means to sit indoors
for many hours, cramped above a desk. Yet out of doors,
the wind may be singing, and my favourite sow may be
preparing to deliver a large litter in the fulness of the
moon." '

And of the *themes* of a writer Kenneth said later (he had
gone to Oxford to speak on the art of letters) : '. . . But
you must please remember that a theme, a thesis, a subject,
is in most cases little more than a sort of clothes-line on
which one pegs a string of ideas, quotations, allusions, and
so on, one's mental under-garments of all shapes and sizes,
some possibly fairly new, but most rather old and patched ;
they dance and sway in the breeze, they flap and flutter,
or hang limp and lifeless. And some are ordinary enough,
and some are of a rather private and intimate shape and
give the owner away, even show up his or her peculiarities.
And, owing to the invisible clothes-line, they seem to have
connexion and continuity. And when they are thoroughly
aired, they are taken down and put away, and the clothes-
line is coiled up and disappears. Now talking of clothes-
lines, I am reminded that Samuel Butler was in the habit,
during his walks abroad, of looking out for any subjects,
that would do for plots for short stories. He never wrote
the short stories, but he collected the plots all the same.
Well, on one of his walks he saw a family wash hung out to

dry. The wind was strong, and the various garments, big
and little, were all behaving in the manner I have indicated,
tossing, and talking to each other apparently, and he
thought what a good idea for a love story. First you would
have the various under-garments of two families hung out
to dry in adjacent gardens. A nightshirt of one family
would be observed, the wind being high, paying more than
particular attention to a lady's nightgown in another
garden. And the nightgown would be seen to reciprocate
the advances of the nightshirt. In due course both would
be observed hanging in a third garden by themselves. By
and by, after a decent interval of time of course, there
would also be seen on that line—a little night garment.
This is meant by me as a parable, which is that my ideas,
illustrations, suggestions, my mental under-garments so to
speak, have now been swaying and fluttering before you
for the last forty minutes. My only hope is that some
garment on my clothes-line may stimulate some train of
thought hanging on the clothes-line in your adjacent garden,
and that the result may be, some day, a little mental nightshirt, or at least the tiniest of chemises.'

I imagine that the years at Boham's (even the War
years), the years prior to May 1920, were among the happiest
in Kenneth Grahame's life. A man lives very close to the
heart of England who lives in the Berkshire downs, and a
morning's walk will take him into and along the very
green artery of her—the valley of the Thames.

So the master of Boham's was glad to be there and I
will leave him, in a crisp December twilight, his hand on
the latch and, while pleasantly anticipating (after ten miles
of lonely downland) tea and muffins, yet pausing to hear
the voice of some cheerful village chorister who goes home
singing, in Christmas mood :

'Then St. George : ee made rev'rence : in the stable so dim
Oo vanquished the Dragon : so fearful and grim
So-o grim : and so-o fierce : that now we may say
All peaceful is our wakin' : on Chri-istmas Day !'

CHAPTER XIII

A CORRESPONDENCE

In the introduction to this book I have said that Kenneth Grahame wrote few letters. Nevertheless there exists, exceptionally, his correspondence with Mr. Austin Montgomery Purves, of Philadelphia. Mr. Purves's letters to Kenneth Grahame have not been preserved but, from 1908 to 1915, letters between the two men were exchanged with regularity.

I am printing a selection of the latter's contributions to this correspondence for several reasons. Firstly, because there are practically no other letters of his to print. Secondly, because they act as an occasional reflector of matters mentioned elsewhere. Thirdly and chiefly, because they are very readable.

Mr. Purves, ' a fine, hearty, jolly-looking man of big build and jovial countenance ', seems to have been the only friend with whom Kenneth Grahame kept in epistolary touch. He was an American business man, a lover of books and music and a well-known collector of books and pictures. He was fond of England and the English. ' Q ', so often referred to in the letters, is Sir Arthur Quiller-Couch the novelist and King Edward VII Professor of Literature at Cambridge. ' Atky ' is Edward Atkinson, Commodore of the Royal Fowey Yacht Club, scholar, traveller, gourmet and *cordon bleu*. Mr. Atkinson was drowned as the result of a yachting accident and in spite of a brave, and almost successful, attempt at rescue made by Bevil Quiller-Couch (son of Sir Arthur and sometimes referred to as the Boy), who was Mr. Atkinson's sole companion when their eighteen-footer foundered. Mr. Quiller-Couch, an Oxford undergraduate, brought Mr. Atkinson, an elderly man and unconscious, ashore through a heavy sea. That is to the black rocks at the spouting base of a Cornish cliff. It was night and a gale blew. At his great personal risk Mr. Quiller-Couch climbed the cliff and knocked up a farmhouse. But, before the rescue party returned, Mr. Atkinson had been washed out to sea. His body was recovered some days later.

Pierre Marot is the fifth, and youngest, son of Mr. Purves and the godson of Kenneth Grahame. Maxfield Parrish is, of course, the American artist. Mr. Saunders is a Berkshire farmer. Jerry is Mr. Purves's coloured valet and the great hand in a kitchen with a lobster. The book referred to, in the letter dated 24th of January 1914, is *Mr. Verdant Green.*

> ‘ *Mayfield,*
> ‘ *Cookham Dene,*
> ‘ *Berkshire,*
> ‘ *3rd Nov.* 1908

‘ MY DEAR PURVES,—Your most welcome and amiable letters continue to reproach me daily, as they bulge in my pocket like a visible bad conscience. I must be allowed to dwell on their amiability, because you have every right to be “ shirty ” to any extent—yet no “ shirtability ” has appeared up to the present date.

‘ The fact is, when one has written letters for many years for one's daily bread, and suddenly finds oneself free of them, a revulsion sets in which must be allowed to work itself off. You will understand and make allowances.

‘ I am most awfully obliged to you for all the solid work you are putting in on behalf of “ the W. in the W.” Your review was perfectly charming, and is bound to be helpful. That the book has given you all personal pleasure is, of course, very good for me to think of. I was greatly interested in the book of your Pageant in Philadelphia that you sent me. It is a fine thing to be a citizen of “ No mean City ”, with a storied past such as yours possesses, and the sight must have been deeply impressive and moving and beautiful. It was well worth doing, and it was evidently done well. I hope that Jack and Ned did not miss it, through being away at their camp. That must have been ripping fun for them—I should imagine that when Pierre Marot heard all about it he simply turned green with jealousy. Our " camp " hasn't come off yet, because I am hoping to manage it after the New Year—in Switzerland to begin with, and then perhaps a drop into the northern part of Italy, for colour and anemones and Chianti and so on.

'We had a beautiful summer here, and now we are having an equally beautiful autumn—still and misty and mild and full of colour. I had a jolly day at Oxford a short time ago. Everything in full swing and the river covered with men doing " tubbing " practice. The old place was just as beautiful as ever, and I bought some youthful ties and some " Oxford sausages " in the delightful market— they are a small species without any skins on their poor little persons—and took a walk down Mesopotamia, and explored many old corners.

'We can't extract any Fowey news from Q., who is probably mighty busy, and neither Atky nor Miss Marsden have given any sign of life for a long time. I wish we could get down there for a bit before the year closes. Perhaps it may yet be possible.

'This is not much of a letter, but look on it as a make-shift and I will try and do better next time. Our kindest regards to Mrs. Purves and all the family, and hearty thanks for all you are doing to help a struggling author to get an honest living, and remembrances to Jerry (I eat a *cold* lobster every Sunday for lunch and mournfully think what might have been if you were all over on this side and lobsters were cheap).

'Ever yours most sincerely,
'KENNETH GRAHAME '

'*Mayfield,*
  '*Cookham Dene,*
    '*Berkshire, England,*
      '*17th Dec.* 1908

'DEAR PURVES,—It occurred to us that you might possibly care to have a copy of the English edition of "The W. in the W.", so I have sent you one, instead of a Christmas card with two robins sitting on a steaming plum-pudding with an intoxicated church in the background. I should like to have sent Mrs. Purves a tiara and each of the boys a steam-yacht or a motor-car, but that will have to be some other Christmas. We are just back from Devonshire and miss the sea and the sunshine. My influenza was apparently a slight one at the time, but the after weakness and general grogginess still continues, and I can only walk a mile or two, and then an armchair and slumber till dinner-time, which is a nuisance. We find deep mud everywhere and leaden skies overhead. But my faithful tame robin was waiting on the doorstep next morning and came for his currant as if we had not been away a day.

'E. is Christmassing for all she's worth. We have had no Fowey news this long while. Well, this is a dull letter, written like Hon'ble Poet Shelley's stanzas "in a moment of depression". But it wishes you all good things, including a Happy New Year, "jointly and severally", for you and Mrs. Purves, and all the boys, and Jerry.

    'Yours most sincerely,
      'KENNETH GRAHAME'

'*Mayfield,*
  '*Cookham Dene,*
    '*Berkshire,*
      '*England,* 27th *July* 1909

'DEAR PURVES,—Your letters, welcome as they are, always hit me on a very sore spot on my conscience—and a spot too that has not had time to skin over properly since

the last one knocked it raw. And yet, do you know, I
do write you any quantity of truly magnificent letters. In
my armchair of evenings, with closed eyes, or strolling in
the woods of afternoons—or with head on pillow *very* late
on a thoroughly wet and disagreeable morning. I see my
pen covering page after page of cream-laid parchment-
wove extra antique. Such good stuff too—witty, anecdoti-
cal, pensive, pathetic—I feel myself lick the envelope—I
see myself running to the post—I hear the flop of the letter
in the box. It's all so *real*—to me—that I was quite surprised to find that you weren't asking me to limit them to,
say, three a week. Please believe that, if they never reach
you, it's not my fault.

'We have had two surprise visits from "Atky" this
summer. He just dropped from the clouds, without notice,
ate a hearty lunch, talked a great deal, and flitted away
again into the outer darkness. He seems to have been very
poorly all the winter, as the result of influenza, which sapped
his strength, but he was distinctly on the mend when he
came here, and is probably all right by now. We were
deeply disappointed to hear from you that there was no
chance of your coming over this summer, but of course we
quite understand. After all one's "affairs" must rank
first, and you want, when you come, to bring an easy mind
with you. And Fowey and the Thames will wait. Meantime, we are amused to hear of the two boys swaggering
about the continent doing the Grand Tour, as it used to
be called.

'Mouse is down at his favourite sea-side resort—Littlehampton, a rather horrid little place, which he adores. I
wish our tastes in places were similar, so that we could
be together ; but in any case E. can't take her bad eye
to the sea just yet, on account of the glare. We are having
a miserable summer, so wet and cold. I have not had
my boat out of the boat-house yet, and have a fire in the
study where I am writing this.

'I must thank you again for all the "cuttings" you so

kindly sent. Most interesting they were, and encouraging. With all regards and remembrances to all of you.

'Yours truly,
'KENNETH GRAHAME'

'Mayfield,
'Cookham Dene,
'Berkshire,
'England, 12th Jan. 1910

'MY DEAR PURVES,—First and foremost, I beg that you will take an early opportunity of conveying to Master P. M. my respectful but very hearty thanks for the beautiful Christmas present that he was good enough to send me. The book is a delightful one in every respect—matter, form and illustration—and Maxfield Parrish keeps up to his own high standard, which is not easy, though we shall never expect less of him. P. M., of course, remembered my fondness for the classical old stories, which are eternally new ; but it was clever of him to choose so well.

'Next, I wish you all a very happy and prosperous New Year, and that all your roseate projects may blossom into full-blown facts—if they do, you will certainly have to be prosperous, and it will be your own fault if you're not happy.

'And then, I want to explain the difficulty I found in answering your last letter, of some months ago, sketching your hoped-for programme for the present year. It found us very busy house hunting and hopeful of being settled in a place of our own by Christmas at least ; and now Christmas has come and gone, and we are as far as ever from a house. And our time is up here, and the owner wants to come back. And until this point is settled, all plans are in abeyance. As soon as I have found something and "moved in", I hope to go on my travels with a light heart. We are both somewhat stale and rusty, and I want to smell foreign smells again and drink wine in the country where it grows ; but we feel it would be wiser to get our troubles over first. However, I do hope they *will* be over, long before you begin to get a move on you ; and then it

16

would be nice indeed if we could stretch our weary limbs under the same marble table outside some sun-bathed restaurant.

'I will get E. to write to you about Tyrol, which she knows—I've never been there myself, but I should like to go. Though I can't talk German I *can* drink beer—and it's handy for Venice.

'Q. is frightfully busy over the election, propagating his pernicious doctrines throughout the west country. We had a nice letter from his boy, who goes into residence at Oxford next week. Atky recently made a sudden flight into Sardinia, an island I've long wanted to visit. He hints darkly at adventures, but as yet I've had no opportunity of pumping him. Your boys must have had a ripping time. I wish some one would take me on a trip like that.

'Well, until we meet, which I hope will now be soon.

'Yours most sincerely,

'KENNETH GRAHAME'

'*Boham's,*
'*Blewbury, Didcot,*
'*England,* 20*th May* 1910

'MY DEAR PURVES,—After exceeding great tribulation we have at last found this little farmhouse, and moved into it a few days ago. Chaos, of course, and we live in a small clearing in a forest of books and furniture, striving vainly to reduce things to some appearance of order. Blewbury is perhaps the most beautiful of a string of pretty and very primitive villages stretched along the northern edge of the Berkshire Downs. It is only about 54 miles from London, but 5,400 years remote from it in every way. This is the heart of King Alfred's Country, "Alfred the Great" who beat the Danes, close by here, about 860, and nothing has really happened since. True, a tiresome innovator, called William the Conqueror, came along some years later, and established a thing called the Curfew bell, which still rings here during the winter months, to the annoyance of the more conservative inhabitants, who say they used to get on very well before these newfangled notions ; but this is all that divides us from Saxon times. We are some twelve miles from Oxford, but its culture does not permeate to us ; if we penetrate as far as Abingdon or Wallingford we are mighty travellers and have seen great and distant cities.

'The village is really a charming one—a mixture of orchards and ancient timbered cottages and clear little streams, and the people are simple and friendly and dignified. The downs lie a mile or two to the south—splendid bare grassy spaces with (so-called) Roman or British " Camps " and " Barrows ". The villages along the edge are all beautiful with fine old churches—ours is a beauty, and not much spoilt. We went to a memorial service for King Edward there to-day and the simplicity and genuineness of it all was very touching. As for this little house, it is a plain Berkshire farmer's house, " unfaked " and unaltered, with no special architectural features, with its orchard on one side and its farm buildings on the other. We are genuinely hoping that you may be able to come and see it—and us, and if you have to suffer any minor discomforts (if for instance we have to " sleep " you " out ", in some dream of a thatched cottage, owing to exigencies of space), I am sure you will bear in mind that Alfred the Great was no better off. I have honestly no fear that Blewbury itself will disappoint you. The Bohams, I may explain, sleep in a row in the churchyard. Only their name remains, attached to this farm and to a road leading from it up onto the downs.

'I wonder whether your plans still hold good, as already related to us ? If so, you will be here about the time that I have hammered in the last tack into the last carpet, and I shall wearily straighten my back and prepare to take a well-earned holiday with you. I suppose you would hardly have time to walk from here, by way of the downs, to Fowey ? Atky says six weeks would do it quite comfortably. That peripatetic personage wrote to me the other

day from Corsica. Each year his " St. Anthony's fever "
seems to agitate his lean limbs more violently. Don't
bring any fine clothes or evening frocks to *us*. We are the
only people here who dine late at all and we keep it dark.

' Yours most truly,

' KENNETH GRAHAME '

' *Boham's,*

' *Blewbury, Didcot,*

' *Berkshire, England,*

' *2nd August* 1910

' DEAR PURVES,—The photos are first-rate. They are
being gradually shown round the village, and are received
with cries of " Law " and " Well I never " and " Fancy
now " and careful identification of every paling and bit of
thatch. The two I like best, pictorially, are the bit of
Leach's farmyard with a Lady hen and a Master pigling
occupying the stage ; and the one of the Barley Mow Inn
with the little white road in the background, running over
the hill to Streatley. But they are all delightful, and breathe
the Blewbury spirit.

' Our great annual social event, the " Fête ", came off
last Wednesday and Society with a big S. was convulsed
from top to toe ; but is gradually simmering down to
quietude again for *another* twelve months. We made £27
for the Church expenses—Mouse as a " costermonger " with
a miniature " coster-barrow ", sold sweets vigorously, and
cleared 17s. 6d. Saunders had a weighing-machine and Mrs.
S. a bran-tub, and made over £2 between them. Dancing
and pyrotechnics closed an event of unexampled brilliance,
which the *Morning Post*, however, has so far failed to
chronicle.

' Yesterday morning we drove over early to East Ilsley
(that village we did *not* go to, the day we were up on the
downs together) to see the big annual sheep-fair, I can't
describe it, but it was one of the most *intoxicating* things I
have ever been at. The noise of dogs and sheep and dealers,
the procession of sheep and men, the droves of flockmasters

and dealers in the most fascinating clothes you can conceive, the pubs all gay and busy, and the beautiful little village glittering with movement and humming with the real Berkshire language, beat any Pageant I have ever seen. And all genuine business too—not an " outsider " present except ourselves. *You ought to have been there.* Mouse was soon in the thick of it, but when I sought him and discovered him bidding at the auction for pedigree rams, I had to haul him out of action.

' Mouse and Saunders have become very good friends and now call each other " old chap " and he goes to tea there when he likes. You seem to have been having a splendid time, both of you, and you won't care to tear yourselves away, even for Venice. The card you sent me of Innsbruck was beautiful, and rather tugged at me. But foreign places all do. We are fixed here for August anyway, and a bit of September. After that—I don't know ; there are possibilities.

' You don't say if the boys have had all the climbing they wanted. Sooner them nor me. Something with a restaurant on its airy summit is quite good enough for me.

' Yours most sincerely,
' KENNETH GRAHAME

' E. is most tremendously obliged for the dental silk, wh. duly arrived.'

' Boham's,
' Blewbury, Didcot,
' Berkshire, England,
' 24th August 1910

' DEAR PURVES,—I have intended that you should find this waiting for you at Philadelphia on your return, as a sort of a greeting from a continent which by that time will seem very strange and far away, in time and space ; but Mrs. Purves's cheery letter, which we read with much delight, has put it in my power to catch your boat, with luck, at the pleasant city of Marseilles—where I once ate a perfectly

whacking and stupendous quantity of *bouillabaisse*. So this
will not be a greeting, but a valediction. Well, you seem
to be quitting in the right spirit ; not damning your luck,
as most of us do at the end of a holiday, but blessing it ;
and by so doing you shall take your holiday back with you
as a keepsake, not leave it hopelessly behind. Perhaps
" Blessed are those who bless their luck " is an eleventh
Beatitude, got dropped out somehow—with one or two
others.

'Thank you very much for negotiating that N. York
draft for me—I sent you a meagre card of acknowledgement
at the time. And many thanks for the colour print of the
" Pan ". You have a fine possession awaiting you—the
god in the best aspect of remote and withdrawn seclusion,
piping to " Water, first of singers ". I am keenly looking
forward to the prints you have kindly promised to send
me (the missing ones, by the way, have never turned up).

'I have your letter of 21st—for which much thanks.
And it is good indeed of you to be sending Mouse a cape
for the storms that daily drench us here. He will be truly
proud when it reaches him—and he will have a dry skin as
well, which a proud spirit cannot give. He continues to be
very happy and contented here. He has had three expeditions to Oxford also, all in beautiful weather ; and in a
fortnight or so we hope to go in again, for the big annual
Fair of St. Giles', which will be a delirium of caravans and
roundabouts and hideous noises. The day after to-morrow
there is another Sheep Fair at East Ilsley, and we hope to
be in the thick of it. So you see, if we don't get to the
Passion Plays and Venices and things, we have our own
little diversions.

'Your hospitable and tempting invitation to come over
and stay with you is *not* being docketed and pigeon-holed,
but is being kept fully in our minds as affecting any future
plans. Meantime I can only say that if at some later date
the thing should prove possible, we shall bring it off, with
much light-heartedness ; and we do not need your assur-

ances that we shall be comfortable, free and happy. That
is the one thing of which we are completely confident.

' And now good luck to you all, and a fair voyage, and an
even keel. And may a prospering wind fill the sails the
Venezia hasn't got, and bring you speedily in sight of the
dear old Custom-house which will tell you that you are really
" Home ".

' Yours most sincerely,
' KENNETH GRAHAME '

' *Boham's,*
' *Blewbury, Didcot,*
' *Berkshire, England,*
' *30th Sept.* 1910

' DEAR PURVES,—Yesterday arrived the packet containing the two beautiful pictures (Jason and Bellerophon),
doubly welcome, i.e. for themselves, and as telling us you
were safely home again, with the rest of the Argonauts—
at least I hope so. I don't know why it was, but the *Venezia*
never appeared in the Shipping News, either as starting or
arriving or doing anything else—she didn't even find an
uncharted rock, apparently. Unexciting sort of vessel.
We sent you a couple of parting screeds to Marseilles,
and hope the *Venezia* condescended to admit them on
board.

' The two prints are exceedingly beautiful things. Imbued
with the true classical spirit, they recall long-forgotten but
haunting Virgilian phrases, and will send me back I think
to that delightful author—if I can find my boyhood's copy
among the debris that still strews the shores of Boham's.
Thank you very much for them and for your promptness in
sending them.

' Mouse's rain-cloak arrived in due course and he was
installed its proud possessor. He highly approves of its
cut and style, and so does his governess, who finds it light
and convenient to carry. It is probably due to the cloak
that, since it arrived, we have hardly had any rain at all ;
and just now we seem to be having a little bit of our lost

summer. This morning Mouse and I went to see Farmer
Saunders and buy some apples—and first we went up a
ladder into the apple-loft, and sampled every sort of apple
and filled our pockets—and then we sat in the parlour and
discussed circuses, and all three of us agreed that they were
the only thing worth living for.

' While *you* have sailed across half the world nothing has
happened here except that the Michaelmas daisies have come
out. O, and St. Giles's Fair at Oxford, which M. and I
visited and had a dizzy day riding around on pink bears,
swinging to the clouds in Dreadnoughts. Next Thursday
is our own fair, which doubtless all the world will attend.

' Yours very truly,
' Kenneth Grahame '

' Boham's,
' Blewbury, Didcot,
' Berkshire,
' England, 18th Oct. 1910

' Dear Purves,—I hasten to acknowledge receipt of your
letter of the 11th.

' I received and read the Maxfield Parrish letters with great
delight and the consciousness of a vivid personality behind
each written word ; and I much appreciated your kind offer
of them for my own keeping. I am, however, sending them
back ; for I feel *very* strongly that a letter has a peculiar
and direct and special appeal for the recipient, which no one
else can entirely share ; and you will like to glance over
these again, on some happy *idle* day that is surely to
come.

' We have been living through a strenuous time of Fairs,—
the tale of Blewbury Fair must await a more leisurely letter
—the glory and colour of it all, the friendly show-people
and their vans, and the maddening whirl of the roundabouts.
I dare not embark on the subject at this late hour of the
night.

' Yours most truly,
' Kenneth Grahame '

' *Boham's,*
' *Blewbury, Didcot,*
' *Berkshire, England,*
' 12*th Jan.* 1911

' DEAR PURVES,—I have been a shamefully long time in acknowledging your beautiful Christmas present—but I have been laid up in bed with a sharp attack of bronchitis, which has interfered sadly with my Christmas duties, and pleasures too for that matter, and other people's also ; but that is over for the present, though I have to sit indoors over a fire and not run about over the downs, as I would fain be doing.

' The book is a charming book, and a fresh instance of Pierre Marot's care and thoughtfulness in choosing for me just the thing I like best.   You are very fortunate to possess those fine and stately pictures, and I like to think that you've got them.   And I've got the book—and thank you very much.

' We have not had much fun this winter—too much wet for gadding about.   But Mouse goes to children's parties and is very happy.   He goes to school after Easter and is much pleased and excited at the prospect.   It is a nice place in Dorsetshire, near the coast, with beautiful bathing and surroundings.   We took a short trip to that part of the country in November and liked it much.

' I have got possession of my " barn "—you may remember the outside of it—I have put a good stove in, and most of my books, and it makes a very decent study indeed, and gives us more room, which we wanted, though you'd be surprised at the way we have " settled in " since you were here and the place was still all straw and packing-cases. The new study also takes *art* very freely and your family bas-relief—the plaster cast—is there, with much else of varying merit.

' The Saunderses were much pleased and flattered to get your Christmas card.   The boy and they continue to be great friends, and he takes tea with them most Sundays. Blewbury hibernates during the winter and you don't meet people unless you go and knock them up, when you find them by excellent fires and they give you ginger-wine in exchange for news.   No fairs, no sheep markets, no riding round on gaily-coloured wooden horses with their names painted on their necks.   But at Easter we shall wake up again, when the gay caravans take to the road once more.   Sometimes we have the hounds though, and Mouse and I had a wonderful bit of luck one morning in November, when the hounds ran into their fox at our very feet and we saw every detail of the kill and the " breaking up " and then Mouse shyly asked the huntsman to " blood " him—do you know the nasty process ?   And this the good-natured man did and presented him with the brush as well, and he was proud indeed.

' With love to you all.

                              ' Yours most sincerely,
                                       ' KENNETH GRAHAME '

                    ' Boham's,
                         ' Blewbury, Didcot,
                              ' Berkshire, England,
                                   ' 7th February 1911

' DEAR PURVES,—Very many thanks for your letter of the 25th Jan.

' We are all four for Cornwall three days hence, if nothing intervenes.   First to the Lizard, for two or three weeks, then, I hope, to Fowey.   I want Mouse to make the acquaintance of my Cornish haunts, and friends, before he goes to school —then he may like to go back there.   So my next letter may be from familiar scenes and contain tidings of gulls and lobsters.   Meantime good-bye and thanks again.

                              ' Yours most sincerely,
                                       ' KENNETH GRAHAME '

                    ' Boham's,
                         ' Blewbury, Didcot,
                              ' Berkshire,
                                   ' England, 15th May 1911

' DEAR PURVES,—Many thanks for your interesting letter of the 21st March.   This reached me when we were established at St. Catherine's House, Fowey, and of course ought to have been answered from that classic spot. But I found the arrangements of the house (which was also very full most of the time) very uncomfortable for correspondence, and I may say here, that we were greatly disappointed in St. C.'s, and the way it is now run. I went there because I thought it would be more simple and homelike for the boy and his governess than the hotel, which I should have preferred ; but there was a skimping and a pinching everywhere, which was not agreeable. Skimping in food, in lights, in chamber linen, in hot water even. Complaints were general, and for my part I shall not go there again. It is indeed becoming a little difficult to find accommodation at Fowey. The doctors have begun to send convalescents there, the G.W.Ry. advertises it assiduously, and although it was still a fortnight to Easter when we left, the place was as full as in summer.

'Well, enough of that side of it, the town itself, the harbour, the river, greeted us with all their old charm. Bigger steamers than ever come up to the "tips", the clay is loaded by electricity, and the work goes on night and day. Fowey is prospering, and new houses have been built, out Point Neptune way ; but the quays and the old town and the harbour-front are the same as ever—the same mud, the same fish heads and guts (apparently). Also the same Q, looking not a day older and even more beautifully dressed than formerly. Mouse was particularly struck with Q's clothes. I think he then realized, for the first time, that Man, when he chooses to give his mind to it, is incomparably the finer animal of the two, and does the greater justice to clothes. (Soldiers and peacocks know this already, of course.) He observed solemnly to me, after contemplation of a certain suit of checks—Irish homespun—that " Q. was his idea of a hero of a novel ". The " Haven " was " done up " too, last autumn, in a new suit of excellent style and taste, and sparkled with cleanliness and colour. Mouse and Foy became good friends at once, and had many teas and walks together, and expeditions to the farm—" Priam's Cellars "

—which flourishes exceedingly. One sunny day we all went over there with a large luncheon basket, and lunched in the open, off " hoggy puddin " and other good things, in a riot of daffodils and primroses, with three big foreign ships— Danes and Norwegians—moored right below us, and all the merry harbour traffic passing busily up and down. They have struck water there—a spring from the rock—and made a tank for water-lilies, and the clearance has made great progress. The terraces of the old garden, that were there hundreds of years ago, show clearly in places.

' Also, we had several expeditions to Rosebank and had two of Atky's " special " luncheons—i.e. mostly fancy *hors d'œuvres* and every sort of sausage—and Mouse had several teas, with gramophone, and liberty to potter about among all the books, and objects. He had not begun sailing, but was busy " fitting out " in the boat-house. He has been doing a lot of carpentering this winter, and that seems to have done him good.

' One specially warm and sunny day I took M. and his governess up to tea at Lerryn, " on a tide ", sailing up and rowing back. There is to me a tremendous sense of *age* about Lerryn—if I were painting some thirteenth or four-teenth century incident, I would be content to take Lerryn water-side, with the old bridge, for background ; just as it is—indeed it has probably altered little since those days.

' Bevil was back from Oxford part of the time, but we didn't see much of him. He was on the water all the time —sailing, sailing, sailing.

' Mouse has asked to be taken back to Fowey some day soon, which is a good sign—but I fancy, on the whole, he liked the Lizard best. To be sure he went there first, and we had better weather there, but the wildness, freshness, and strangeness of the Lizard, its grandeur and sparkling air, probably impressed him more than the slightly sophisti-cated Fowey ; and he liked the simple, friendly people, who were all so nice to him and let him run in and out of their places, and had him to tea, and called me " Mr. Kenneth ", as I was known to them four-and-twenty years back. But the cliffs are not really safe for children, so I shall not hurry to take him back till he's a good deal older.

'By the way, I thought "Lady Good-for-nothing" excellent, and quite in Q's best and finest manner.

'Since we got back from Cornwall we have been very busy fitting M. out for school and getting him off. The joy and pride of a complete new outfit of clothes—including even "Eton" jacket and trousers for Sundays—no doubt mitigated the pangs. At any rate he made the great plunge last Monday, going off very manfully and composedly and, from what we hear, he is falling into the ways of the new life very well. It is very quiet here now without him.

'I hope your influenza is all over by now and that P. M. has emerged from the trial all new and shiny, and that the boys continue on their wild careers without check or hindrance. Blewbury is slow in waking up after the winter, but the farmers are all busy and happy, for it has been grand farming weather for weeks and both fruit and crops look most promising. The place itself is a mass of blossom and colour.

'The enclosed lobster is for Jerry, in memory of the past lobsters that died nobly in a good cause. Alas, I never see a lobster now in this inland village. If I were to meet one walking on the downs, I would fall on his neck with tears of joy, and I would lead him gently home, and we would not part again, never, never.

'With warmest regards and the best of good wishes from both of us to all of you.

'Ever yours sincerely,
'KENNETH GRAHAME'

'Boham's,
'Blewbury, Didcot,
'Berkshire,
'England, 16th Aug. 1911

'DEAR PURVES,—Thank you very much indeed for the beautiful Maxfield Parrish colour print you sent me—the pie picture. It is a noble piece of colour, and I am glad indeed to possess it. Of course it ought to have been acknowledged long ago—and your two letters—and there is also Mrs. Purves's letter to E. and the two *Print Collector's Quarterlies*, the five magazines, and the gift of photos.

' We never expected you to write at all during your terrible heat-wave. How thankful you must have felt that the boys were away. Here we have been having a bit of a wave too, in our own small English way. People have been crying out, of course—but, to me, it has been the most glorious summer that I remember. I never saw such colour in the crops—burnt to a fierce tawny red. What is getting serious is the drought—practically no rain in these parts for two months, and no sign of it. The farmers are hard put to it to find food for their beasts, and sheep are fetching wretched prices in the market.

' We are staying on here quietly, for the present, for Mouse's summer holidays. He seems quite happy and contented here which is as it should be. When he is older, perhaps, he may find it a bit dull. He brought home good reports, and says he liked it from the first day.

' We had several pleasant trips to Oxford before the hot weather set in. Since then it has not been possible to make any expeditions—at least it was possible, but it would not have been very wise. I take a siesta, foreign fashion, from 2 to 4, and later, get up on the downs, where there is generally a breeze. I hope soon to get some boating on the Thames ; but since I last wrote to you, our life has been most uneventful. Not even any fairs as yet. Owing to the coronation, when we poor country folk spent all our hoarded pennies in decorations, &c., the dates of all the village fêtes and fairs have been fixed for us late in the summer as possible, to give us a chance of saving a few more pennies for shows and roundabouts. But when we get our harvest money, we shall be rich again, and the fun will begin. Then we will ride on noble steeds of wood, with their names painted in gold on their necks (they are all named after famous racehorses of old time), and shy for cocoa-nuts, and swing till we are sick —at least I shall be sick.

' Well good-bye for the present. This is not a real letter. Perhaps later I shall have something solid to tell you about. Some wild village orgie—or " harvest home ".

' Yours most sincerely,
' KENNETH GRAHAME '

' Boham's,
' Blewbury, Didcot,
' Berkshire,
' England, 20th Sept. 1911

' DEAR PURVES,—The sad news of the deplorable tragedy at Fowey has no doubt reached you ; but you will naturally be anxious for all particulars, so I am sending all that appeared in the *Western Morning News*, in case no one else has done so. We have not yet had any letters from Fowey about it. Please keep the cuttings if you want to.

' I loved Atky—in perhaps a selfish way first of all because all his special " passions " appealed to me—boats, Bohemianism, Burgundy, tramps, travel, books, and pictures—but also, and I hope and believe chiefly, for his serene and gentle nature, his unfailing good humour and clear, cheerful spirits, and his big kind heart. But *you* know all these qualities of his as well as I do. And you are mourning him too.

' Again and again, in imagination, I get my boat at White-house Steps and scull up the river by the grey old sea wall, under the screaming gulls, past the tall Russian and Norwegian ships at their moorings, and so into Mixtow Pill, and ship my oars at the little stone pier, and find Atky waiting on the steps, thin, in blue serge, with his Elizabethan head ; and stroll up the pathway you know, to the little house above it, and be talking all the time and always some fresh whimsicality. I had a letter from him a very few weeks ago, telling of a Yachting Dinner they had just had—he, apparently, in the Chair—and his spirits seemed as buoyant as ever.

' Well, I will not write more just now. I feel as if we had all suddenly grown much older. All, that is, except Atky. He couldn't do it, he didn't know how.

' Yours, KENNETH GRAHAME '

' Boham's,
' Blewbury, Didcot,
' Berkshire,
' 8th Feb. 1912

' DEAR PURVES,—Nothing that we had this Christmas delighted us more than the Dennison box of notions. Sending off parcels is no longer an agony and a running about all over the house—rather a delicate delight.

' We are alone here once more, Mouse having departed school-ward, undaunted and in high spirits. We have excellent accounts of him and his progress. I had a line from Q. just the other day. The Boy had been elected to the " Leander " Boat-Club—the premier rowing club of England—which I suppose is a great compliment for so young an oarsman. He stroked one of the two trial eights this year, but he is not in the " Varsity " crew—at least up to the present. I fancy he may be a trifle light as yet —those boys run to such a size nowadays. On Latin and Greek and such trifles the father was silent.

' We have been having some bitter weather lately, but it's all gone now for the present, and Mud is King once more. We hang on for a bit, and go South when it is nearly sure to be fine.

' We had rather an interesting time in Brittany in the late autumn and saw a lot of new country and new things, but, to me, that is not the South and therefore—nothing. You've got to have the Alps to the North of you before the air begins to have the right feel in it.

' You see I've no news,—and indeed this is the dead time of the year here. Even the farmers have little to do.

' I hope Mrs. Purves and the rest of you are well and

lively, and having lots of opera and such good things, which your noble city provides so plentifully.

'I will write you a better letter next time—perhaps something will have happened—just now we're hardly thawed out after the recent frost.

'Yours most sincerely,
'KENNETH GRAHAME'

'*The Fowey Hotel,*
'*Fowey,*
'*Cornwall, 8th July* 1912

'DEAR PURVES,—First, let me formally acknowledge receipt of your two letters, 25th May and 8th June, and of the copy of the *Century*, with its charmingly written appreciation of Maxfield Parrish and of the treasures which decorate your new room. We have been away from home for some five weeks—first Dorsetshire, in a little old sea-town called "Lyme Regis", chiefly known through being enshrined in one of the novels of Jane Austen, and then, for a fortnight, here. Fowey is prosperous, cheerful and full of smiling faces. More steamers up the river than I have ever seen and the jetties working all night as well as all day. Many inquiries after you all, from all classes, and a general feeling of having come home. Q. and miladi are going very strong, the Boy has been at home for a week, but is off again to camp as an Artillery man. Phelps walks down the road at precisely the same hour every day and Canon Purcell enters the Club at 6.45 p.m. as usual—and begins abusing the Government, and the Regatta is beginning to loom very large on the horizon. So you see that, whatever happens in outlying portions of the globe, Fowey holds on to its own old way and always will.

'We have been up to Rosebank—a sad sight rather, with its empty rooms and bare walls. Miss Marston is still there, alone, but has taken a flat in London, whither she will move in the autumn. The place is for sale, not to be let, and I don't think it will sell in a hurry—it's not everybody's house. The pictures sold badly—the water-colours were much faded

17

by the sun and spotted by damp, and the dealers in a body stood aloof. But the books did well. The enormous stock of clocks, barometers and binoculars (I believe he had 45 telescopes alone) fetched very little. We have been having consistently beastly weather throughout, and have to-day rather suddenly determined to get home to-morrow, starting by an early train. So this letter will be a bit truncated, from pressure. I will try and do better next time; and in Berkshire I may remember some more " Fowey bits " to tell you. Meantime, we want to hear all about the Hospital Fair, and the dresses, with nothing left out. And I don't see why we shouldn't meet near Paris, next year—and here too, with luck. Fowey and Paris have both their good points.

'Yours ever sincerely,
'KENNETH GRAHAME'

'Boham's,
'Blewbury, Didcot,
'Berkshire,
'England, 8th Aug. 1912

'DEAR PURVES,—Your letter of the eighteenth of July has been before us for some days, and all its talk of next year seems to bring your migration to these shores once more very near indeed. After all, in the month of August, when lamps are once more lighted for dinner, "next year" is a pretty near thing, isn't it? Certainly we ought to be able to come together in Paris or elsewhere, wherever you settle upon eventually, and as for Fowey, that ought to be a sure thing. We don't want much tempting to skip off down there. You won't find any change to speak of, a shop or two has moved or blossomed out, the cloak shop has shifted further into town, but Varco will still greet you from his shop door at the corner. Miss White will smile at you through the fruiterer's window a little lower down, the hotel bus, crashing down the hill, will shave your toes as you skip for safety into the little bar-door of the Ship, and when you reach Town Quay, and sit on the same old garden-seat out-

side the " Institute ", with the same old men on either side
of you, it will be as if you had just closed your eyes there
for an afternoon nap and opened them again.

' We met Climo one day in the street, as usual hawking
a basketful of delightful, blue-black squiggly lobsters. We
had some lobster talk and made a sort of a rendezvous
later, on the other side, to renew the subject, but we quitted
prematurely and it never came off.

' Q. is more full of work than ever at present. A book
of original verse coming out, another anthology, and a novel.
You really mustn't take it to heart, by the way, if they don't
write to you. They never write letters to anybody. For
myself, I don't think I have ever seen so much as a pot-
hook or a hanger of her Ladyship's ; as for Q. I sometimes
have to bother him, for introductions, or information of
some sort, and when he replies, which he always does
promptly, he gives me a half-sheet summary of the latest
gossip—in shorthand. I fancy that professional writers
nearly all hate letter writing. The *style* is different and
that makes it difficult for them. The amateur finds it
easier. Lamb was good at it, to be sure, and Edward Fitzgerald—but in a sense they were amateurs.

' Well, I am getting prosy, and had better stop. All good
wishes to all of you.

' Yours very truly,
' KENNETH GRAHAME '

' *Boham's,*
' *Blewbury, Didcot,*
' *Berkshire,*
' 11*th July* 1913

' MY DEAR PURVES,—Many thanks for your letter of the
3rd. Of course we are immensely disappointed to hear of
the very small probability that exists of your being able to
get to England ; and we are deeply sorry to hear that you
are so pulled down and all the rest of it. But I want to
say at once and right away, that what you are doing is
absolutely the right thing, and the only thing, and the thing

to make you fit and well again in the shortest possible time.
You have got to " slack " as if you were in for a prize for it.
Not only must you not think to-day of what you will do
to-morrow, but you must not think in the morning of what
you will do in the afternoon. In fact, you mustn't think
at all, but sit in the sunshine and let things just happen
before your eyes and don't ask yourself why they happen,
or any other conundrum. Nature will do her work all right,
if she's given the chance and a free hand.

'We shall probably start for Fowey on the 16th or 17th
as we have got to be back here about the 26th, to get ready
for our journey to the Highlands in the following week.
We continue to have excellent accounts of Mouse in every
way. I wish we could bring him to Fowey with us, but that
may not be.

' Yours most sincerely,
' KENNETH GRAHAME '

' Boham's,
' Blewbury, Didcot,
' Berkshire,
' 12th December 1913

' DEAR PURVES,—Ever since our return from Scotland I
have been reminding myself almost every day that a letter
was due from me to you ; and lo, here is Christmas almost
on us, and the letter still unwritten. Fortunately I have
other letters still more overdue, and that reflection somehow
seems to cheer me amazingly. I wanted particularly, first
of all, to thank you most warmly for your very kind, thoughtful invitation to Mouse to come and see something of
Holland under your auspices. Had he been kicking his
heels here, at a loose end, I would have jumped at the
opportunity ; but the fact is, it would have abruptly cut
his Highland holiday off suddenly, and the boy was so enjoying every hour of it, and so eager to be allowed to stay there
till the last possible day—which indeed was what we did
—that I hadn't the heart. I wish you could have been with
us ; we were in places which were almost fantastically

beautiful, even for the Highlands, and some of it only recently opened up to travellers.

'I was greatly pleased when I heard about Q. and the new Book. It is [1] just one of those graceful and delicate compliments which it is such a pleasure to receive and such a privilege to be able to pay ; and it will bind you to Fowey by yet one more golden link. The book has been exceedingly well noticed over here, I am glad to see. I sometimes think he is at his best in that sort of work.

'I wish you had been with us the day before yesterday, when we were returning from London after a day's Christmas shopping. It was " Cattle Show Week ", the annual orgie of the country farmer in London, and our carriage was crammed with a jovial crew of Berkshire farmers, their wives and children, laden with toys for the children left at home. They all came from two primitive little villages about five miles from here, and when we parted at Didcot we had invitations to visit them all and see their houses—no one apparently lives in anything later than Elizabeth, and they feed their pigs out of Staffordshire slipware dishes and chop wood in the woodshed on Jacobean stools with carved legs —at least that is what I gathered, in the course of the journey. This country really gets older and more primitive the longer one lives in it, and the Berkshire farmers are, in a sense, a race apart—prosperous, well-to-do, living a jolly life, but among themselves, and intermarrying among themselves and keeping up their old habits and customs.

'I wonder if you ever read *The Scouring of the White Horse* by T. Hughes, the *Tom Brown* man ? It was written, I suppose, about fifty years ago, and gives, in a small way, a rather faithful picture of life in these parts—as it is now, because of course here fifty years amounts to just nothing at all.

'I was calling lately on a farmer in a neighbouring village, and I asked him about a certain house supposed to be

[1] This in reference to a dedication by Sir A. Quiller-Couch to Mr. Purves.

haunted—we have lots of haunted houses about here. He said he wanted to investigate the legend himself, so he went to the oldest inhabitant, but found him scornfully contemptuous. " Ghostesses ? " said he, " I don't hold with no ghostesses. Cos why ? Lookee here. If so be as they've gone to the *right* place, they don't want to come back ; and if so be as they've gone to the *wrong* place, whoy, damme, they won't *lat* un." Probably a chestnut, but he said that was what the old fellow said.

' When we went to Newbury Fair a month or two ago —and a very jolly fair it was—I went to see a very beautiful old house which is now after many vicissitudes in the hands of a furniture dealer. (It is right on the " Bath Road ", so they get a lot of motor-car custom.) He showed me an old room they had recently reopened ; it had become unpopular and been bricked up because a certain highwayman had hanged himself there in the eighteenth century and seemed unwilling to quit the scene altogether. The staple he hanged himself from is still there all right. The house had a secret chamber, or " Priest's " Room, as well, but I preferred the Highwayman's room, it was practically untouched since the incident, and much more " grooly ".

' We have a house near here where, on one night in the year, an old woman knocks at the front door, and on being admitted walks quietly upstairs and disappears. They always let her in all right. They don't mind. When a thing has been going on for a thousand years or so you begin to get used to it. I wish we had something of the sort at Boham's, but though we're old, I'm afraid we're not " classy " enough, the house being a simple one of the farmer type.

' I hope you continue to have good accounts of Jack. At any rate he is in " Christmas Country ", as one always regards Germany somehow, and that is a sort of consolation for his absence.

' Well—I must bring this rambling screed to a close. You know all our good wishes and best thoughts are with you,

you fellow citizens of Fowey, which is " no mean city ", and perhaps some future Christmas we will have a private joint-stock lobster-pot of our very own, and haul it up and eat the proceeds thereof on Christmas Day.

> ' Yours most truly,
> ' KENNETH GRAHAME '

> ' Boham's,
> ' Blewbury, Didcot,
> ' Berkshire,
> ' 24th January 1914

' DEAR PURVES,—That was a truly noble volume that you were so very kind as to send me this Christmas, and thank you ever so much for it.   It is a remarkable book—I never possessed a copy of it before—I read it, I suppose, before I was twenty and never since—when it arrived I began turning the pages over and found myself insensibly immersed in it for the rest of the evening.   That's just it, I suppose—it's pre-eminently *readable*—and that's a spell many writers would give a thousand pounds to discover. Perhaps it's the only thing that really matters.

' The holidays are just over, and we are in a state of unnatural peace and calm.   The day before yesterday I took Mouse up to town, had him " vetted " by the dentist, filled him up with a solid British Luncheon at Simpson's in the Strand, and fired him off by train along with two carriage-fulls of comrades in misfortune all adorned with a somewhat forced gaiety.   Boys don't like going back this term, because it's the dullest of the three, and there is nothing particular to look forward to, and Christmas holidays mean many domestic joys and much home comfort, after which school looks a little bare and blank.

' The portrait of P.M. that you sent with the book was much admired by everyone here.   He is a credit to the lot of us.

' We are rejoiced to hear that you are really so very much better in health.   This must make your whole outlook upon things very different.   But you must take life a bit easy.

" Rundownedness " is quite a specific complaint, and a bad one ; and it's apt to be the patient's own fault too.

' This is only a brief and very belated note to thank you warmly, which I do once more, for your kind and much-appreciated present.

' With all regards, and every good wish for the year now fairly launched.

' Yours very sincerely,
' KENNETH GRAHAME '

' Boham's,
' Blewbury, Didcot,
' Berkshire, England,
' 18th Feb. 1915

' DEAR PURVES,—We have been genuinely distressed at learning from your recent letters of the very poor time you have been having in the matter of health, and can only hope that the slightly more cheerful note in Mrs. Purves's postscript is still justified. And then on the top of it you had business troubles and worries—it all seems very hard. Well, one can only remember that troubles mostly pass, sooner or later, and that, when one has sailed into smooth water again, perhaps the pleasant harbour and its sunny shores look more smiling and peaceful on account of the breakers left behind.

' We very deeply appreciate all the kind and sympathetic things you say about our position in this appalling war. I was pretty sure how you both would feel about it, but your kind words made pleasant reading. Your people may feel sure, that their many manifestations of sympathy—and by this I mean both *instinctive* sympathy and *reasoned* sympathy, for there have been many evidences of both—sink deep here, and will not be forgotten. The English are taciturn and ungushing—also their papers often say foolish and tactless things—but they remember all right.

' It is strange, isn't it, and also most puzzling, how a great and prosperous nation can pour out its blood and treasure simply for the privilege of being Slaves—and of Enslaving ?

' Our little village has played up well, sending some seventy men out of a total population of less than 500 souls. I think there has been a certain amount of nonsense talked about the recruiting. From all I have seen I should say that men have come in splendidly—and are still coming in ; and good stuff too. We missed getting down to Fowey for a few weeks after Christmas as I had counted on doing, so I'm not in a position to give you any gossip from Town Quay, for though I've heard from Q. once or twice, on business, he was quite silent as to local affairs, except as to recruiting, which had been taking up all his time. So you probably know more about the place than I do, for you see a local paper and I don't. Also I don't go into Oxford as of old. One misses the boys, and it's sad to see the river deserted, and have nobody playing the garden-ass or the giddy-goat. Oxford has played up well and no mistake.

' In London, when we run up for the day, things seem to me to be going on very much as usual. Of course we are not there at night, when things may be quieter than of old, but during the day it seems as busy and bustling as ever. I generally go to some sort of afternoon performance, and it is exceedingly difficult to obtain seats.

' The " veterans " of Blewbury have started a Volunteer Defence Corp, and we drill, in the evenings, in a beautiful great timber-framed thatched barn—like my own, only three times as big. The rats run in and out of the thatch along the rafters, and the barn cat, who ought to be attending to them, sits on wheat sacks and reviews us with great delight. He is having the time of his life, for he thinks that these drills are specially got up for him, to brighten the monotony of his long dull evenings. The corps have elected me their Commanding Officer—the cat concurring—because they said I was the most martial-looking of the crowd, and there I agree with them ; they were careful to add, however, that it wasn't for any other reason whatever, and that also I can fully understand.

' E. keeps pretty well.

' In normal times we should now run away somewhere where it was dry and sunny, with a cheerful restaurant or two in the foreground ; as it is we have to stay at home and talk about the places we would have gone to if we could.

' I hope the boys are all flourishing and doing well in their respective pursuits and careers. P.M. will, I suppose, be careering schoolwards daily, and fairy tales are laid aside for facts. We also wish to be warmly remembered to Jerry, who would really weep if he knew how long it was since I saw a lobster, and we are of course anticipating a really better account of yourself, for your case is one that has always responded most hopefully to a complete rest, which is what you talk of trying, and which, after all, is a cure for nine maladies out of ten.

' Mrs. Purves, I note, keeps up her indomitable spirits, which are worth exactly £1,000,000 a year.

' Yours most sincerely,
' KENNETH GRAHAME '

Mr. Purves died shortly after this last letter was posted.

CHAPTER XIV

FOLLOWING THE SUN (PART I)

THERE was no true comparison of course for, to Kenneth Grahame, Cornwall was the place, the only place, whither the jaded went when weariest. Cornwall was as certain as Heaven was certain when a man was weary of earth.

But at intervals he wanted that ' Old Master ', the sun —wanted ' beggars, fleas and vines '. And he went to Italy for all four of them. And of the sun he wrote :

' *Solis et artis opus :* thus smiled the friendly legend from the dial upon me sitting among the vines hard by the swift Rhone ; and there was something cheery in the text, no less than in the feel of the warm sun striking hard between my shoulder-blades. For a month past I had been impaled on an Alpine peak ; set hip to haunch, too, with an athletic, unperceptive humanity, the male part of it mostly in orders ; hounded about by guides with the eyes of wolves ; and insulted by blatant boards in advertisement of " Lawn-tennis ground and English Chapel ". And it was but now, as I sprawled in flowers, that I began to realize how the mind may starve and pine in glacial surroundings. Poet and novelist alike are wont to insist on the superiority of nature in a large-paper copy, with a plenitude of margin, totally uncut, and the merest dribble of text. They think small things of you if they catch you stretching in soft grass, with the dumpy duodecimo you are so fond of— the little fat book crammed full of human life, a Rabelaisian chuckle oozing from its every well-thumbed page. Yet Nature is capable of brutalities, as well as man ; and in her excessiveness, be it in volcano, glacier, earthquake, or whelm of snow, she must—if we are to look facts in the

249

face—be evened with the colliery, the leprosy of suburban brickfields, the devastating network which the railway-spider ejects abroad.

' " There is surely," saith Sir Thomas (of Norwich), " a piece of divinity within us ; something that was before the elements, and owes no homage to the sun." We have all of us far too good an opinion of ourselves to deny the pleasing impeachment. And yet, after fully allowing for the divinity, we are conscious of a residuum of very solid stuff, that must needs look thankfully to the sun as very master and lord. *Solis et artis opus :* 'tis the work of solar heat and Nature's fashioning thumb, and it will ever throb sympathetic to anything that, like itself, is of Art and Him ; to anything the effect of him St. Francis hailed as Brother Sun. Nay, it is frankly glad to lay by its divine element and own its debt to the old maker that draws out us funguses in this damp alluvial under-world, and ripens us till we rejoice to be alive. For, like Hesperus, he also bringeth all good things : as I realized when, in strolling through the little town, sweating and happy, I chanced upon a real cat. True, she fled my approach on the wings of terror. Still, she was no vision, but good honest cat. In the courtyard of the hotel, a grave old mastiff bitch smiled permissively, while the children lugged forth her puppies one by one, and the merry brood of younglings tumbled in the dust together, two-legs claiming no vantage over four-legs. And later, when the bedroom candle flickered timorously down the passage—was there not, in yonder painted chamber, the most authentic and the most bloody among ghosts ? Aloft there, these several elements had not been. Cats may have their failings, but they are not born fools, and before those icy altitudes they prefer a level where the mellow shine, as it soaks into their fur, recalls a happy past to them, and they behold themselves walking divine in Egypt, duly worshipped as they should ever be. And as for ghosts, what self-respecting spook could put up with the ceaseless clumping of nailed

boots, at one in the morning ?   Along a corridor that should
rightly—at that hour—have been all his own ?   Even the
poor human worm had been used to turn in his sheets, and
sleepily damn the clumpers ere he snored again ; and, a
sensitive spectre in his place had been driven wild.   It was
annoying to reflect that all the while I had gone lingering
on above the snow-line in the futile expectancy of getting,
somehow, " braced ", the sun was saving up these genial
comrades for me here !

'We forget too much that, like all good fellows, he is
essentially responsive.   Treat him well, and he will treat
you well.   Consequently, we abuse him for nine months of
the year as an absentee, and the three others we challenge
him with umbrellas and straw hats, insult him with statistics
in *The Times*, accuse him of unnatural alliances with gipsy
comets : behave, in fact, as if this sober-sided and steady-
going director of our very limited company were himself of
the race of these same bushy-pated eccentrics, and portended
woe ! Now, if we would only meet him half-way : if we
would treat him to sun-dials, loggias, patios ; dot our
Regent Street pavement with little green tables ; stud our
walls with bits of Robbia's craft so apt and strange, he,
being our brother and our helper, would call more regularly
than he does, and stay a little longer every time.   Truly,
here, as everywhere, we persist in the shy British mistake
of leaving all the overtures to the other party.   As I sat
there, the old fellow was silently at work on a masterpiece
of his, in an environing wilderness of clustered grapes.
They on their part were imbibing and storing his every
particle : so that in each fast-mellowing globule a tricksy
spirit was making ready some day to spread his filmy wings,
and flash through the brain of man, kindling as he went
—what high thoughts, what passions, what poems yet
undreamed ?   The potentiality of the place was overpowering.   Was it not by sun-gendered sprites of just such a
nativity that our own rare Herrick was finely touched to
his fine issues ?   And might not this vine-clad slope be

the cradle of a thought that should create an epoch ?   If
it should hap, His were the gift, and His the glory !   The
great poet, singer, artist, our master, ever original and ever
new, whose cult and whose system shall not have their day
nor cease to be ! '

Kenneth began these southern truancies when quite a
young man and he saw Rome in the days of the *contadini*
and when, in the Piazza di Spagna, still lingered some of
the characteristics that Shelley knew.   Still on the Spanish
Steps were to be seen the *ciociari* and *ciociare*—the models
who, loafing picturesquely, waited some Angelo who might
hire them and meanwhile ogled English tourists and sold
them gay flowers of all colours.   A trove of one of these
early Italian visits is a plaque, a blue-and-white della Robbia,
a Madonna and child, picked up in Tuscany to be treasured
for years and to have a final resting-place between the
windows on the outside wall of 5 Kensington Crescent.
There it still is, unless the house has been pulled down
since last I passed by.   It was an aesthetic joy to Kenneth
and a source of displeasure to Sarah Bath who came of
chapel folk.

In post-war years Kenneth Grahame's chief concern in
Rome was to find unorthodox places wherein to eat and,
afterwards, to wander among palaces and churches hoping
ever that in the firmament of Rome some new and exquisite
shooting-star might, on his turning an unfamiliar corner,
disclose itself to him in the vaulting shape of a hitherto
unknown fountain.

For he loved running water, from a yard of pump splashing into a horse trough to a ton of sparkling Thames tipping
into Whitchurch weir pool, and he could truly say : ' Water
first of Singers ', or

> ' Water brown, water bright—
>   Pearls and swirls that sever ;
> Running water's my delight
>   Always and for ever ;

> Let it from the chalk go peep,
> Let it from the limestone leap,
> Let it off the granite steep
>   Pour, or from the mill be ;
> Sunshine's daughter,
> Running water
>   Was and ever will be.'

But fountain water was the best of all especially if it
ran to the expression of a rare fancy in chaste and chiselled
stone and leapt, in Roman sunlight, against some inspired
background. Then was he enchanted indeed. And, best
of all the lyrics in marble, he loved the delicate and jocund
grace of the Fountain of the Tortoises—the Fontana delle
Tartarughe. Its frivolous jets, its sponsoring tortoises (to
whom bare, bronze youths for ever give ' leg-ups ' into the
brimming basins) delighted the eternal boy in him. He
loved too *The Barcaccia*—the boat that Father Tiber bore
to the foot of the Spanish steps on the waters of the great
flood of 1598. Pietro Bernini translated that shallop into
stone and, into it and out of it, runs the Trevi water—the
best water in the world ; (so men say who know not, of
an August day, the small fern-fringed spring that bubbles
out of the granite on the high, purple rigging of Battock
in Angus).

There was also the Fontana di Trevi concerning which
there is a legend fostered by the romantic (and also by the
Municipal Authorities who periodically shut off the water
to cleanse the basin). The legend is that those who leave
Rome and who desire to return to her must throw a coin
into the basin by moonlight and over the left shoulder.
And by moonlight Kenneth Grahame would sometimes, of
his good nature, accompany a party of pretty American
girls who desired to throw their dimes into the water and
be sure of a trip to Europe next fall. He would sit, a silent
figure, in that shallow amphitheatre of stone which sweeps
about the fountain, lulled by the cool splash of it, by the
semi-silence of the night, and by the intonations of the
nymphs.

Another fountain that ' kept still the poet's dream ' was that system of four that have, since time began, perpetually played in the great square of Peter. It is said, I know not on whose authority, that the Kaiser, after attending a Papal Function at St. Peter's, paused without to inspect his guard of honour. This duty accomplished, he waved an imperial hand towards the sparkling and immutable four and he said, ' And *now* they may turn the water off.'

Kenneth Grahame met most of the eminent archaeologists of Rome and, learning of them, became an excellent guide to the more unusual sights of the city. Miss Beatrice Harraden has said that he seemed ' to be able to make the past and the present known to his companion without appearing to transfer the information from himself to the one benefited '.

But Rome, to him, was not entirely the place of fountains, quaint eating-houses and the grandeur of the Past. He was wondrous fond of toys and sweets ; the marrons-glacés of ' The Golden Gate ' were never to be passed by unbought, and it was a serious sorrow that he was rarely in Rome during the hot weather, during the delicious season of the cream and the water ice. There were, however, for consolation, the vendors of paper-butterflies and of floating-geese, the latter artfully launched in the basin of the Medici fountain, the former fluttered in the air (oh, but alive) by the magician who dealt in them until they were transferred from his skilled fingers to the hot and chubby paws of small purchasers. Whereupon the bobbing geese (they were never ducks) and the tremulous butterflies became, to the woeful disappointment of the cherubs who had parted with their pocket money, as devoid of animation as a tinned tongue.

When in Rome he lived at the Hotel des Princes in the Piazza di Spagna, the centre of English life in Rome since the days when travellers, who did the ' grand tour ', used to park their carriages in the square. He loved the sunshine on the Spanish Steps, a ' song in stone ' he called them, even when unadorned by the baskets of the flower-

sellers and the colour and fragrance of rose and violet, lily
and carnation. He would climb to the top notes of the
song and find there the Trinità de' Monti and the Pincio.
And he would sit and see sometimes the glory of Rome,
but more often would he watch the swans in the little toy
lake below the water Clock playing ' up tails all ' just as
did the swans below the bridge at Whitchurch.

Among the restaurants that he was happiest in and
whither he took the friends he wished to entertain, was
the Ritrovo dei Poeti—the Meeting Place of the Poets.
Wandering in the flower market he found the little wine-
shop whose lintel bore this intriguing title. He entered
and found the place to be as good as its word. Although
partly filled with capacious market women greasily eating
macaroni and washing it down with tumblers of raw red
wine, there sat apart, sipping, sipping, a company of a
picturesque and even a romantic appearance. A group
they were of dark young men with unkempt locks and
blue or bristly chins. They wore floppy ties and wide
sombrero hats ; so like the Café Royalists of Regent Street
were they that Kenneth began to fumble for the half-crown
that one or other would, recognizing him, forthwith borrow.
They were quite obviously poets.

But to be certain he inquired of the market women.
These daughters of Flora laughed loudly and derisively.
' Poets ? ' they cried ' *Dios*, no indeed, they are a party
of Neapolitan umbrella-menders—if he looks outside the
Signore will see their bundles and their baskets upon the
steps.' And so it was. But Kenneth, anxious that the
Ritrovo dei Poeti should be justified in its name, invited
to lunch with him there, a real poet, the American
Ambassador, Robert Underwood Johnson, and, himself to
make a second (it takes two poets to make a Ritrovo), the
thing was, for all time, accomplished. And the red Gensano
wine was pronounced, by both bards, to be admirable.

He would haunt also the Ristorante Concordia and eat
fettuccini Concordia—the flat macaroni which is the attrac-

18

tion of the place. He found his host there to be an ex-
Garibaldino and that the restaurant cats were friendly and
sociable. There was also the restaurant run by Russian
refugees where a Russian Princess, in diamond earrings,
made the omelette which an Archduke served to you. And
when you asked for the bill you were begged not to mention
it. So you dropped what you thought was right into an
earthenware pot and went out into a squalid street where
socialists and soldiers continually shot at each other.

Kenneth Grahame took small part in the social activities
of Rome ; he was a lion who had little wish to be lionized.
Yearly, it is said, towards the end of their stay, Mrs. Grahame
would lead her husband to a table covered with visiting-
cards and suggest that some of the calls might be returned.
Yearly he would answer, ' I have no cards with me. Have
you ? ' ' No.' ' Then let's leave it over till next year.'
And that was the end of that.

But in spite of this aloofness, he had one friend in Rome
whom he visited again and again, and that was the Bambino
—the sacred Bambino, the miracle-wrought, the miracle-
working, Babe of the Ara Cœli. (Now did not St. Luke's
self return from Paradise, as lately as in medieval times,
to paint that little face so finely sculptured in the sacred
olive wood by another saint, temporarily restored to earth
for that very purpose ? Why, of course, yes.)

The Bambino (' that good little fellow ', Kenneth Grahame
would affectionately name him) is just the size of a real
infant. He lives in a crystal case sunk behind the High
Altar. There He stays save when He is brought out to
be seen by His adorers or to heal the sick. For as a curer
of illness the ' good little fellow ' is *facile princeps*. Accompanied by three priests, He will go in His carriage-and-
four to attend the houses of sick people, to lie, for a moment,
beside the sufferer and so downstairs again to be driven
home to His Church of the Ara Cœli by His respectful
ministers. His head is crowned with the tiara given Him
by the Canons of St. Peter's. His dress blazes with gems ;

His little person drips with gleaming chains of pearls and emeralds and blood-red rubies. Upon His wrist winks, in brilliants, the most adorable little diamond wrist-watch. At His feet lie His letters which reach Him from all parts, letters from the sorrowful who beseech Him for a miracle, letters from the grateful who rejoice that a miracle has been done.

There was once a wicked countess who coveted the Bambino for her very own. So she caused a facsimile to be made of Him in secret. She then feigned a sickness and implored a visit from the Holy Child who, with His gorgeous attendants, duly arrived at the palace of the wicked one. Then when the Babe lay, as prescribed, upon the bed, the priests, on the plea of the ' patient's ' sudden and desperate illness, were pursuaded to step into the ante-room. In a moment the change was made.

Anon the holy men drove home in the golden carriage-and-four. But it was the toy, the gemmed simulacrum, who sat facing them on the front seat.

In the middle of that night there was some one who sobbed bitterly outside the great door of the Church of the Ara Cœli. The sleepy vergers at last heard and, *clank*, *clank*, they turned their big keys, they threw open the heavy doors. There, in the cold white moonlight, stood a little jewelled figure, the exquisite little form of the True and Heavenly Bambino, crying ever so bitterly and beseeching, His little hands outstretched, to be restored to His own.

But what became of the kidnapping countess I do not know and perhaps it does not matter. For has not Kenneth Grahame personally said that in all the best stories there is naught except essentials ? But the Bambino was his friend and, upon his writing-desk at Pangbourne, still stands, where it has always stood, a beautiful likeness of the ' good little fellow ' who was at Kenneth Grahame's elbow until the end.

In Rome, in 1921, the American Ambassador, Mr. R. U.

Johnson, asked him, ' Will you not let your mind play
about the subject of Keats and write a five-minute tribute
to him for the centenary of his death which will occur on
the twenty-fourth of February ? You can readily find
some special topic, such as Nature in Keats's poetry—anything that strikes you in thinking of him. We are relying
on Sir Rennell Rodd and yourself to represent England in
the Anglo-American celebration of this poignant event.'

The answer was in the affirmative and the talk was
delivered. The actual speech I cannot find. But its gist
said how easily John Keats might have heard his nightingales
on the rural heights and twilit copses of the hamlet that,
in those days, his native Hampstead remained. As ' a
tribute ' it was a great success and the speaker, preserving
strictly his time limit, caused his audience to ask for more.
Thus it happened that the English Ambassador, Sir Rennell
Rodd (now Lord Rennell), addresses : ' Dear Sir (*sic*)
Kenneth Grahame ' and induces him, knight or no knight,
to deliver ' a discourse or a lecture or a reading ' at the
Keats–Shelley Literary Association. Of this I am fortunate
in having the MS. Its title is ' Ideals ' and its readers may
decide for themselves which of Sir Rennell's three alterna-
tives it exactly represents :

' Among the various instincts which govern this poor
human nature of ours, in its affairs of social converse, I
suppose one of the very strongest is the passion—for in
some cases it really amounts to a passion—for imparting
information to other people.

' So very violent is this morbid craving, so universal, so
unsparing of either age or sex, whether of the imparter or
the impartee, that it is difficult to say what might not
become of a world in which it should succeed in obtaining
the mastery—what attempts at mutual extinction, what
bloodshed, might not eventually ensue. Fortunately the
race is gifted with another powerful instinct, another passion
almost equally overmastering—the sullen dislike we all feel
for being fed with facts, our dogged determination not to

be made the vessels for their storage, the demand we all automatically make that they shall be instantly taken away and dumped—if they *must* be dumped—on somebody else.

' This instinctive repulsion of ours seems to apply, strangely enough, to facts alone, to the things that really are and that really matter, and not at all to the things that really aren't and that really don't matter. For it is undeniable that we will listen long and listen gladly to any quantity of fiction—and not necessarily first-class fiction either. Poetry, too, we can stand—at least some of us—to almost any extent ; and neither poetry nor fiction need be new and unfamiliar. Indeed we have usually a special welcome for old friends. The one thing we do not want, apparently, is truth—truth in the guise of solid facts and figures. Almost any fiction will do, so long as it is really fiction. To speak out quite honestly, we like jolly lies and plenty of them.

' Many thoughtful persons have doubtless ere now noticed, and perhaps deplored, the existence of those two rival passions ; and philosophers will have recognized that the second of these—the revolt against information—is, after all, merely one of those sound instincts by which the human race defends itself against possible extermination—that it is a sort of moral phagocyte. For our purposes to-day, however, it will suffice if we content ourselves with the simple reason, that we dislike facts so much because they insist on taking up the place and the time of other things that we like better.

' This aversion from the acquiring of exact information is most glaringly evident in the case of the very young ; but perhaps this is only because it is on their hapless heads that the information-hose discharges its stream of contents with the greatest force, directness and continuity, and because they are weak and defenceless, and also less skilled and subtle than we are in evading it. Children as such, indeed, do not reject the acquiring of facts as such, in anything like the same degree as we fact-weary ones of larger growth—as any of us well knows who has been cornered suddenly by some child of seven who has acquired a mastery of, let us say, All the Flags of All the Nations, and insists on telling us them. As a matter of fact, children are far more patient, far more receptive, than we, under the sousing, pitiless hose of information. Indeed, curiosity being the main motive-power of a child's mind, the passionate need for knowing the how and the why of everything will often drive him to acquire laboriously such a mass of facts on one subject or another as should put us elders to shame—which it frequently does. No, the child has no such strong distaste, as we others have, for information in itself, but there are moments when even he rebels ; and the reason for his attitude must be sought elsewhere.

' I suppose that the most obtuse, the most conventional of schoolmasters, finding Smith Minor's receptive faculties tightly closed against information on the subject of, say, Greek grammar, is not such a fool as to suppose, either that he is wilfully obdurate (which is indeed unlikely, Smith being quite ignorant of the subject and therefore without prejudice or prepossessions, for or against), or that Smith's mind is an empty chamber, free of all furnishing, the door of which merely sticks and refuses to open. No, he knows his Smith too well for that. The trouble to the master is, that he knows Smith's mind to be fully occupied already. As he puts it himself, the boy, just when he ought to be attending, is always thinking of something else.

' That, M'lud, is my client's case. Smith is thinking about something else. And about something far rarer and braver, we may be quite sure, than even the most irregular of verbs.

' Of course Smith's mind may be unworthily occupied— with cricket averages for instance ; but this is not so usual as is commonly supposed. Away from the actual games themselves, a boy's mind is by no means so taken up with them as some of his depictors would have us believe. What, then, *is* he thinking about ?

' We may adopt the Socratic method of inquiry, and

begin by asking ourselves what he is *not* thinking about. Well, of course he is not thinking about his work ; we have agreed as to that already. Nor is he thinking about his indifference to work, his consequent place in his form, and whether the Governor will jaw him and make him swot during the holidays ; for these would be obvious thoughts, and dear Smith never wastes the precious hours of class-time in thinking of the obvious. Neither—when we proceed to judge him by our baser selves—is he likely to be thinking about women, for instance, their merits and demerits ; because he knows nothing whatever about them, and what's more, he doesn't want to. For the same excellent and sufficing reason, he is not thinking about the various methods, honest or otherwise, of making money. No ; in place of occupying itself with all these things, that seem so natural to us, his mind is up and away, in a far, far better world than this, a world wherein matters are conducted as they should be, and where he is undoubtedly the best man there and is being given a fair chance at last. He is, in fact, pursuing his ideals, and his mind is fully occupied with them. If the real had anything half so fine to offer him, the real would doubtless get its chance with him ; but, as we all know, it hasn't.

'But now I seem to hear the objection, that I have deceived you, that I have let you down. At the mention of ideals, you looked for me to trace and follow some of those rare and passionate visions which have taken our great ones by the hand and led them from crag to crag, from height on to further height, till they have reached Olympus itself and brought back to level earth some of its sacred fire. And instead of this I am offering you, it would seem, the wayward, self-indulgent daydreams of an unconcentrated and purposeless boy—dreams he will grow out of or will shake off when the time for action is at hand—dreams which are no help to his self-development, but a real hindrance. Ah, but can we, dare we, attempt to draw a strict dividing line between the wayward dream and the high purposeful ideal, to pronounce exactly where one leaves off and the other begins? Is it not indeed of the essence of both, that we are carried away by them into an intenser, finer, clearer atmosphere than this earth can possibly offer? Most of such visions, it is true, come to nothing; only a very, very few achieve actual concrete results. But this is only because actual artists, shapers, makers, are scarce, while dreamers are many. It is no disparagement of the dreams themselves that only a very few of the dreamers have the power, or rather the gift, to harness their dreams with mastery and bend them to their imperious will.

'And when we are tempted to speak somewhat contemptuously of the wayward fancies of a boy, let us ask ourselves seriously whether we ever entirely lay aside this habit of mind; whether we do not all of us, to the last, take refuge at times from the rubs and disappointments of a life where things go eternally askew, in our imaginary world where at any rate we have things for the time exactly as we want them? I hope to pursuade you that this is really so—that in each and all of us the real and ideal planes, so to speak, are co-existing and functioning constantly side by side.

'In childhood, the simplest and most usual form of ideal may be described as an image projected by the young mind on a sort of white screen of its own—the image of some*thing*, some*body*, or some*where*, which on the one hand it knows doesn't and can't exist, something frankly impossible to realize, and which it is therefore free to make as wilfully fantastic as it pleases; or on the other hand it may be a case of some thing, place, or person shortly to be seen, and of which it would fain construct a simulacrum beforehand. Of this latter class of ideals, two things may with certainty be predicted—that they will be fantastically unlike the reality when it arrives; and that they will almost certainly be far finer, nobler, and better, that is because they are ideals.

' Let us take the very simplest case we can think of—
the case, let us say, of an inland-bred child who is told
that next week he is going to the sea.   That child does not
say to himself, " Very well ; next week and not before, I
shall know all about it, about this mysterious wonder, this
thing of such divine possibilities.   Till next week, therefore,
my mind must remain a blank on the subject, my judgement must be entirely suspended."   No, he forthwith proceeds, every minute of the intervening days and almost
every minute of the nights, to project on his mental screen
images of all he fondly hopes the sea to be, of all the strange
new delights he dreams of finding there—all wildly fantastic,
all utterly unlike the real thing, and all of course far more
beautiful and bewitching than any actual sea-coast that
was ever foaled.   That is why so many children appear
to be disappointed at their first sight of the sea.   " Is this
all ? " they say.   You see, there was so much more on
their screen !

' Or take another equally simple case—the expected
arrival of some hitherto unseen relation—let us say a Grandmother.   Again the child does not say to itself, " All right,
when grandmother actually comes along, and not before, it
will be time to size her up.   Probably she will be a fair to
average grandmother.   It doesn't do to expect too much
in these days.   At any rate, I must just wait and see."
No, emphatically.   On the mental screen is immediately
thrown a fairy grandmother, unfairly and unnaturally
gifted and shaped.   That is why some children appear to
be disappointed at first sight of their grandmothers.   For
the consolation of any grandmothers who may have been
hurt by some such cool reception, may I remind them that
their only rivals were their ideal selves, and in such a contest
it is surely no shame to be worsted ?

' Of course the fantastic quality of these mental-screen
pictures that I am insisting on may be more or less so,
according to the amount of information the child may
already possess on the subject, either from oral information

or from reading. There is a good instance of this in that very popular book of a year or two ago—*The Young Visiters.* The child-author had evidently never been to London herself, but must have heard a good deal about it from others, from time to time. Much of this she probably forgot, but certain things, certain salient things, naturally stuck in her memory. Accordingly the London that her heroine reaches is mainly a compound of the Crystal Palace and the private apartments at Hampton Court, lightly tricked out with an hotel, a hansom-cab, and a policeman. It is an ideal London, of course—does it not include unlimited strawberry ices and a Prince of Wales always accessible to persons of very low extraction? And yet, though ideal, not so very fantastic a London, after all!

' The most usual form, however, which this dream-habit takes is that of the possible acquisition of personal property, in the shape of presents. Almost anything is possible in a present; and a child reaches this world so very naked of everything of its own, that with the first dawn of consciousness comes the passion for private ownership, and even an old jam-pot that is shared with none other is encircled with a halo all its own. The approach, therefore, of every Christmas Day or birthday means much wistful dream-creation of ideals that rarely materialize—could not, indeed, be materialized, many of them, outside of the *Arabian Nights.* The real things that do in fact materialize, those presents which we purchasers carry homewards at nightfall, weary of foot and dubious of mind, or smugly self-satisfied and confident, as the case may be, are sometimes, alas!—through nobody's fault, I most readily admit —very far removed from the pathetic, timid (yet greatly daring) hope of the recipient. Let us be very thankful, we elders whose duty it is to do the right thing on these occasions, that we do not know—that fortunately we can never know—the full beauty and wonder and magic of those presents we *ought* to have given!

' In such young ideals there is often a fashion, and the

fashions are apt to change from time to time. When I was a small boy, both I and most other boys of my own age and period, the mighty mid-Victorian, were wont to indulge in a day-dream of wildest audacity, to wit, that on some wonderful morning one would be awakened by the sound of a pawing and a crunching of the gravel outside, that one would spring from bed with beating heart, would fling wide the lattice-window and looking down would see on the carriage-drive a neatly attired groom holding the bridle of a peerless pony, a cream-coloured pony—it was always cream-coloured—with a long flowing tail (it always had a long flowing tail). I find, after delicate and tactful inquiry among boys of the present generation, that much the same daring dream is apt to haunt them as birthdays draw near —with a slight difference due to the change of fashion mentioned above. They too hope to be awakened by that same crunching of gravel outside ; they too expect to spring delightedly from bed and fling the casement wide. What their enraptured eyes, however, are now to look down upon is a peerless cream-coloured motor-car with a long flowing wheel-base ; or at the very least, a snorting and quivering young motor-cycle. The visions, you see, are essentially the same ; and doubtless the latter is as rarely realized as ever the former was.

' Now you will have noticed that each of the instances I have given were taken from the fancy-realm of childhood ; deliberately so, for the reason that the child-dream is the more simple, clear-cut, and vivid. But I will now ask you to believe that these instances might nearly as effectively have been taken from the mental processes of one of ourselves. It is true, that for *us* mystery and awe and wonder spring up no more at the mention of sea or lake or great mountains ; but which of us, even to-day, when about to visit some new far-distant city or country, does not form, sometimes deliberately but usually almost unconsciously, a picture of it, more or less vivid, beforehand ? And do we not nearly always find in our past imaginings, when we take the trouble to refer back to them, just those two touchstones of the ideal—a fantastic unlikeness to the real thing, together with a special beauty nowhere to be actually found? I suppose that all of us here can remember our coming to Rome for the first time in our lives, and the preconception of the place that we brought along with us. Do we not all remember, when we reached Rome at last, the same two things—the absence of that strangeness which I have called the fantastic element and which somehow we cannot keep out of our imaginings, and secondly, the slight touch of disappointment that even the beauty of Rome was not just that particular beauty that we had caught a glimpse of through the magic casement of our idealism?

'To pass to the next of my simple instances—the occasional (only occasional), slight disappointment of the child at first sight of the long-expected relative. Of course by this time *we* are well aware of the superlative and abiding charm of our grandmothers; or else we have learnt by sad experience not to expect very much from any of our relations. But indeed this instinctive craving for a finer type of humanity than we actually find around us is the most widespread of all forms of idealism, and is very significant—indeed enormously significant. Some little time ago the natural explanation would have been, that in our nature, now sadly degenerate, there still lurked some sub-conscious recollection of a better age when we were to our present selves as our present selves are, say, to a marmoset. To-day we do not admit degeneracy; and therefore hold it to be but a part of the mysterious subliminal " urge " which has thrust us up from protoplasms to marmosets and such, and from them to ourselves of to-day. The fact remains, that the feeling is there, in the man and woman as in the child, and we can put this to the test at any time by examining our own feelings as regards our hero of the hour, be he statesman, soldier, poet or what not, when met in the flesh at last. Would we not nearly always—now I am asking you for great frankness and a most naked self-examination

—would we not nearly always have liked him to be—well, at least just a little different, a little finer, a little more after the pattern we could so easily have made him ourselves, if we had only been the Almighty for five minutes? Well, it is just because we are all idealists, and all paint our dream-heroes instinctively as finer than they are, that we can recall to mind so very few heroes we could not have improved upon. Indeed, I suspect that it is only popular actors who successfully pass the test, and face the daylight as confidently as the footlight.

'The Greeks, who were in a way greater idealists than we, were also idealists of a more practical sort. By this I mean that, having arrived at their ideals, they were satisfied with them, and thereupon proceeded to set them forth, to display them, nay more, to perpetuate them as the final ideal in bronze, marble, and so on. In their theology and their literature, again, still satisfied with the ideal they had arrived at, they produced the demi-god—the man made perfect as they saw perfection, very flesh of our flesh, always essential man and yet a god too, or at least a *divus*, one whom, while hailing him at times as a brother, you were also free to worship as a god—if you wanted to. Now we Northerners would never have done all these things, even if we had had the particular genius or technical skill; because *we* are never satisfied with our ideals, never reach even a temporary finality, must always be breaking our moulds, re-fusing our metal, entreating our public—which is of course the world itself—to wait a little bit longer, till we can give them the real thing at last. And meantime we give them nothing—or at least so very little! This, I think, marks the eternal difference between the South and the North; and to bear this in mind may be of some assistance to us Northern students on our way through the galleries of Rome.

'Which is the method of idealism of most benefit for the race? That of the South, which arrives, attains, achieves, and then—well, remains there satisfied, advancing no more, but yet bequeathing so great a legacy? Or that of the

North, which never arrives, achieves but little, yet knows no limit to its flight ? It is a big subject, but one we must not pursue to-day. It is enough for our purpose to realize that we are all of us, young and old alike, always (though perhaps unconsciously) on the look out for the half-gods, hoping to come upon them at last in the forms of our heroes. Only, *we*, know a little too much, while children never despair. And so the disappointment, alas, is usually the child's ; yet not always. Their standard being less rigid, they find their half-gods more easily than we do ; and I hope we have all of us enjoyed, in our time, looking on at the innocent and pretty spectacle of a child in the full tide of his hero worship.

' We come now to the last of my illustrations—the child's ideal of personal property, of those wonderful possessions which he dares to dream may possibly come his way, through the medium of some happy stroke of Fortune, of an Arab jinn suddenly emerging out of a bottle, or of a fat and elderly godfather suddenly emerging out of a train. Now it may be perfectly true, that a cream-coloured pony no longer says very much to any of *us* at our time of life. But—but—now remember, we are in the confessional to-day—but—how about that cream-coloured motor-car ? And is not that car of our dreams a Super-Rolls-Royce, and is there another one on the high roads of Europe that can compare with it for speed, for perfection of springs, for immunity from break-downs ?

' Then again, there are some men to whom I should much like to put this question privately, as soon as I knew them well enough—at about what period of your life—was it when you were, say, 30, or 40, or 50—that you sadly but finally laid aside that vision of the ideal steam yacht—the wonderful vessel in which you were wont to visit all the ports and harbours of the world, to lie off tropical islands or breast the long Atlantic rollers, all on the same evening, over the last pipe or even when snugly in bed ? But perhaps you have never really laid up your steam yacht, you

still stick to it through thick and thin, and you always mean
to ?   If so, you are fortunate indeed.   Never let it go.   It
costs nothing, it has no rivals while afloat ; but once it has
struck on the rocks of fact and foundered in deep water, it
can never be raised to the surface again.

' This class of vision, which in the case of a child I call
the dream of ownership, in adults frequently takes the form
of asking oneself what one would do, if one came unexpectedly into a large fortune ?   I mean how would one
spend the money thus happily and easily acquired ?   I do
not suppose there is any one who has not played with this
dream at one time or another, and whose dream has not
been composed, as usual, of the two elements of the fantastic
and the ideally beautiful, dreams of altruism and of world-
reform.   Fantastic they do not seem to be at the time, all
those splendid larks we are planning to have ; and as to our
world-reforms, why, there would be little trouble or sorrow
left anywhere if dream-notes could be honoured on presentation.   But supposing that, once in a way, the fortune
does really happen to come along, and you find yourself at
close grips with a Banker, a Solicitor, and a Stockbroker,
seated opposite you at the same table, grimly determined
that you shall not make a fool of yourself if *they* can prevent
it—how many of your fantasies and your altruisms will
those matter-of-fact gentlemen leave you possessed of, when
they have quite done with you ?   Well, we can only hope
that, as in the old fairy tale, a few gold coins will be
left sticking to the bottom of the bushel-measure, and
that so your idealism may not have been altogether in
vain.

' But perhaps the most usual shape which the cream-
coloured pony assumes in grown-up dreams, is that of the
ideal house, estate, country property, always just the right
period of architecture, just the proper soil, just the correct
distance from town, and furnished, equipped, staffed and
managed, just as we, and we alone of all people, could do
the thing if we had the chance.   Now this is never an ignoble

dream, for nothing responds so generously to care, love, and expenditure, as a noble house or estate, or fastens itself so closely about the roots of the heart.　In this dream, fantasy almost disappears but beauty has fullest and finest play. Few unworthy desires find room for growth here, and one may even end a wiser and a better man after the enjoyment of a mansion only built in cloudland.　Sometimes, indeed, it is no question of ideal sky-building at all ; for the place may be in actual existence, may even be ancestral, and long known and loved as such, and passed away from us perhaps by some hard turn of fortune but be still within reach and possibly some day obtainable—and then your dream may be in truth a noble ambition, shaping and driving you towards fine ends, as all true ambitions must.

' This contemplation of the ideal house, the house of our secret dreams, leads us by a natural step to the subject of the dream-city, the City Celestial or the New Jerusalem as dreamers of old time were wont to call it ; and here we find ourselves at once on a wider platform, and on firmer and surer ground—if one may use such terms of dream-architecture reared in cloudland.　For here the child rarely busies himself.　The subject is too ambitious for him, and he generally knows but one town familiarly, if that.　The grown man on the other hand, and the grown mind—indeed the best and rarest minds of each generation—have never been ashamed to occupy themselves constantly and openly with this game of ideal-town-planning.　To our forefathers, as I was saying, the New Jerusalem remained really visionary, literally in Cloud-land ; and it is of such a Celestial City that we get occasional glimpses and flashes in the writings of such poets as Crashaw, for instance.　But in the early sixteenth century we have Sir Thomas More, the keenest and most penetrating mind of his age, devoting a whole book to the working out of the practical details of such an ideal city as might be given actual earthly shape and form forthwith, if Tudor Statesmen would only have the necessary moral courage and vision for the task—for you will remember that the governance of the rest of the island of Utopia is based on that of the capital city, and shaped and directed from it. Again, in the pleasant prose romances of William Morris, there is nearly always an ideal city, of which not only are all the details given with almost wearisome particularity, but sometimes we are supplied with an actual plan, with (I think) points of the compass and a scale. This is doing the thing properly, for if a real city calls for such guidance, how much more an ideal one? Camelot was another ideal city, and Tennyson once at least turns aside from the incidents he calls his Idylls, to draw a vivid picture of the city of magic that Merlin built for Arthur. But you can all remember instances for yourselves; my point is merely that we need not be ashamed of dreaming on from our ideal house to our ideal city, when we find ourselves dreaming in such good company.

' But may not the dream habit be a possible hindrance to the practical side of life? This is a fair question, and a serious one, because it is the most dangerous thing in the world to affect to despise or ignore the so-called practical side of life—in other words life itself, as it has got to be lived. The answer is, of course, that there are no two sides to life. Life is not like the Public School of to-day, with its classical and modern " side ", and you choose, or your father chooses for you, probably wrong in either case, which side you had best " go on ", as their jargon has it. Life has only one side to it, and can only be lived in one way; but, as we all know, that way demands constant re-actions and recuperations. Accordingly, from time to time we go to the hill-tops, or to sea-coasts, or into retreats, or we (some of us) go on the spree, as it is vaguely but pleasantly called. It is all the same—all re-action in one form or another. Well, dreams are but re-action from life, and the easiest, the most accessible form of healing re-action that there is. For your hill-top may disappoint you, and your sea-coast be too stuffy or too expensive, but the mountain air of dreamland is always recuperating, and there Apollo

19

and all the Muses, or at least Pan and his attendant Fauna, await you.

' What, then, is the conclusion of the whole matter ? Is it not that we are all idealists, whether we would or no ? And that we are all idealists, chiefly by virtue of our waking dreams, those very imaginings which we are so ashamed of, and so reluctant to speak about, which we sternly discourage in others, but which all the same we secretly cherish to the very end ? For in these dreams we are always better than ourselves, and the world is always better than it is, and surely it is by seeing things as better than they are that one arrives at making them better. This indeed is what " vision " means, and one knows that " without vision the people perish ". Not—stay as they are ; not even—go backwards. But—perish, from the anæmia of no ideals.

' But now you may say again, as at the beginning, that I am playing you false ; for I was asked to try and entertain you, and here I am almost preaching—the favourite vice of English writers. Why should I talk, you may fairly say, about making the world better, instead of frankly claiming that dreaming and idealizing are in themselves the most delightful pursuit in the world, far surpassing even the shooting of big game in Africa so invariably resorted to by disappointed heroes of lady-novelists ? Why not simply urge that ideals should be resolutely pursued for their own sake, however far they may lead us up into the empyrean of thought, and quite regardless of whether they may finally result in actual achievement in terms of this world's work ? Well, that is a perfectly fair objection ; for, after all, possibly the present world is neither very much better nor very much worse than it has always been, and possibly never will be. But I would submit that after all it comes to very much the same thing, whether we think of ultimate consequences to the world or not. For if we are perfectly honest with our-selves, we must admit that we always do the thing that we really like doing, for the sake of the doing itself. If in addition we achieve something definite, so much the better,

for ourselves and for the world.   If not—and it is not given
to every one to achieve—at least we shall have had our
ideals.'

Perhaps, to talk of ideals, the post-war Rome that Kenneth
Grahame knew in his later years was not the ideal Rome.
It had lost its old charm without yet acquiring the modern
order and grandeur of open spaces and new forums, mount-
ing into the sunlight, which Fascism has brought about to-
day.   Yet I think (though no record remains) that the child
who once declaimed Macaulay to the windy pines of Windsor
missed little in the Land of the Lays that would please him
—neither the lower reaches of Tiber, down to Ostia, the
forests of fir and pine beside the sea, the lakes of Bracciano
and Nemi, nor the still waters of ' reedy Trasimene '.

CHAPTER XV

FOLLOWING THE SUN (PART II)

IN the ledger wherein Kenneth Grahame, when young, wrote
down his youthful thoughts and verses there is occasionally
a quotation. Among the latter I find this one from his
Horace :

> 'Solvitur acris hiemps grata vice veris et Favoni,
>   trahuntque siccas machinae carinas ; '

which he translates, rather roughly, thus :

> 'Gone are the snows and April come is she
> The West wind blows and, down loud beaches, we
> Once more our prows propel to their blue sea.'

No doubt the *Mary Ellen* was in his thoughts when he
wrote and yet it may not have been so ? He may have
had in mind some of the blind unreason of his ' wayfarers '
for ' lands that are warmed by another sun ' (*not* the Cornish
one), he may have been dreaming of shores where the young
Persephone arrives soon after Christmas.

Anyhow, as soon as he parted from the Old Lady and
her exacting service, he would yearly fit four springs into
one year. A sort of solar pub-crawling, a movable feast
of flowers which, beginning in early February with a waft
of almost nuptial lemon-blossom in a Sicilian orchard, saw
secondly the wistaria at a Roman window and a dazzling
cherry-tree on the Campagna, and came thirdly to Orta
in the season of Narcissus. And so home, just when the
swifts arrive at Pangbourne and the mays and lilacs push
through in the lock-keeper's garden beyond Whitchurch
weir-pool.

It was in Tuscany that, as a youth, Kenneth first fell

in love with poetry and the South. Some relatives had a
villa among the blue hills and there he spent a holiday. It
was there that he saw first the large, mild-eyed oxen, their
horns wreathed with flowers and vines, placid yoke-mates
who drew Vergilian wagons heaped high with purple grapes.
There he saw the dark-faced, bare-footed youths tread out
the vintage in the tireless old fashion in vogue in the days
of Auster, when—

'In the vats of Luna,
This year, the must shall foam
Round the white feet of laughing girls
Whose sires have marched to Rome.'

And there he saw the fierce watch-dogs in the courtyards
eat grapes as though, said he, they were the very pards of
Bacchus. So, likewise, in Venice he was more amused than
surprised when he met three enormous mastiffs who adapting
their diet, it seemed, to their domicile ate the blades of
oars. The dogs lived in a beautiful garden in that rather
gardenless town. The garden was separated from the canal
by a broad hedge of ilex. The passing *gondolieri*, merry
souls, would playfully thrust their oars through the hedge.
Whereupon the great dogs, seizing the blades, would crunch
them up as though they did but eat biscuit.

Kenneth leaning upon his window supposed that oars
were cheap in Venice? The watermen assured him that
the amusement of three parties (themselves, the mastiffs and
el illustrissimo Signore) was cheap at any price. Once, leaning
far over from his window the better to see the tug-of-war,
he dropped his pocket-book of bank-notes and a mastiff
seized it and seemed to be about to bolt it. But, like any
Shylock, the ban-dog went behind a camelia tree and there
he buried it. And presently its rightful owner, coming
downstairs, dug it up again.

Florence is in Tuscany and in Florence are the pictures
of Fra Angelico and other godlike men of old. And, said
the dogmatic young Englishman, Italy has the noblest

artistic past in the world yet that nobility is crowned by *Il Beato Fra.*

Among the early thoughts that Kenneth has jotted into his confessional ledger I find this one : ' The smells of Italy are more characteristic than those of the South of France. A change of smells is as cheering as a change of air, cooking and custom.' This entry interests me as it shows a glimmering or germ of the truth of smells which Mr. Kipling was later to make his own in *Lichtenberg* and *Some Aspects of Travel.*

But when I think of Kenneth Grahame's attitude towards Italy I am, in spite of myself, partly reminded of John Leech's ' jowly ' little boy of the 1850's, he who when offered sixpence to say what he most admired in ' that temple of industry ', the Crystal Palace, replies without hesitation, ' veal-an'-'am pies an' the ginger-beer, give us the sixpence '.

For, again and again, crops up throughout the records that I have of his Italian wanderings, an artistic love of the table and the bin. There was, for instance, the red Gensano wine so jovially tippled at the Sign of the Ritrovo, in the Campo di Fiori, that most manly stuff which went so well with white Parmesan cheese and Mortadella sausage. Simple things all but oh, how excellent !

And born of them, somehow I see the poet who enjoyed as one of the good companions in Stevenson's archaics :

> ' Brave lads in olden, musical centuries
> Sang, night by night, adorable choruses,
>   Sat late by alehouse doors in April
>   Chanting in joy as the moon was rising ! '

And again I am reading of him, how that driving with a party in Tuscany he happened upon a village fair. Fairs and circuses were always occasions to Kenneth, but this fair beat any Berkshire ' Veast ' by far. For here, beside the high road, sat vagabonds who roasted chickens on spits over wayside fires of wood. The ravishing smell of the roasting went to his head like music. The call to eat was irresistible. And the chicken that ensued was pronounced

to be the best ever man tasted since Noah came out of the
Ark.

And, later, I find the big man drawing his chair in to a
salad so marvellously coloured (red and gold it is and mottled
in cool greens and purples) that for a moment he hesitates,
his horn spoon lifted, to disturb such a masterpiece.   The
moment was, I suppose, but a brief one.   Fresh sardines
too and sweet potatoes compete for his attention, upon
another occasion, with a cathedral—and successfully.   For,
as he said, cathedrals knew how to wait—this one indeed
had already waited five hundred years.

And at Bologna he sees with interest the Mortadella sausage
alive upon the hoof in lovely babyhood.   So chubby and
so rosy are those little cock-nosed piglings that they remind
him as they run of those pink-sugar mice' with the string
tails that 'one used to buy in Torquay'.

And, in Perugia, he shows a Lamblike enthusiasm for
porchetta.   *Porchetta*, the whole hog, the full-grown pig,
stuffed with rosemary and, on saints' days, roasted whole in
gargantuan ovens.   On these red-letter mornings Kenneth
Grahame, strolling, would stop on cellar steps and, peeping
down into bake-houses, would sniff luxuriously and, later,
linger where on long tables, a pig to a table, the *porchetta*
was exposed for sale.   He was the ready purchaser then, and,
come dinner-time, the true, full-fed appreciator of Perugia
and its saints—St. Francis and St. Bartolommeo and the
rest of them.

In Naples his attentions are divided between the Castel
dell Ovo, the embodiment of the enchanted egg on which
Virgil (the magician) made the safety of the city to depend,
and 'a most delicious lunch' at one of the neighbouring
trattorie; 'fresh anchovies and a most delicate white wine'
are as unforgotten as are the frescoes by Giotto in the chapel
of the Castel.

Perugia, Siena and 'sweet Assisi', cities set upon a hill,
were always the loadstones to him.   In the latter city the
thornless roses, the roses that lost their thorns under the

benign influence of St. Francis, were 'just the roses for
St. Andrews' Lang'. And he quoted :

> 'Had cigarettes no ashes
>   And roses ne'er a thorn
> No man would be a funker
> Of burn or whin or bunker
> There'd be no need of mashies
>   And turf would ne'er be torn
> Had cigarettes no ashes
>   And roses ne'er a thorn.'

And, being in Florence at the time of the *Palio* in Siena,
a party was made, a motor-car hired and the *fiestas* attended.
The *Palio delle Contrade* are famous feasts. They are held
in the public square, the Piazza del Campo, in July and
August annually. They date from the Middle Ages and
they commemorate victories and the Virgin. They were
initiated as bull-fights. But, in the sixteenth century, races
on mounted buffaloes were instituted and the bull-fighting
ceased. Since 1650 the festivities have centred round a
pageant and a fancy-dress horse race, three times round the
stony and precipitous square, to win a *palio*, or banner.

Siena is divided into *contrade*, or wards, each one having
a distinct title—The Giraffe, the Goose, the Wave and so
on—each one with a chapel and a flag of its own. And each
one living up to the truth laid down long ago by the schoolboy Kenneth Grahame in the *Chronicle* of St. Edward's
School in Oxford, namely that 'it is very difficult to feel
friendly towards a rival'.

There are seventeen *contrade* and, yearly, ten of them,
chosen by lot, may enter one horse to compete for the *palio*
and be galloped lame on the pavement of the Piazza.

A lady who went with the Grahames to Siena that summer
day writes of the outing : 'It was a lovely drive in the
cool of the morning and, though we reached Siena early, the
steep narrow streets were already full and grey-and-green
soldiers were everywhere diverting the traffic. Bands of
performers, in costume, waiting the word "go", strolled

here and there in the medieval designs, velvet, satin and lace,
of Michael Angelo. Windows and balconies, in the immense
grey square, were " hung with garlands all ", the stands
were crowded and gay, the sky was blue as cornflowers,
carabinieri, mounted and on foot, were noisily clearing the
course and, just as we got to our seats, the bells in the
Campanili began to ring. In the distance one heard fifes
and drums and then the processions trickled round the
corner and into the square.

' Each *contrada* has its own procession and its own
thirteenth-century costumes. Each marched, men-at-arms,
halberdiers, drummers, " nimble and naughty " pages, behind its own cognizance. To each procession were two
gonfalonieri, bearers of banners, defiant fellows who tossed
their enormous gold-fringed standards aloft juggling with
them, in challenge, as easily as winking, and flapping them
like signallers on Salisbury Plain. The dresses were as rich
as stained glass windows—green and white, blue and scarlet,
black and yellow. The banners were stiff with bullion and
slashed with flaming colours. The processions saluted the
Archbishop's balcony and moved to their stone seats above
the Palace steps. There they broke like kaleidoscopes and
sat down glowing like a garden of flowers.

' Marching eight abreast in gala, the children followed
linked up by garlands of laurel. Lastly came a four-horse
wagon. Its postilions wore green livery and the tall caps
of the Middle Ages. In the wagon was the *Palio* itself—
great and old and splendid, guarded by mounted men in
helmets and bronze armour. The belfries clash and are
silent. There is an interval for refreshment.

' And now the ten runners (previously blessed by the
Archbishop before the Cathedral's altar) face the starter.
They are of all kinds but mostly indifferent. They start
and are flogged indiscriminately by their jockeys and by
the spectators. Hoofs clatter " as if Cheapside were mad ".
The race is awarded to a horse who, having unshipped his
rider, finishes first. On second thoughts this decision is

reversed. Jockeys, whip-slashing, attack other jockeys, a
dozen free fights ensue and I hear Mr. Grahame say, half
to himself, " Lisheen Races, second-hand". A horse, called
Lola, has won for the *Contrada* Girafa.

' The jockey is one Melone who has refused, we hear, to
"nobble" Lola for a bribe or even to pull her. " *Ne anche
per millione* " (not for a million), said the impeccable Melone.
Or so declared the men of The Giraffe. These go shouting
of victory now, " *La Girafa e granda, arriva al terzopiano !* "
(The Giraffe is so high that it can see into third-floor
windows.)

' Mr. Grahame was a noticeable-looking man anywhere
and here, among that Southern crowd, he seemed remarkably
so. Heads turned his way and a courtly priest approached
him and, bowing, paid him the compliment of begging that
he and his party would eventually accept the hospitality
of his house which overlooked the street where the winning
Contrada was later to celebrate victory with a dinner.

' Kenneth Grahame was as pleased as a boy and named
himself " the man who found the key in the horse's ear ".
" And who might he be ? " I asked. He told me a French
fairy tale about a seeker who sought " a golden key on a
green silk cord " which unlocked all doors. It was to be
found in a far city, in a secret stable, and hidden in a horse's
ear.

' The feast that we had been invited to witness was laid
(a fortnight later) in the main street of the *Contrada* of the
Girafa. Tables were laid, so as to form one continuous
" switch-back " table in the centre of the narrow, hilly
street. It was spread with white cloths and embellished
with flowers and regiments of wine flasks. At one interminable end sat Melone, the winning jockey. At the other
stood Lola, the winning mare. She wore a necklace of
green apples and seemed, on the whole, to be enjoying herself. The illuminations made the warm night as bright as
day. Great moths fluttered and swooped, a hundred bands
played, the fun was noisy and grew noisier. Our host

handed round china bowls of sweet biscuits and glasses of
sweet wine. We got back to Florence nearer five than
four in the morning.'

' The golden key in the horse's ear ' was one of Kenneth
Grahame's conceits. By it he explained his welcome in
places where the tourist is not usually *persona grata*. He
was familiar, for example, with the Bassi in Naples (those
' under-structural ' dwellings where the poor live, with their
wretched livestock, in a common gloom) and at Capri of
the Quail he was on jolly, gossip terms with old women
porters who would ' remember back ', to please the Englishman, to the very times of Tiberius. In Palermo ' the key '
unlocked the heart of a little, desiccated keeper of a wine-
shop whom Kenneth christened ' Mr. Venus ' vowing that
he was the identical taxidermist of *Our Mutual Friend.*

In the tavern under the four judas trees the ' Barone '
(Kenneth was prompt to receive courtesy titles in Italy—
the English ambassador dubbed him knight, as we know,
and here, in Palermo, he was Baron) would sit and sip the
gold Marsala till closing-time, pledging the aristocrats of
the place—the tailor, the tinker, the candlestick-maker.
And then, bowing his *buone notte* to the company, he would
stroll to feel ' the Boulevart break again to warmth and light
and bliss '.

If a stranger enters that wine-shop to-day and calls for
a beaker of the best he will be served from the choice of
the ' Barone ', from the cask still known as the Cask of
the Englishman.

Palermo is the place of puppet shows and to one of these,
given specially for children, Kenneth Grahame, as the English Interpreter of Childhood, was earnestly invited. The
show bore the promising nursery title, *The Damnation of
Judas.* And when the hero hanged himself and was finally
engulfed in an inferno of flames, the little audience, which
had been twittering like a flock of delighted sparrows
throughout, went wild with enthusiasm. Judas was encored
again and again ; indeed, said the guest, had Judas betrayed

his Master a hundred times, he would not even then have
satisfied fully the demands of his admirers. ' Mr. Punch,'
said Kenneth Grahame, ' will have to take a back seat.'

This Art of the Marionettes is one that holds the heart
of the artist. He may throw it aside for a better-paid
employment, but the strings of the *Fantocci* are round
his heart and they draw him back to the booths as surely
as the sea calls the sailor.

Once at Syracuse, as Kenneth brooded (like the good
Arcadian that he was) over the deep tranquillity of the Fonte
d' Arethusa, two pretty girls near him asked their duenna
who Arethusa might be ? She could not say, but Kenneth
Grahame could and did. And to a pair of little princesses
he told, standing bare-headed and mighty courtly, the old
legend of how a frightened nymph became first a spring of
running water, then, as a secret river, how she fled under
the sea and, lastly, how she rose again in safety to make a
happy ending just where the present party stood.

And at lovely Taormina ' the key ' admitted him to the
orange groves where the jewelled lizards run in that bit
of long-ago England which is still the house and estate
bestowed on the first Lord Nelson by the King of the two
Sicilies. There the English modes of the time of Trafalgar
were observed in their continuity. And there old manuscripts and relics were examined by the author of *The
Twenty-first of October* as likewise was some ' admirable
white wine ' which had been forty years in the dark and
now trickled into the big monogramed goblets ' like molten
sunshine '. Somebody quoted as he raised his glass, ' " It's
Trafalgar Day," said Selina.' ' " And nobody cares " ' ,
Kenneth Grahame capped him and set his beaker down
empty.

Taormina is full of saints and superstitions. Two of the
former were black. ' Comme votre chapeau noir,' a Cockney
linguist told a French girl at table d'hôte. He spoke of
San Philipo—Neri and he was right. A journey was made
to the shrine of the saint which is perched on a high rock.

It was the feast day when San Philipo comes forth on a litter, borne, at break-neck speed, by fifty bearers. A slip, a stumble on the part of any one of these latter, means failure of the crops. To-day no stumble was made and all was therefore well.

So San Philipo proceeded to ' cast out devils '. Those ' possessed ', young and good-looking wenches all of them, were bidden to kiss the saint and be restored. One refused —for a time—pouting and flouncing. ' What's wrong with her ? ' asked Kenneth, looking at the sullening minx. He was told that she would not answer when spoken to, that she was, in fact, possessed by a devil of dumbness. ' " Mum-saucy ", that devil's called in Berkshire,' said he.

To country fairs he went when opportunity served, for, though the unthinking (but unthinkable) cruelty to the live stock exposed for sale revolted him, he could yet listen to cheapjacks and enjoy their jests and chaffer with the witty vendors of inanimate merchandise such as paper butterflies and flowers. Of the latter, once he said to their stout and good-looking contadina, ' Your bouquets, Signora, are fine enough for a church.' ' For a *church* ? ' flashed she, ' but they are fine enough for a *salon*.'

Perhaps the best bit of keyholing on the part of the ' golden key ' was to admit its bearer to the appeal court of Palermo where Paolo, the brigand, was appealing against a sentence of one hundred years' imprisonment which (since capital punishment is not to Sicilian taste) he had received for numerous malefactions, including thirteen proved murders.

Paolo was an archdeaconal looking man of middle age, and of a portly habit. His complexion was as apple-blossom, he was heavily manacled and he was surrounded by a bristling guard which he kept in smiling humour by his cheerful sallies and witty conversation. There was no public in court except Kenneth Grahame to whom one small soldier was allotted as sufficient personal protection for a man so large as he. There were the judges (to each

of whom ten bayonets made bodyguard) who, eventually
granting Paolo's appeal, reduced his sentence to one of ninety
years. There were counsel for and against ; and to each
advocate a guard of five soldiers sufficed. The well of the
court was filled by an army corps. In the dock stood, of
course, the urbane Paolo who, presently, overjoyed by his
success, became more amusing than ever and was finally
led back to jail by an escort now convulsed with laughter.

I will take yet one more incident of the ' golden key '.

It was a rainy day in Brittany ; and the *Landes* are
forlorn when it rains. A wedding was in process and the
guests, hand-in-hand, capered through the wet streets of a
little town pausing before each wine-shop on their itinerary
to execute a set dance. The men wore glossy, black, short-
jacketed suits and low-crowned black hats, wide and heavy
of brim. The women also wore black dresses banded, on
sleeve and skirt, with black velvet. They were coiffed with
the elaborately goffered Brittany cap and an otherwise
sombre scheme was enlivened, a little, by gala aprons of
flowered brocade—rose and gold, silver and blue, green
and lavender.

These folk danced woodenly and without spirit, their
faces seemed as melancholy to Kenneth as ' seven years
of famine '. They went on their way to a private dance-
room where the main festivities were to be.

As at Siena so at Pont Aven. Some one noticed the tall
Englishman and, addressing him as ' Mon Colonel ', invited
him to take a part in the revels. Within doors matters
became a little more cheerful. Even so, however, the party
was only too evidently a frost.

But of a sudden there was among the guests a dumpy,
slatternly, not so young woman with a vacant, turnip face.
Her sleeves were rolled up above her fat, red elbows. She
wore no goffered, snowy cap. Her coarse, untidy hair
strayed, in fiercest carrot, from under a check duster bound
about her head. No gala apron was hers but, around her
ample middle, a sack was draped. And yet a glossy-suited

swain hastened to take her rough hand. And a miracle
came. This almost grotesque figure suddenly assumed the
attributes of a *première danseuse* so agile was she, so gay,
so animated, so graceful. Her eyes sparkled, her lips smiled.
She was beautiful. She was a lyric. And the whole party,
inspired, followed her, first with verve then with abandon
and delight.

'Mon Colonel' was charmed and, during an interlude,
he sought and obtained an introduction. The sylph apolo-
gized for her lack of wedding clothes. 'You see, Monsieur,
I was making my dishes, my arms were in the water when
they fetched me. They *had* to fetch me because the dance
was not going, oh, not going at all. And when that is so
I must come and dance with them for then all goes well
indeed. For I love to dance and it is I who make others
love to dance. In rain and sun I have danced over every
stone in Pont Aven. I am not always so graceless in my
toilet, but to-day they would not, *could* not wait. No
moment might I have to change my apron, no moment to
put on my cap.'

'Mademoiselle,' said Monsieur le Colonel, 'your sister is
my old friend.' 'So, Monsieur?' 'Your sister Thalia—
for surely you are Terpsichore's self?' She dropped him
a smiling 'reverence' and a partner claimed her. 'And,
well—anyhow she didn't *deny* it,' said Kenneth Grahame.

CHAPTER XVI

' A DARK STAR '

WHAT follows is the last address that Kenneth Grahame delivered. It was spoken within a stone's throw of the Thames and to an audience that came from near and far to fill a village-hall to overflow. It was the only occasion upon which I, his biographer, had heard him speak in public. He was over seventy years old. Yet when he stood up under the arc-light he was as upright as a man of half his age and his voice was musical, far-reaching and young. He named his address ' A Dark Star '.

And this is what he said :

' I have often wondered vaguely, as from time to time I read fresh estimates by the critic of the moment upon the great masters of the past, or who are passing now, why it is that finality in this sort of criticism seems so rarely to be reached, and how it can be possible for the new critic of each succeeding age to put forward a revised estimate and to gain some acceptance for it. Surely, I would say to myself, the best critics of the day, the leading minds of a poet's generation, ought to be able to lay down such a definite criterion once and for all, that it should afterwards be unassailable. For after all, the things that really matter are quite definite. Sheer absolute merit, sheer quality, is definite. When we open a certain book of plays at random, and come upon such a passage as—

> " Night's candles are burnt out, and jocund day
> Walks tiptoe on the misty mountain tops,"

or we turn a page or two and read—

> " Unarm, Eros, the long day's task is done,
> And we must sleep,"

when we light on such passages, and Shakespeare keeps
letting fall such consummate trifles as these with a careless
facility that almost frightens us, so entirely effortless it seems
to be—we don't argue, we *know*. We just say to ourselves,
" Well, there you are ! That's *it* ! "

' Then again originality is quite a definite thing, it can be
proved, indeed, by exact quotation ; and as for novelty,
which is much the same thing but not quite, being on a
lower plane, it is the most easily proved of all. Three
instances of novelty, as such, occur to me, which I give in
their historical order—the " faked " poems attributed to
Ossian, which in the eighteenth century, by sheer novelty
of treatment, almost carried by storm the best critical
opinion of the day, with the exception of the sturdy Dr.
Johnson and a few others ; and then there is the case of
Martin Tupper, whose Proverbial Philosophy, couched in a
diction and versification which at least were something quite
new to the reading public, had an enormous vogue. Well,
these two books are long dead, and rightly so, being instances
of novelty and little else. But in my third instance, that
of Walt Whitman, we note a difference. Here we had
novelty indeed, but we had, as well, original genius of a high
order ; and it is interesting to note that here the novelty
was of little assistance to the poet, for many readers who
loved the matter were repelled by the form. Still, Whitman
is an instance of what I mean by the appeal of novelty as
distinguished from originality of genius.

' If, then, these tests can be so easily applied, and if real
genius emits a radiance of its own that hardly demands a
test at all, how is it that when the great critic A. has said
his say and classified his man, thirty years later critic B.
comes along, and thirty years afterwards critic C. each with
a new estimate, and I am bound to say an estimate which
often seems an improvement on its predecessor, more
especially the one that is nearest to our own generation.
And yet sheer quality, as such, remains the same through
all the ages, and you can take a pencil and mark the passages

20

of sheer poetic beauty in the *Iliad* or the *Æneid* as easily as you can those in, say, *Childe Harold*, by Byron, or the *Excursion*, by Wordsworth, or say, *The Ring and the Book*, by Browning.

' It seemed to me, pondering on these matters, that there was some missing element in all such criticism, or else in the matter criticized, always there, like radium, for instance, but not recognized or not sufficiently recognized—at any rate not kept constantly before the mind of reader or critic as it should be—and it was my business to try and find out what that was.

' But I did not find the task so very easy. I thought and thought, but what I wanted would not come to the surface and become visible, though I was sure it was lurking there all the time.

' I knew it was there, because I could perceive the effects though I could not identify the cause. Now I seem to have read somewhere that astronomers have found that there are certain dark stars—stars, that is, which for some reason neither emit nor reflect light. They are in fact invisible, and are only known to be there by the influence, the attraction or repulsion, that they are observed to exert upon the bodies that are their neighbours—their contemporaries in space, if I may so express it. It is, in fact, by that pull or push that the astronomer weighs them, measures them, gradually sizes them up, so to speak, and eventually gives them place and name among the hierarchy of heaven. Something like that was to be my task—to identify the invisible cause of an irregularity of movement among my literary planets.

' Then again you will remember how Socrates, with his pupils grouped around him in some shady grove in Athens, or by the banks of the babbling Ilyssus, would propound to them some such question as this very one, and some pupil would reply, " I think, Socrates, that what we are seeking may be defined as so-and-so." And Socrates would reply, " Well, that being so, we may fairly conclude that

it is also so-and-so, may we not ? " And, his pupils assent-
ing, he would gently lead them on, by easy steps, until he
had involved them in a palpable self-contradiction. Socrates
would then say, " Well, supposing we begin again, and first
ask ourselves what it is *not*, and so, by elimination, arrive
at what it really is ? " Now, something like that we have
already done to-day. We have agreed that what I have
called the missing element has nothing to do with the
sheer *quality* of the writer, nor with that form of genius
which we call originality, nor with novelty, for these things
we can identify and define. By leaving them out, then, it
is easier to run to earth the fox we are really after. (There
is some slight mixing of metaphors here, I know, but, as
some eminent person has said, the man who never mixes
his metaphors never mixes anything—or words to that
effect.)

'Well, I got my fox by his brush at last and pulled him
out, and though he is not much to look at, I think he is a
genuine *canis vulpes*. What is usually missing, I think, in
criticism or estimates of past writers, is a proper recognition
of the special contemporary appeal which almost every good
writer has for his own actual contemporaries, the subtle
liaison, the bond between themselves and their actual contemporaries only, and never between the writer and later
generations. Other bonds there are, of course, and plenty,
between them and posterity ; never this particular one.

'Perhaps I may also speak of it, this thing that I call
the "contemporary appeal", as the "incommunicable
thrill". Other thrills there are, which may pass downwards
through the centuries, but this particular one cannot be
communicated by one generation to its successor. This
thrill exists for its own generation alone.

'Of course you may reply, "Oh, but we have always
known *that*. We have always realized that a writer, whatever he may pretend, writes for, and at, his contemporaries
and not posterity, and that his appeal to *them* must therefore
be closer and more intimate than to later readers." Well,

that may be. But is it always steadily borne in mind by those who estimate past work afresh, brushing aside contemporary judgements, that to themselves there is and must be something missing, something *they* can never hope to recover, and a very real thing too, something you have no business to ignore, as it is too often ignored disdainfully— the contemporary appeal. Of course it is true that good literature is an almost imperishable thing which continues to glow and to palpitate through the generations that succeed its birth ; but I am afraid that it is also true that literature which reflects very strongly the special taste of the day, such as the classicism of the eighteenth century, may become a sort of *hortus siccus*, a collection of pressed and dried flowers, in which the colour is still there, and the form, and you can recognize the petals, and stamens, and count them, but the first bloom and iridescence is gone for ever. But it was not gone for its contemporaries. *They* got that, but they cannot hand it on. Still, it was there at the time and, when it can be identified, it will prove to be a fine and precious thing, and poets are entitled to credit for it.

' I wish I could present my thesis to you in more concise and clear-cut terms, and with more comprehensiveness than is to be found in the phrases " contemporary appeal " and " incommunicable thrill " ; but if you will let me give you a few illustrations of what I really mean, my contention will perhaps begin to make itself more clear.

' Here is one. I remember reading in some memoir or autobiography or other—I cannot lay my hands on my authority at the moment—how on a certain night in the year 1850 a group of young men were assembled in the rooms then occupied by Rossetti, in Chatham Place, by the Blackfriars Bridge, long ago pulled down. They were all young, all budding poets or artists, and the occasion was, that one of them, through his friendship with some printer or publisher, had been promised that night, as a special favour, an advance copy of a book of poetry that was to be published

next day,—a book called *In Memoriam* by one Alfred
Tennyson, a young poet then rapidly rising in public favour.
The emissary was sitting at the publisher's office at the
moment, and the group were eagerly awaiting his return.
It was past midnight when he entered at last, waving the
magic volume over his head. The best reader was then
selected, and the remainder of the night was spent in the
reading aloud of these poems to a silent, enthralled, spell-
bound audience. It was broad daylight, the author tells
us, when the meeting broke up at last, and he and his friends
walked homeward along the Embankment, all still silent,
still strangely moved and shaken, as if by some new
revelation.

' Now I am not going to criticize *In Memoriam*, one way
or the other. I will only ask you to observe that if the most
ardent Tennysonian now living, and there are still a few
such, had by some singular chance or accident never read
In Memoriam and it were put into his hands to-day, he would
be surprised and delighted indeed, he would lose no time
in possessing himself of its contents, but I do not think he
would deliberately devote the hours of the night to something that could as well be tackled in the morning ; and I
think also that, while delighted, he would also be critical.
He would compare, and analyse, and dissect this dead
specimen of a past generation. Those boys of 1850, for
they were little more than boys, never criticized. They
were as it were drunk—drunk with the contemporary appeal,
drunk with the incommunicable thrill.

' Remember also that Rossetti and his followers were not,
strictly speaking, Tennysonians at all. They were the
founders of another school of poetry, a school that very
soon drifted far away from the Tennyson idiom. *But*—
they were contemporaries, that is the point of the story.

' I will give you another instance, and a very similar one.
This time I am going to put in the witness-box my own
grandmother. When my grandmother was a young girl,
living at home with her parents, in London I think, though

I cannot be sure of that, one night a certain mild excitement was caused in the house by the arrival of the Edinburgh Mail. Now the Edinburgh Mail of those days was carried by a coach and four horses, and took some four days to get through with luck and travelling hard, so its arrival was something of an event. Well, there were the usual business letters for the father, and the long letters of gossip —Edinburgh and Glasgow gossip—crossed and re-crossed for the mother, and there was besides a dumpy package tied up with string, bearing the label of the well-known publishing firm of Ballantyne, and on this, the girl, my grandmother, fell with a shout of triumph, for she knew it could be nothing else but an early copy of the very latest Waverley Novel— I forget *which* of them it was now—a book waited for throughout the length and breadth of England with an intensity which seems strange to us now. So when the girl took her bedroom candlestick and climbed upstairs to her little room at the top of the house, she managed to carry the precious parcel with her, intending to start on the book the following day, as early as her domestic duties, which came first in those days, would permit her. Arrived in her bedroom, she said to herself, " I wonder if it would be very wrong of me if I just took a peep at the first page, merely to see how the story begins ? " So she stretched herself on the hearthrug, with her candlestick on the floor beside her, and cut the string of the parcel. And the hours slipped by, and the candle burnt low, and the grey dawn began to filter in past the blind, and still the girl read on. And the candle guttered in its socket, and the dawn gave way to full daylight which took the place of the candle, and still the girl read on, entranced, bewitched, possessed and held spell-bound by a touch of the wand of him who was already known as the Wizard of the North.

' Now let us suppose, if it is not making too monstrous a demand on your powers of imagination, that there was actually in existence to-day some young person who cared a straw for Walter Scott's Works and who, by chance, had

never read one of the best of them. Supposing it came into
her hands, she would be delighted indeed, but it would be
ridiculous to suppose that she would lie on the hard boards
of her bedroom floor all night, like my poor little grandmother. Indeed a great part of her interest in the thing
would be that which one takes in a literary curiosity. She
would not be handling a real live pulsating thing, of which
you could almost hear the heartbeats. But my grandmother *was* ! For her there was the contemporary appeal,
the thrill at its height. You see, she was one of Walter
Scott's contemporaries.

'Let us take another instance, and this time we will go
a little further back. In Boswell's *Life of Dr. Johnson*, under
the year 1777, we find him, Boswell, corresponding with a
certain critic on the *style* of Dr. Johnson's book, *Journey to
the Western Islands of Scotland*. You will remember that
Boswell took Dr. Johnson a tour through Scotland to try
and cure him of his prejudice against the Scotch, which he
did not succeed in doing, and when they got back they each
of them wrote a book about it. The critic in question had
" praised the very fine passage upon landing at Icolmkill "
but proceeded to disapprove of " the richness of Johnson's
language ". Boswell then proceeds to quote the criticized
passage, in full, in justification of its author :

' " We were now treading that illustrious island which
was once the luminary of the Caledonian regions, whence
savage clans and roving barbarians derived the benefits of
knowledge, and the blessings of religion. To abstract the
mind from all local emotion would be impossible, if it were
endeavoured, and would be foolish if it *were* possible. Whatever withdraws us from the power of our senses, whatever
makes the past, the distant, or the future, predominate over
the present, advances us in the dignity of thinking beings.
Far from me, and from my friends, be such frigid philosophy,
as may conduct us, indifferent and unmoved, over any
ground which has been dignified by wisdom, bravery, or
virtue. The man is little to be envied whose patriotism

would not gain force upon the plain of Marathon, or whose piety would not grow warmer among the ruins of Iona."

'Boswell continues, speaking for himself : "Had our Tour produced nothing else but this sublime passage, the world must have acknowledged that it was not made in vain. Sir Joseph Banks, the present respectable President of the Royal Society, told me, he was so much struck on reading it, that he clasped his hands together, and remained for some time in an attitude of silent admiration." So far Boswell.

'Now I want to say here, and at once, that when Sir Joseph Banks clasped his hands together and remained for some time in silent admiration, Sir Joseph Banks did what was only just and right. For it is indeed a fine passage. Written though it be in the rigid, frigid, somewhat ponderous style of the period, it is sonorous, well-balanced, beautifully restrained, and even deeply moving. English literature owes a great debt of gratitude to Johnson, and to others like him—if indeed there be any others like him—who have set themselves a severe and lofty standard of writing such as this ; for such standard is a sort of fixative which keeps our language from slipping away, as it always has a tendency to do, into a careless slovenliness and inexactitude of expression. We do not read them now, neither their style nor their matter please us longer, but their works remain to show us with what earnest care, with what reverence and regard, the English language used to be treated by those who thought themselves worthy to write it. But what I want you to notice just now is that if you were to read this passage to " the present respectable President of the Royal Society ", whoever he may be, he would probably say, " Yes, that is an admirable specimen of a formal and laboured style of writing, now happily long past." *He* would not clasp his hands together—why indeed should he ? *He* isn't a contemporary, and if he remained silent for some time, it would probably be not from admiration, but from boredom. *He* is not moved by the contemporary appeal—*he* would feel no thrill. But Sir Joseph Banks, his predecessor, *did* and hence he acted in the manner Boswell has so faithfully recorded for us.

' Here is another instance, from the same source. Boswell tells us that Johnson's *Life of Richard Savage*, the poet, is (I am quoting now) " one of the most interesting narratives in the English language. Sir Joshua Reynolds ", he continues, " told me, that, upon his return from Italy, he met with it in Devonshire, knowing nothing of its author " (this was in Johnson's early days) " and began to read it while he was standing with his arm leaning against a chimney-piece. It seized his attention so strongly that, not being able to lay down the book till he had finished it, when he attempted to move he found his arm totally benumbed."

' You see, poor Sir Joshua came off rather worse than Sir Joseph. The respectable Banks only suffered a temporary paralysis of the vocal organs, but Reynolds had a limb put out of action in this his first encounter with the irresistible eloquence of Johnson. I have never read this *Life of Savage* myself, so can express no opinion on the matter ; but I do not remember ever having heard or seen this masterpiece quoted or referred to by any modern critic or writer or speaker. Yet Reynolds, who was a writer himself as well as a consummate artist, was as sound a literary critic as any of his critical generation.

' Another criticism of the same book, written at the time of its publication, concludes with the following passage : " His reflections open to all the recesses of the human heart ; and, in a word, a more just or pleasant, a more engaging or a more improving treatise, on all the excellencies and defects of human nature, is scarce to be found in our own, or perhaps any other language."

' That criticism, though anonymous, was believed by many to be written by no other than Henry Fielding himself. Now when you get two men of the calibre of Joshua Reynolds and Henry Fielding writing in this manner, you simply dare not ignore them. They carry too much metal.

'Before I leave the subject of Johnson I would ask, is
he not a good illustration, in another manner, of the value
of this now lost "contemporary touch"? Johnson was,
by the unanimous voice of his age, the greatest writer of
his period. There was no question about it. Gibbon was
writing, Goldsmith was writing, Fielding was writing, and
many another; but every one awarded the palm to Johnson.
And he was also a *voluminous* writer. To-day, these writings
are all dead—dead and buried, and have been so for many
a long year. The "thrill" has died out of them, and, if
Johnson's posthumous fame depended on his writings alone,
his name would be rarely heard. Johnson lives to us now,
and very vigorous he is too, solely by virtue of his sayings
and doings, chiefly his sayings, his table-talk, as reported,
and very scrappily and imperfectly reported, by Boswell,
Thrale, Sir Joshua Reynolds and one or two others. Now
you will find all these diarists and recorders from time to
time bursting out in the same way, "Oh if I had only put
down more of this wonderful conversation, Oh if I could
but remember more of all that he said that night—if I
could but convey to my readers some of the fire and power
and energy with which he treated this or that subject, then
future generations might form some faint idea of what a
man he was." It is the thrill incommunicable over again.
There were evenings at the Literary Club, when Johnson
had been taking the floor and was in specially good form,
when the members—distinguished men all of them—would
walk home, silent and deeply moved, just like those youngsters after that first reading of *In Memoriam*, only able to
gasp out at intervals, "*What* a Man!", or words to that
effect. But they all agreed, that it was impossible to give
to posterity anything more than the merest echo of the real
Johnson. And we know that they were right. Only his
contemporaries could feel the real, the authentic, thrill.

'Here, however, it is interesting to note, that it is just
in our delight in these scraps and fragments of talk, whenever evidently reported faithfully and verbatim, that we

seem to get nearest to his contemporaries' feeling about him ;
and yet we know that that appreciation was based on his
writings, not his talk, because naturally only a very few of
his host of admirers ever even set eyes on the man.   His
writings, however, do not help us a bit, in the way that his
reported talk does, to get into the skin of his contemporary
admirers.   They might of course help us if we ever read
them, but we don't and won't—I might even say we can't.
I suppose the explanation is that, as compared with collo-
quial talk, *all* writing has a touch of artificiality about it,
and the Essayists of the Eighteenth Century deliberately
pushed this artifice to an extreme—almost as far as the
short-lived Euphuists and Gongorists of the Sixteenth Century.   They meant to be artificial, and they were.   Really,
at times, with Johnson you are not quite sure when you are
reading English and when you are reading Latin ;   for
example, here is a sentence from the Preface to the *Dictionary*
singled out by Boswell for our special admiration :   " When
the radical idea branches out into parallel ramifications,
how can a consecutive series be formed of senses in their
own nature collateral ? "   The enraptured Boswell, heaving
up his either hand, like the child in Herrick's poem, declares
this sentence to be " the perfections of Language ".   And
so it is, in a way—the eighteenth-century way.   But not
our way.   They deliberately thought that the more English
resembled Latin the better it must be.   So thinking, they
lost all flexibility ;   we, for our part, cannot and will not
stand an *in*flexible language.   The great crime of the
Eighteenth-century Essayists was that they sinned deliberately, sinned against the light.   For they were no pioneers,
like Dante or Boccaccio, in Italy, blazing a track through
a forest primeval, letting light and air into a dark jungle.
No, they had before them, or more strictly speaking, behind
them, the splendid corpus of work turned out by those
sixteenth-century writers we roughly summarize under the
name of the Tudor Translators, including, of course, the
compilers of the Authorized Version of the Bible, writers

of an English vivid, virile, picturesque and, above all, flexible, such as has never been written before or since, and they turned their backs on it all for the sake of a narrow Latinity, cramped and hidebound if, often, sonorous. To them the Elizabethans were barbarous, their style Gothic —Gothic spelt with a k or a que—and their penalty is that their translations lie piled on the floors of dusty garrets, while we can, and do, read to-day, with increasing delight, the distinctly less accurate, but always vivid and virile, translations of Sir Thomas North, Sir Thomas Urquhart, John Florio, and many another. It is strange indeed to reflect, that neither Boswell, nor Sir Joseph Banks, nor perhaps even Sir Joshua Reynolds himself, would have troubled to so much as glance at a page of those high histories which so delighted men like Sir Walter Raleigh or Sir Philip Sidney. It is strange too to consider that it was at this very period of arid Latinity that the passionate and romantic Ballads of the North Country—what we speak of as " The Border Ballads "—were beginning, for the first time, to assume literary shape and form. These things, I say, are strange, we can only recognize them, and wonder, and pass on.

' To return to my subject, after all what I am really asking for is only that critics of to-day, and readers too for that matter, should recognize the force of this contemporary appeal and its reality, and in judging past work, should try and make themselves as contemporary as possible, so to speak, in the hope that they too may catch some faint vibration of the particular thrill. They will be the more likely to do justice to their subject. I was privileged recently to listen to a young poet delivering his *apologia*, or defence of the work of his particular school of poetry, and very interesting it was. To be sure I did not know that any one had attacked him, but he appeared to be on his defence, and in the course of such defence had to say something slightly disparaging about both Tennyson and, I think, Swinburne. This he was perfectly entitled to do, nor was he in the least unfair or even severe ; but as I listened

I could tell that he was making no allowance for, indeed
probably did not realize, the special appeal of these two
poets to their contemporaries, who included many men just
as good as himself. Indeed, he would probably, if chal-
lenged, have refused to admit that such contemporary appeal
possessed any value for the critic. Poetic merit, he would
probably have said, is absolute, not relative. It either
exists or it doesn't. The passing of a generation or two
cannot affect it. Well, that is true, but my point is that it
is not the whole truth. There is a good deal of talk in the
scientific world at present about something called Relativity.
Well, I am afraid that what I am claiming is something like
Relativity in poetic merit. That is, that the actual measure-
ments of this merit may vary under varying conditions of
time or space. But this is much too dangerous a subject
for me, a layman, to dare to pursue it further. To take
the case of Swinburne first. Now I dare say that when
our young poet was in the nursery, and the nursemaid had
corrected him on account of some youthful indiscretion, such
as even young poets sometimes commit, that she added
to the punishment some sarcastic remarks about the lilies
and languor of virtue as compared with the roses and rapture
of vice ; and I dare say the young poet, between his sobs,
would cry out, " O for heaven's sake, Mary Ann, not that
stale old *cliché* again." And rightly, for by that time it
was a stale old *cliché* and in the mouth of every nursemaid.
What should he know, by that time, of the wonderful thrill
that shook the reading world when the " Ballad of Dolores "
made its appearance in the sixties ?

' How undergraduates of *both* universities, even Cambridge,
rushed to each other's rooms to shout it and declaim it,
how they whooped and chortled over it, or dreamed and
moaned it, in their sleep, how they parodied it and how,
alas, they tried to write similar poetry with very indifferent
success. " Thou wert fair," this new poet sang,

> ' " Thou wert fair in the fearless old fashion,
>   And thy limbs are as melodies yet."

Limbs, if you please, in the sixties ; up to then, there had
been no limbs in England. Not a single limb. Now we
have very little else, but it doesn't really seem to make much
difference, at least not the difference we thought it would
make in the sixties, when poor Swinburne got all the blame
for it. Then there was the rest of that wonderful " First
Series " of *Poems and Ballads*, with its haunting, almost
odorous atmosphere, and its medievalism which was yet a
new medievalism ; and, much about the same time, *Atalanta
in Calydon*, with its ringing, dew-sprinkled choruses, beloved
by dons and scholars even more than they were by undergraduates (because they were good enough to be set for
Greek or Latin verse), those two books made a special appeal
to their delighted audience of the sixties which they have
never made to any later one. And of all this our young
poet should have been well aware, from the report of others,
and probably was aware, only, not perhaps counting such
appeal as a literary virtue in itself, he was not inclined to
give its inspirer any credit on that account.

' To turn to Tennyson. Doubtless our young poet, when
he was playing as a boy in the garden, and wanted his sister
to come and have a game of lawn tennis, occasionally yelled
through the window, " Come into the garden, Maud ",
because that was a very common catchword of that period.
(Of course I don't mean to imply that his sister's name really
was Maud.) For by that time a catchword was all that it
was. No trace was left by then of the—I may almost call
it strong wave of emotion, mingled with controversy, which
flooded the literary world on the appearance, in 1855, of
Maud—not for the story, which is naught, nor for the
philosophy, which is, if I may say so, naught-er, but for its
wonderful singing lyrics—" O let the solid ground ", " Birds
in the high Hall-garden ", " Go not, happy day ", " O that
'twere possible " and, above all, " Come into the garden,
Maud ", which the best critics of the time hailed as a perfect
specimen of a flawless lyric, capable of standing the severest
test that meticulous criticism could apply. And indeed it

would be difficult to suggest alteration, substitution, elision,
or change of a syllable in this passionate yet most restrained
lyric. What recollections it brings back, even to quote a
line or two of it :

> ' " All night have the roses heard
>   The flute, violin, bassoon,
>   All night has the casement jessamine stirr'd
>   To the dancers dancing in tune,
>   Till a silence fell with the waking bird,
>   And a hush with the setting moon.''

But fine as the sheer *quality* of this poem is, its contemporary
appeal was, by all accounts, transcendent. This is the
second time to-day that I have had to produce Tennyson as a witness, and this is not because I am specially
addicted to Tennyson above other poets, but because
Tennyson, in a quite remarkable way, gave voice to the
thought and feeling of his own period, to an extent, I believe,
never known in any other English poet. I should like to
read you a short passage which I came across lately, in
Mackail's *Life of William Morris*, illustrating this. It is a
quotation from some reminiscences written, some thirty
years later, by a man who was an undergraduate at Oxford
in 1855 :

' " It is difficult for the present generation to understand
the Tennysonian enthusiasm which then prevailed both in
Oxford and the world. All reading men were Tennysonians ; all sets of reading men talked Poetry. Poetry
was the thing ; and it was felt with justice that this was
due to Tennyson. Tennyson had invented a new Poetry,
a new poetic English ; his use of words was new, and every
piece that he wrote was a conquest of a new region. This
lasted till ' Maud ', in 1855, which was his last poem that
mattered. I am told that in this generation no University
man cares for poetry. This is almost inconceivable to one
who remembers Tennyson's reign and his reception in the
Sheldonian in '55. There was the general conviction that
Tennyson was the greatest poet of the century, some held

him the greatest of all poets, or at least of all modern poets.
I would add that we all had the feeling that after him no
further development was possible, that we were at the end
of all things in poetry."

'There the quotation ends. But I want you to notice
that last sentence. Many years ago, I found myself sitting
at dinner, or rather at the close of dinner, next to Francis
Turner Palgrave, the poet better remembered as the com-
piler of the well-known anthology, *The Golden Treasury of
Songs and Lyrics*, perhaps the best-known and most popular
anthology of English verse. And I remember his turning
to me and saying : "Now, you are a good deal younger
than I am, and I want you to tell me, is there any real merit
at all in any of these new writers whose names I hear so
frequently, there is a young man called Stevenson, for
instance, and another called Kipling. Is there really any
lasting worth in what they write, or are they just the fleeting fashion of the day ? " Well, I did my best to give him
a résumé of the qualities of these two writers, and I ventured
to suggest that, if he could spare an hour or two, some
evening, to the works of either or both of them, I thought
he would not find his time had been wasted. He only shook
his head rather sadly, " My interest in English Literature,"
he said, " stopped short at Tennyson. He was to me the
culminating point, and I didn't care somehow to go on any
further. I have never read the later writers." You will
find the same sort of idea—this idea of the finality of Tennyson—in books such as Edward FitzGerald's letters, and in
various Memoirs and Reminiscences by famous men who
were contemporary with Tennyson or slightly older. They
all wanted to stop there. They didn't want any more,
they didn't, indeed, see how there *could* be any more.
Now by this time I think we may consider Tennyson to be
pretty fairly ranked and placed. However high his merit,
he is not Shakespeare and he is not Dante. But when a
poet can make so tremendous an appeal as that to his own
age, surely he is entitled to some special good marks for

that thing alone, in addition to the marks he earns for intrinsic merit. And these men, who held Tennyson so high, were no fools. Brilliant men, nearly all of them, and just as good critics as those of the present day. But really to attempt to justify the taste of the Mid-Victorians is considered to-day to be an offence in itself, just because they wore side-whiskers and crinolines, I should say, of course, side-whiskers *or* crinolines, because naturally they didn't wear both at the same time. But I dare not say more on this subject, as, although I wear neither, I am a Mid-Victorian myself.

' I may, however, just add that I am frankly puzzled by this special claim to finality, put forward by Tennyson's contemporaries on his behalf. I don't remember it being made in the case of any other poet. When Wordsworth, for instance, had somewhat slowly succeeded in getting his merit recognized for what it was, you never find the little band of enthusiasts who had championed his cause from the first, claiming that they did not want, or, indeed, expect, any further progress in English poetry. When Byron, again, took the literary world by storm in a day, when Johnson dominated it for years, when Pope was hailed, by his contemporaries, as easily the leading expression of contemporary taste in verse, or, to go further back if you like, to Shakespeare and even to Chaucer, who stood almost alone in his time, still you never find any of the special backers of these poets proclaiming that they never wanted anything better, and, what's more, wouldn't read it if they got it. I say again I frankly can give no explanation of it. Is it possible that there was more than a touch of self-complacency in the composition of the Mid-Victorian—self-righteousness, as we should call it in another connexion ? Or is an even simpler explanation the right one, namely that they were suffering from satiety, from a sense of Repletion ?

' In this connexion, I am reminded of something I once read about George Eliot in her later years. An acquaintance told her that he proposed to bring so-and-so to call on her

21

the following Sunday, adding, " a very interesting person, whom you will be glad to include in the number of your friends ". George Eliot, however, did not seem to be enthusiastic at the prospect before her, and merely observed plaintively, " Don't you think that we have most of us got *enough* friends ? " And I remember how that esteemed writer and gentle spirit, Walter Pater, having, in the kindness of his heart, undertaken to dine with an undergraduate at his lodgings, felt it his duty to admire warmly everything that the lodging-housekeeper's taste thought most fitting in decoration—the oleographs on the walls, the repp curtains, the veneered walnut furniture and so on. This continued till the end of the meal, when the dessert was placed on the table in a service of more than usual Mid-Victorian atrocity. Pater was heard to murmur, " *Pretty* plates, *pretty plates*—only they must not make any *more.*" Perhaps then the Mid-Victorians were merely thinking that, for the time, they had had enough poets, that Nature mustn't make any more, that they wanted a rest ; for there certainly were a lot of poets knocking about, in those palmy days.

' For instance, among many others, there was Robert Browning, who, in that same year, 1855, published his *Men and Women* in which some of his most famous work appeared. But I am dragging Browning in here, in order to be able to remark, that there never was a great English poet who had less of that quality which I am calling the contemporary appeal than Browning. As Browning's thoughts were peculiarly his own, so was his language ; and really it was not till his admirers, very sensibly, formed a Society to, so to speak, unload Browning stock on the market, that he could be said to have got a real public hearing. The experiment was entirely successful. The public always like a Prospectus with a good list of Directors ; and Browning was thenceforward accepted as a recognized National Poet. Now it is interesting to note, unless I am quite wrong, that since the time I speak of (the Browning Society was founded in 1881) Browning's position with the

British Public has hardly changed at all. As soon as they eventually placed him at all they placed him high, and he remains at the same level. Had he possessed more of that quality of the contemporary appeal, he would certainly have been ranked higher in the forties and fifties, and if we hold that it is a poet's business to appeal to his own generation first, and future generations afterwards, we shall reluctantly have to refuse to Browning those special extra marks which we are allotting to-day. George Meredith was in much the same boat as Browning, intensely individual (I am speaking here of Meredith the poet), thinking his own thoughts and expressing them in a special language of his own that he was determined to use and no other, he was like a man writing for his own private enjoyment only, and he was never in close enough contact with his contemporaries (except a few of them of course) to evoke that answering thrill. But, I can hear you say, do not these two instances go to shatter your own argument ? For if you admit, as no doubt you will, that both Browning and Meredith at their best reached a higher level than Tennyson, and yet never gained that contact with their contemporaries that you seem to value so much, doesn't it amount to this, that your " appeal ", your " thrill ", is merely popularity—popularity, the cheapest thing on earth, the thing most unworthy of notice or regard on the part of any serious writer ? Now in my reply I would ask you to observe, that in the few instances I have taken as illustrations of my theme, I have confined myself to writers of such assured and acknowledged position in the world of letters as to make them independent of mere popularity, even if they possessed it. There were scores and scores of other writers, men of fame in their day, whom I could have quoted as instances of intense con- temporary popularity, if that had been what I was after, writers, too, actually more " popular " in their day than the great men I have quoted. Indeed, of these last, Scott was perhaps the only one who was really " popular " in the widest sense. He was read by high and low, educated

and ignorant alike.   Johnson, as a writer, was only " popular ", naturally, among educated people, and as for Tennyson, why, he never, in spite of " The May Queen " and
" Locksley Hall ", achieved a tenth part of the " popularity "
of Longfellow. No, popularity is not the same thing.
Moore was a good example of a popular poet. A writer
of verse always melodious and refined, free of the slightest
trace of subtlety or profundity of thought, a man personally
popular in himself, knowing everybody worth knowing and
going everywhere, the darling of the humblest parlour that
could run to a cottage piano on account of his *Irish Melodies*,
he was popularity embodied. Nor is *vogue*. Vogue differs
from popularity in that vogue always contains some hint
of *fashion*. One reads so-and-so because the best people
all read him. It's the thing to do, that's vogue. Samuel
Rogers was the great instance of vogue in the last century.
Rogers was rich ; Rogers entertained ; and Rogers wrote
of his travels in Italy, and the Grand Tour in Italy was still
the fashionable thing and he could afford to have them
illustrated by Turner.

   ' Before leaving these occasional instances of really great
poets who nevertheless made little or no contemporary
appeal, one cannot refrain from glancing at the case of
Keats, in some ways the most singular of them all.   One
would have thought that a generation which, wearying of
classical severity and perpetual Latinism, had already begun,
however reluctantly, to welcome that change of thought
and manner of expression represented best by that group,
then known as the Lake Poets, or " Lakers ", would have
welcomed Keats in his turn as only a fuller and more sensuous
development of the new manner. But it was not so. The
change, the rate of progress, was too rapid for the public,
Keats was ahead of the taste of his time, and it was not
until a generation later that public appreciation began to
place him on that pinnacle where he has since remained.
But it was then too late for any one to feel the contemporary
appeal, the real authentic thrill. By then Keats had become

a classic, and a classic is something we criticize and even dissect. We feel our *own* thrill, of course, but that is not the same thrill that would have gone through the whole reading public of, say, the year 1820, had Keats instantly come into his own.

'But the latest example of this sort, in date, that I dare to quote is that of Samuel Butler, author of *Erewhon* and several other now very well-known books, who died only as recently as 1902. Butler, for reasons which were partly his own fault, for he refused to tackle the public and the book-market in the same way that other men did, certainly made no contemporary appeal. His first book, remarkable, original, and also amusing, as it was, fell flat as regards the public, and thereupon Butler deliberately declared that he would write no more for his contemporaries to read, but only for posterity. This is how he puts it—I quote from the well-known *Notebooks of Samuel Butler* : " If my books succeed after my death . . . let it be understood that they failed during my life for a few very obvious reasons of which I was quite aware. . . . I had money enough to live on, and preferred addressing myself to posterity rather than to any except a very few of my own contemporaries. . . . I have addressed the next generation." Those are his own words.

'Now you would scarcely think, would you, that it was in the power of any writer to say who should read his published works and who should not ? It is for the reading public itself to settle that, and the reading public is both wilful and capricious and, above all, resents being dictated to on such a matter. Supposing the public had said, " We're *going* to read *Erewhon* and *Erewhon Revisited* because they are jolly good books, and we don't care a hang for what old Butler says " ; what could Butler have done then ? The odd thing was, that it all fell out exactly as Butler had predicted. During his life, except from the very few who knew, he received little public notice or appreciation. Directly after his death, the next generation

—the *very* next generation, as he said, not any dim and misty future generations, took him up warmly, especially the young reading men, and I think we may say now that every thoughtful young man has read, or is reading, the works of Samuel Butler. Had he been living and writing now, there would have been plenty of contemporary thrill, so far as any one could thrill at all about such a rather cold-blooded and very perverse, though brilliant, writer as Butler. As it was, like that very different person, Keats, he just missed his market by some thirty years.

' Just one other illustration that I came across the other day in support of my claim that this contemporary appeal should be treated as an enduring fact of value, and not merely a fleeting opinion of the moment. Sir Arthur Quiller-Couch, King Edward the Seventh Professor of English Literature at Cambridge, writing on a kindred subject, the special appeal, not of books, but of certain places, has the following passage : " Even their worst enemies will admit that Oxford and Cambridge wear, in the eyes of their sons at any rate, a certain glamour. You may argue that glamour is glamour, an illusion which will wear off in time ; an illusion, at all events, and to be treated as such by the wise author intent on getting at truth. To this I answer, that, while it lasts, this glamour is just as much a fact as *The Times* newspaper, or St. Paul's Cathedral, just as real a feature of Oxford as Balliol College, or the river, or the Vice-Chancellor's poker and, until you recognize it for a *fact* and feature of the place, and *allow for* it, you have not the faintest prospect of realizing Oxford." You see I am only claiming for certain books what Sir Arthur claims for certain places : that unless you recognize a certain element for a *fact* and *allow* for it, you will not fully *realize* the book.

' Now as I draw near to my conclusion, I seem to hear some of you saying, all this is distinctly depressing, for what you maintain amounts to this, that in the case of many masterpieces of bygone days, *we* must not expect to detect the finest essences, to savour the fullest bouquet, because

the time for that, you say, is over and gone. That, indeed,
is true enough, but then we have our consolations ; when
a genius arises to-day, who makes also a particular appeal
to his own times, why it is we who get the full benefit of
that, as against succeeding generations. We have no right
to expect to have it both ways ; to expect to sit in the
first row of the stalls on the first night of all the masterpieces
of time as well as our own. Another consolation is, that
there is a range of poets, who, from a certain joyous quality
blent with freshness and simplicity, never have dated themselves and apparently never will. Their appeal is probably
as fresh to-day as when their works first appeared. I have
no time to-day to do more than indicate the names of a few
of that happy band. Herrick is I think the most striking
example ; Robert Burns, Shelley, perhaps Andrew Marvell,
have this dateless quality ; and of course there are others
which all readers will like to supply for themselves.

'I hope, then, that by this time I may have succeeded,
by observing and noting, after the astronomical fashion,
the action of an invisible object on its neighbours suspended
in literary space, in making evident the existence of my
" dark star ", as I have called this influence, the contemporary appeal, which unrecognized or not sufficiently
recognized, has so often affected, even deflected, literary
judgement. Illumination of the surface, full visibility, we
could not hope for ; that was postulated from the first.
By force of the evidence alone can the thing be perceived.
And though I fear that many of you will say that this is
no solid body but rather a will-o'-the-wisp, yet there may
be some who will be inclined to admit, not only that this
is a real little planet enough, too small to be seen, though
big enough to disturb and deflect others, but also that there
may be other such asteroids poised invisibly in our literary
firmament, and awaiting detection. As long as the canons
of literary criticism remain so vague, so varying, so easily
disturbed, the discovery of such " dark stars " must help,
however slightly, to make critical judgement more exact,

and the mind of the reader more easy and, I may add, more interested. The professional critic may be left to look after himself, but each one of us owes to the reader, and especially to the young reader, every help and assistance, however small, it is in his power to bestow.

' One last word, I fully recognize that everything I have said to-day in the course of our rambling talk, for it has only been a talk after all, though a very one-sided one, is highly controversial, and I suppose there is hardly an opinion I have expressed which some one or other of you would not be disposed to question or at least to qualify. Believe me, all that does not matter one bit. It is never the differences that matter; it is the agreements that matter. And we are fully agreed on the essential greatness of those past masters of literature, on whose work I have touched to-day, and profoundly grateful to them for the legacy they have bequeathed to us.'

As we went out into an October evening some of us looked back. The lecturer stood, white head and shoulders high, among those who congratulated. He seemed as one who heard with a polite indifference.

CHAPTER XVII

'SWEET THEMMES, RUNNE SOFTLY TILL I END
MY SONG'

ALASTAIR GRAHAME died in 1920 and in 1924 his parents
left Boham's and came to Church Cottage, Pangbourne.
Pangbourne, as is Blewbury, is in Berkshire, but otherwise
the two villages are not alike. Blewbury is on the downs,
Pangbourne beside the Thames. Blewbury remains ancient,
Pangbourne tends to become modern. In Blewbury the
traffic is confined to the sheeted thoroughbreds who pass,
once or twice in twenty-four hours, as demurely as any
Victorian 'crocodile'; all day, through Pangbourne, the
Oxford road roars unceasingly. Blewbury is 'archaic',
Pangbourne is 'arty', almost as Hampstead is, and the
summer river is gay there with pleasure craft, from the
steamboat for fifty to the cushioned canoe for two. Pangbourne possesses a Literary, Dramatic and Musical Guild,
and Blewbury makes do with lark song and sheep-bells.

But, standing one day on top of a Blewbury down,
Kenneth Grahame saw the silver of Thames water ten miles
away. And in a waterless land, of a sudden, he was home-
sick for the River. And therefore he came home there again
to 'end his song'.

For he loved the Thames and he loved also a garden.
And Church Cottage was within three minutes' walk of the
river and its garden was no cottage garden at all (not that
Church Cottage was a cottage) and its lengths of manorial
lawn ended in an amphitheatre of smooth turf backed, in
half circle, by huge old jackdaw-haunted elms. A secluded
and dignified place suggestive of pastoral plays and, inci-
dental to its dignity, of Kenneth Grahame himself. Its

tool-shed was unique too—the old village lock-up, a squat, circular building with a pepper-pot roof and a grille-window ; once the temporary abode of drunks, disorderlies and similar malefactors, now it became the place of spades, forks and potatoes.

There was, of course, no ' approach ' to Church Cottage though it was (and is) what auctioneers describe as ' a small gentleman's residence '. Its owner, its amphitheatre, and its door-bell were its three most noticeable features. The door-bell was a great, ship's bell purchased at Falmouth. It bore the name ' Rosarian ' and its tone was, so it seemed to me who am unaccustomed to ships' bells, of a quite singular beauty and as musical as the hounds of Hercules.

There was also an upper garden, a close of tall red poppies, peace and flowering fruit trees. At certain hours this terrace was a favourite resort of its owner. Therefore the elderly gardener was requested to respect, at such seasons, his employer's privacy—' Mr. Grahame wanted to be free to sit there and think,' he was told. ' And what likelier place for free-thinking could he want ? ' agreed the good fellow, leaning upon his spade.

And sometimes, when tired of thinking, he would make a lyric there to the address of one or other of the birds in the leaves. Here, for instance, is one with a cock bullfinch for theme, a bullfinch who was not, of course, dead except by license of poetry :

QUIS DESIDERIO ?

(To a Dead Bullfinch)

Wanting now the song of you,
Piper gay in vanished Springs,
We, the lovers long of you,

Lay you now where no bird sings.
Hushed the flutings strong of you :
Very still those striving wings.

Little Orpheus, say, for you
Did some small Eurydice
Chirp below, and pray for you ?

If indeed some lyric-she—
Bride one happy May for you—
Dwelt with dark Persephone,

Then it scarce seems wrong of you
If you fled and left us here
Tuneless all the silent year,
Wanting still the song of you !

And so the summer days went by, and yearly, as we have
seen, Kenneth Grahame followed them leisurely south with
the sun and the swallows and only came home again when
the big apple tree, outside his library window, stood as pink
and as white as an April bridesmaid.

They were quiet years those ultimate ones spent by the
river—the years of a man who is now well enough content
to sit in the shadow and see the view down the valley.   For
the days began to mark him down.   The silent twenty-mile
tramps must become strolls of a mile or so, no more.   Meals
too must be restricted to what, for a trencherman of his
inches, seemed the ridiculous minimum.   Both deprivations
were borne with philosophy and without complaint beyond
a boyish, rather pathetic, ' *Do* let me have something to eat,
Bourdillon ? ' whenever his doctor called.

Yet, though one placid day was much like another, life
was still the jolly thing—old books and bindings, birds in
the garden, a stroll, the dressing of a salad, the summer
pageant of the boats.   And occasionally routine would be
varied by a voyage down-river to Mapledurham to take tea
with two friends of whom he was fond because they were
young and lived, by letters, in a caravan and gave him,
surreptitiously, cream ices to eat which tasted better now
that he had been forbidden them (and vanished quicker)
than ever before.

Occasionally also the Literary Dramatic and Musical Guild
was not to be denied.   Its local lion must roar.   And, being
a good-natured lion, he quite often did.   A lecturer would be
introduced by him in a ten minutes' speech that filled the
village-hall.   Or perhaps a picture show would be declared

opened—and the art of the painter depicted from a finely
original aspect. Moreover, it was to the Guild and its
supporters that the last of Kenneth Grahame's rare lectures
was delivered—that ' Dark Star ' which was the subject
of the previous chapter.

Pangbourne is not far from Oxford and to Oxford, always
dearly loved, Kenneth Grahame would go to enjoy a fair
or a market, or, *laudator acti*, to decry the cut of the modern
undergraduate's trousers, to poke about in Gothic corners,
to purchase the latest necktie for his personal wearing.

For he was always interested in his clothes. To the end
he was as delighted by a new and successfully tailored suit
as is a débutante supposed to be by her first party dress.
To a lady who wished to choose a tie for him he said, ' A
man's tie and a man's tobacco are what he alone can choose.'
In this case however he accepted the deputy, approved her
choice and, I am told, actually wore the same.

Children ran in and out. Annabel, as epicure as Kenneth himself, pleased him well by her genuine appreciation
of the picnic basket he had packed (in *The Wind in the
Willows*) for the Rat and the Mole. Before she went
to school she had made Kenneth vow to her that he would,
when the holidays came, lecture to the Pangbourne children on animals. But Annabel died during her first term.
And her friend, without Annabel to listen to it, never gave
his lecture at all.

On the 25th of June 1932 the Lewis Carroll centenary,
held at Bumpus's book-shop in London, was attended at the
urgent wish of its promoters. Of the younger generation of
writers present many looked at Kenneth Grahame (thus the
youth of the hamlet may have gazed curiously at the returning Rip Van Winkle) and wondered who the big, white-haired
man might be—' Kenneth Grahame ? *Surely* he's older than
that ? '

On the evening of an ensuing week, the evening of the
5th July, he came home from the holiday river ; he mixed
his salad, enjoyed it, and soon he took *The Talisman* and

went to bed. And presently, *The Talisman* fell to the floor, for Kenneth Grahame was gone to sleep. He was in his seventy-fourth year.

When a famous man is passed from us his fellow men speak of him and make his many memorials. Some say this and some say that. Some speak with a personal love, many with beauty, all with reverence.

Of innumerable letters I will quote three only, that of a child :

Pangbourne Lodge

' DEAR MRS. GRAHAME,—I hope these flowers will comfort you as I am sorry you are unhappy.

' Love from

' PENELOPE '

And from that of Miss Ann Spencer Watt (who had lived, as maid, with Mr. and Mrs. Grahame for many years) I take these words : ' I've so often compared other people with Mr. Grahame and wondered why there were so few real Gentlemen in the world.'

Lastly, in a letter, written by Mr. Graham Robertson, I read :

' . . . he wrote what he wished when he wished and he wrote no more than he wished, and this very fastidiousness will probably win him an enduring name.

' The pictures of Leonardo da Vinci are less prized for their beauty than because only about five of them exist ; if the lost poems of Sappho were found it would be a serious blow to that lady's reputation ; in fact nothing can obscure an artist's merit like over-production. In Kenneth Grahame's work there is no need to winnow the wheat from the chaff ; he has left us nothing but the purest golden grain, and his mere handful of writings have swept round the world on a gathering wave of love and admiration for the man who would give nothing short of his best, and whose best is, perhaps, about as near perfection as may be compassed by our poor mortality.

And a River went out from Eden

(*From a drawing by W. Graham Robertson*)

' Now he has gone from beside the much-loved river. Now he has traced to their source the windings of another river, that River that " went out from Eden ".'

Of printed words these which Sir Arthur Quiller-Couch, writing from Fowey, addressed to the Editor of *The Times*, seem to express, in obituary, all that is called for here concerning Sir Arthur's old friend and to be, in epitome, what I have meant this book to be—a picture of Kenneth Grahame :

' In the obituaries of Kenneth Grahame one misses (though friendship may be exacting) full recognition of his personal charm and the beauty—there is no other word—of his character. This, of course, could be divined in his books, few, yet in their way, surely, classical ; but he avoided publicity always, in later years kept deeper retirement under a great sorrow ; and so, perhaps, as these books must by their nature have attracted many readers towards a further intimacy of which he was shy, a word or two about him may be acceptable to them and pardonable by his spirit. One does not, anyhow, wish to go out of this world without acknowledging one of the best things found in it.

' He came to these parts and to this house (from which he was afterwards married) a little more than thirty years ago ; convalescent from a severe illness. Lazy afternoons at sea completed his recovery and made me acquainted with a man who combined all enviable gifts and yet so perfectly as to soften all envy away in affection. Noble in looks, yet modest in bearing ; with flashes of wit that played at call around any subject, lambent as summer lightning, never hurting, and with silences that half-revealed things beyond reach of words, he seemed at once a child and a king. Withal he was eminently a " man's man " and keen on all manly sports : a man, too, who—as Secretary of the Bank of England—knew much of practical affairs and could judge them incisively if with amusement, while his own mind kept its loyalty to sweet thoughts, great manners, and a quiet disdain of anything meaner than these. I must remember him as a " classical " man, perfectly aware of himself as " at best a noble plaything of the gods ", whose will he seemed to understand through his gift of interpreting childhood.'

INDEX

319

Printed in Great Britain by
Butler & Tanner Ltd.
Frome and London